MADAME PH.D.

GROWING UP BLACK IN DC AND BEATING THE ODDS

NETTIE'S DC STORY OF PERSEVERANCE, HOPE, AND DETERMINATION (PHD)

> To Shirley Carswell:
> This book is dedicated to those on whose shoulders I stand and to the sons and daughters of the institutions I have served. I hope you enjoy reading my story & labor of love!
> — Gwynette Ford Lacy
> 1/23

Gwynette Ford Lacy, Ph.D., MBA

Copyright © 2022 Gwynette Ford Lacy, Ph.D., MBA.

All rights reserved. No part of this book may be used or reproduced by any means, graphic, electronic, or mechanical, including photocopying, recording, taping or by any information storage retrieval system without the written permission of the author except in the case of brief quotations embodied in critical articles and reviews.

This book is a work of non-fiction. Unless otherwise noted, the author and the publisher make no explicit guarantees as to the accuracy of the information contained in this book and in some cases, names of people and places have been altered to protect their privacy.

Archway Publishing books may be ordered through booksellers or by contacting:

Archway Publishing
1663 Liberty Drive
Bloomington, IN 47403
www.archwaypublishing.com
844-669-3957

Because of the dynamic nature of the Internet, any web addresses or links contained in this book may have changed since publication and may no longer be valid. The views expressed in this work are solely those of the author and do not necessarily reflect the views of the publisher, and the publisher hereby disclaims any responsibility for them.

Any people depicted in stock imagery provided by Getty Images are models, and such images are being used for illustrative purposes only.
Certain stock imagery © Getty Images.

Photo section created by JRE Kustom Printing

ISBN: 978-1-6657-1372-6 (sc-color)
ISBN: 978-1-6657-2042-7 (sc-black/white)
ISBN: 978-1-6657-1374-0 (hc)
ISBN: 978-1-6657-1373-3 (e)

Library of Congress Control Number: 2021920775

Printed in the United States of America.

Archway Publishing rev. date: 04/01/2022

This book is dedicated:

To my family, friends and those on whom shoulders I stand

To my Great, Great, Great Grandmother:
Sookey Jubeter, a South Carolina Slave

To my Parents:
James Monroe Ford and Gloria Etta Wright Ford

To my Grandmothers:
Bellinger Golden Wright and Mabel Ford Chisley

To the Loves of my Life:
My Husband, George Corinth Lacy, Jr., Esq.,
My Children,
Gharun Stephen Lacy and Gayna Georgette Lacy
Grandchildren,
Juliana, Logan, and Lexington
and
Godchildren

To my Sister: Valeria
and the rest of my family

To my teachers, mentors, classmates and friends at:
DC Public Schools
Eliot Jr. High School
McKinley Tech High School
Lincoln University (PA)
George Washington University
University of Wisconsin – Madison

To Alpha Kappa Alpha Sorority, Inc.
Especially Epsilon Nu Chapter, Lincoln University
and the Divine Nine Greek Sororities and Fraternities
Especially Kappa Alpha Psi Fraternity, Inc.

To my colleagues, students and mentees of:
Howard University
University of the District of Columbia

and to
All of my other past and future students and mentees

CONTENTS

Introduction ix
Chapter 1   The Early Years 1
Chapter 2   Bullied for Being Smart 17
Chapter 3   The Transition to Honors: River Terrace to Eliot ... 29
Chapter 4   On McKinley, On McKinley, Victory Is Our Aim ... 47
Chapter 5   Hail, Hail, Lincoln! 89
Chapter 6   A New Beginning as Husband and Wife 169
Chapter 7   Newly Wed and Working 197
Chapter 8   On Wisconsin? 253
Chapter 9   Two Affirmative Action Badgers 265
Chapter 10 A Road Less Traveled 285
Chapter 11 Home, Sweet Home and Baby Makes Three 313
Chapter 12 New Baby, New Job, New House = Crazy! 333
Chapter 13 Hell's Kitchen vs. the Mecca 347
Chapter 14 Sick or Crazy? My Defense 357
Chapter 15 It's Never Over, Until It's Over 367
About the Author 385

INTRODUCTION

Every Ph.D. has a story. This one's mine. This is my story of how I beat the odds: how an underprivileged black girl from the inner city of Washington, DC, grew up to obtain a Ph.D. Some people don't even know what a Ph.D. degree is. A Doctor of Philosophy degree (Ph.D.) is the highest academic degree one can obtain in one's professional field. Historians, scientists (such as chemists, biologists, and pharmacists), and in my case, MBAs (those with a master's in business administration degree) can all seek a higher degree in their field, called a Ph.D. Medical doctors, anthropologists, and sociologists can also seek a Ph.D.

The Ph.D. is considered a terminal/research degree and qualifies a person to teach at the college or university level. Ph.D. holders are usually graduates of large universities. Instead of standing up, getting applause, and sitting down, they are the ones called to the stage. Their names are called, they are given their degrees, and they are congratulated by the president of their university and others. That's how important a Ph.D. is.

People are often curious about what would motivate a person to seek the highest academic degree that exists, the Ph.D. Some people think you have to be a genius, super-smart, or just plain crazy to put in all the hard work and time it takes to climb to the top of the food chain of educational attainment. Others believe you have to be from a high socioeconomic rank, super-rich, or well-off financially to even think about obtaining a Ph.D. because it is so expensive.

None of that applies to me. I believe that you have to be smart enough to do what it takes and crazy enough to put in the time and go through with it—what experts call an "affinity for high achievement." The rest is all about *perseverance, hope, and determination.*

My case has been very different from most Ph.Ds. As I travel around the country, when people read my résumé or bio and see my first and last name, they often expect to meet a white Irish woman, or someone with a French background, my first name being French and my married name being Irish. When an African American woman shows up, they are often a little surprised. Or when people read that I am a native Washingtonian and attended DC public schools for my basic education, I am often asked what motivated a person of my "background" (or what gave me "the gall") to seek the highest degree that is possible to obtain in the world. I don't fit the profile. I don't fit the mold.

So here is my story—the story of how the great-great-great-granddaughter of a female slave named Sookey Jubeter became the first and only African American female to earn a Ph.D. from the University of Wisconsin–Madison in her specialized business field of industrial relations. She goes on to become the first African American female Ph.D. to be tenured and become the chair of the Department of Management in the School of Business at Howard University. She also held several high administrative posts at Howard and is now a national/international consultant, trainer, and motivational speaker.

My story is about a young black girl who overcomes tough times, a broken home, bullying, and the mean streets of inner-city Washington, DC—who survives and thrives despite her background and gender. This is a story about a black girl growing up in the 1960s and '70s with all the joys and pains of the times: the civil rights movement, government politics, the Vietnam War, protests and marches, assassinations, and riots. Yet it is also a story about the triumphs, music, and college life of those times, DC Go-Go, and a great love affair.

This is a story about finding oneself in the 1960s and '70s; about Afros and dashikis; about studying and hard work, stress and strain, illness and pain; and about finding the answers to life and creating a life that matters. It is a story about race, the racial divide, and racial and gender inequality, yet it is also about racial pride and tolerance. It is a story about *perseverance, hope, and determination*—another kind of PHD.

ONE
THE EARLY YEARS

ARE GENIUSES BORN OR MADE?

THERE IS A long-running debate among researchers as to whether a child is born smart or whether intelligence can be taught. I believe that a little of both is true. In my case, I am told that I was a very smart, precocious child from the very beginning. Before the age of two, I could talk and spell quite well. One story is that in an attempt to break me from drinking from a bottle, my babysitter hid it on a windowsill under a shade. One sunny day, seeing the silhouette of the bottle under the shade and having heard others spell the word *bottle*, I said, "I want my bottle," spelling out the word. So, are smart people born that way or can they be made? I believe a little of both is true.

Doctors and scientists agree that long-term memories begin to develop in early childhood, around three or four years old, and that although our short-term memory begins to wane as we age, our long-term memories tend to last. My earliest memories are just as the scientists say. I remember our small family, chasing the American dream.

To give credit to the theory that smartness is often inherited, the smartest person I knew at an early age was my father. His name was

James Monroe Ford (yes, after the fifth president of the United States), and he was born and raised in La Plata, Maryland, in rural Charles County. It is believed that his family members were descendants of slaves who belonged to George Washington or to George Washington's family, some of whom carried Washington as their last name. Therefore, a lot of the boys in Daddy's family were named after presidents of the United States. After slavery, Daddy's ancestors moved across the Potomac River to Southern Maryland and became sharecroppers. Daddy worked for one of those sharecroppers in his youth.

Daddy graduated from La Plata High School at the top of his class during a time when many black men never finished high school. He enlisted in the army and served for two years at the end of World War II. He was trained as a technical mechanic and worked on army jeeps and electrical equipment. He used to say that he "didn't like that man's army," so he didn't stay beyond the required two years.

After the service, he moved to Washington, DC; met my mother while she was still in high school; and got married. Together, they had two daughters—my older sister Valeria and me, Gwynette. My father named us after his ancestors. We were teased a lot as youngsters about our relatively unusual names. Therefore, like most kids from "the hood," we adopted nicknames. Valeria became "Vee," and I became "Nettie." Valeria was born three years before me. She, too, is very smart and has a Ph.D. in her own right, which lends itself to the hereditary argument.

My mother was smart too, but in a different way: street smart. Part of the first generation in her family to be born in DC, my mother was the fifth child born to Fred and Bellinger Wright, who moved to DC from Jim Crow South Carolina in the mid-1920s for what they thought would be a better life for their children. My mother's birth name was Gloria Etta Wright. She chose to get married right out of high school, to her mother's displeasure, as a large percentage of black kids did during those days, especially in DC, when people said that you could get a "good government job" without a college degree. She bought into that.

That was also an era when men were the breadwinners, so that's where she placed her bet: on finding a good man and getting married, although she always said that she planned to work, too, and she did. She thought that a two-income household would get her where she wanted to go in life, so that's the road she took. She married James Monroe Ford and had two girls.

I remember my father being very smart in math, which may be the reason my sister and I later tested near the genius level in math. The truth is, given his race and the lack of opportunities for black men during the Jim Crow era, like many smart black men of his time, he was relegated to getting a job at the post office—a good government job. However, having served in the army as a technical mechanic, he was entrepreneurial enough to do mechanical and electrical odd jobs as a side hustle, such as fixing cars and TVs and small electrical appliances for neighbors, family, and referrals, to make a pretty good second income. By most accounts, our little family was better off financially than many in our neighborhood. As a family, we were on our way to achieving the American dream.

I was my daddy's tomboy and little helper. At about three years old or so, because I had undiagnosed juvenile arthritis and couldn't stand for long periods of time, I would sit on the curb next to Daddy's toolbox and hand off small tools and screws, as requested. Daddy's favorite beverage (and mine) was beer, and I was known to say, "I can drink a whole can of beer. If you don't believe me, just ask my daddy, or better yet, just watch me." Then I would chugalug on a can. Daddy taught me my numbers and how to add them, and I would practice counting and adding while helping him.

TIME CHANGES THINGS

But time passes and things change, and so do our dreams. My parents' marriage began to crumble. I remember Daddy being home less often and both parents staying out and coming home late. I remember phone calls where people would hang up immediately when I would answer the phone. "Hello, hello. Who is this?" And then there were arguments—loud arguments and tough-to-hear arguments.

One day, I was on the wrong end of a beer can. My dad came home late, after dinner was over. He asked my mother to fix him a plate. She did. To him, his dinner seemed cold, so he said to her, "This is cold. Can you heat it up?"

I often got bloody noses as a child, and no one knew why. Mom and Dad would often place cold beer cans on my forehead to get the nosebleed to stop. With me on her hip and Daddy treating one of my bloody noses, my mother dumped the plate onto his lap. Having a can of cold beer in his hand, Daddy hurled its contents toward her. But it missed her and got me, getting beer all over me.

That incident and others that followed were turning points in my life that I attribute to my theory that high achievement often depends on how motivated a person is to achieve against all odds, good and bad. That incident contributed to the end of the Ford marriage and the beginning of some difficult days and years for my mother.

My mom and dad separated in 1956, when I was five years old and just about to start kindergarten. I had just returned from a trip with my maternal grandmother to South Carolina. I guess all the drama took place while the two of us were gone. Because my granddad worked on the railroad and my grandma was his widow, she received two free passes to go anywhere on the train once a year. She would take one of her thirteen grandchildren on a trip with her to visit her half-brother, Sankie, in South Carolina, just before we started school. That year, it was my turn.

That trip was my first up-close-and-personal encounter with "Mr. Jim Crow." *Jim Crow* was the name given to a group of laws passed in the Southern states, designed to keep blacks separated from whites—a segregation tactic. At one of the train stops was the first time I had to drink from a "colored" drinking fountain and use a "colored" toilet. When I attempted to play with a little white girl my age on the train, her mother took great offense and pulled her away from me. My grandmother pulled me back closer to her and set me down, as if I had done something wrong. I didn't know what I had done!

I didn't think much about the incident, for I was only five years old. But that was all my grandmother talked about when we got back to DC: Nettie's encounter with "Mr. Jim Crow." The story my grandmother told seemed odd to me, because I didn't remember meeting a man by the name of Jim Crow. To me, discrimination and bigotry in DC wasn't as overt and blatant as it was in the Deep South. It was more subtle and undercover, so I didn't have a clue what was going on. I was only five years old!

When I returned from that trip with my grandmother, my mother announced that we were moving and that my father was not coming with us, and that was that. No explanation, no discussion. Although I missed him, I got over it quickly. I didn't miss the arguments and the fighting.

My dad came to visit us about once a month, paid his child support, and checked our homework. He was happy that his daughters were smart and always told us that we could be anything we wanted to be. He never told us that there would be limitations placed on us because we were female, or black for that matter. He loved his two daughters dearly. We meant the world to him, and he was so proud of us.

We weren't allowed to discuss anything about our parents' marital status at school. Mama didn't want anyone at school "in our business." She didn't check "separated" on any of the forms that came in from school, either. I often wondered why not. Now that I think about it, I think she was right, because back then there was still a stigma about broken homes, and teachers and administrators often treated children from broken homes differently, as if they were less than. At least, that's how it seemed to me.

Mama moved the three of us into a large one-bedroom apartment in Northeast Washington, on 20th Street. The apartment was two blocks from where the Washington Stadium (the future home of the

Washington Redskins) would be built, which eventually became RFK (Robert F. Kennedy) Stadium after his assassination. The bedroom was big enough to fit a large bed that my mother and I shared, a twin bed that my sister slept in alone, and two dresser drawers, plus closet space. It was a bit cramped for three females. The three of us shared one bathroom, with very few of the arguments that you would normally attribute to three females sharing one bathroom. My mother saw to that. My sister and I had an allotted time in the bathroom, as we weren't teenagers yet.

My mother was a tough cookie who believed in tough love. She made it very clear that she needed to work in order to keep a roof over our heads and food in our bellies. Times were hard, but Mama made a way out of no way, as she had learned from her mother. She worked hard so we could have. We didn't have much (as Stevie Wonder sings about), but she taught us to be grateful for the things we did have.

LATCHKEY KIDS IN THE 1960S

My sister and I were latchkey kids long before there was a name for it. We didn't have formal babysitters, but we had each other, our immediate and extended families, our neighbors, our school family (with teachers and administrators who really cared back then), and our church family, all of whom really looked out for the Ford girls. We were on our own until Mama got home, so we made the best of it.

The kids in our neighborhood walked to Henry T. Blow Elementary School together, literally a mile, from 20th and C to 19th and Benning Road, NE, in a section that is now called Capitol Hill Extended but was far from what it is today in the late 1950s and early '60s. I guess you would call us free-range kids today, as were most of the kids in our neighborhood. We walked around alone or in small groups to and from school, to the movies, or to the one recreation center that existed in our neighborhood.

Mama worked full-time as a currency examiner at the US Bureau of

Engraving and Printing, the agency within the Treasury Department that prints US currency and postage stamps. Over her thirty-five years of employment there, she worked in both divisions (currency and stamps) and on every major shift: the day shift (7 a.m. to 3:30 p.m.), the evening shift (3:30 p.m. to 11 p.m.), and the graveyard shift (11 p.m. to 7 a.m.). She also worked a lot of overtime, whenever she could get it, especially when new currency and stamps would come out. She did that so she could do the best by her girls.

The three of us looked out for each other, although Mama often reminded us that *she* was the boss. Mama looked out for her girls, and we looked out for Mama. And literally, sometimes we were her lookouts.

My sister and I didn't need an alarm clock. When Mama worked the day shift and we heard the door shut at 6:15 a.m., we knew it was time to get up to get ready for school. But first, we would run to our bedroom window and watch Mama cross the street and walk to the corner of 21st and C Streets, most of the time in the dark, to catch "her ride" with her coworker Johnny—carpooling, as it was later called. It was a nice ride, too, a "Deuce and a Quarter" (a Buick Electra 225), up-to-date and very, very clean. We would watch out for Johnny's car to turn onto C Street and pick Mama up for the ride through Capitol Hill to the Bureau. Then we knew she was safe, and on her way to work. There was no subway back then. My mother was "chauffeured" to work in a nice clean ride, with two lookouts or wing-girls. We could give the Secret Service a run for their money.

Then it was time to get ready for school. With a combination of some new clothes that Mama got from working overtime, after getting them out of the layaway (pay as you go) from Morton's and Lerner's Specialty Stores (those would be equivalent to Target and JCPenney today); hand-me-downs from family members and friends; and finds from the swop meet, we were the best-dressed kids and the envy of our neighborhood—which often got us into trouble with the bullies in the hood. Sometimes my mother dressed us alike, often buying us the same dress in our different sizes. Since we weren't twins, eventually she stopped that practice.

On weekends, Mama would wash, starch, and iron our pretty little dresses for the week and line them up one by one on the doorknobs and doorframes. All we had to do was pick out a dress to wear for the day and, after bathing, put it on. We were not allowed to wear slacks, jeans, or tennis shoes to school back then.

One day, one of my teachers pulled me aside and asked me, "Who does your mother's laundry? You're always so nice and clean."

I answered with a puzzled look, "My mother does her *own* laundry."

Then the teacher said, "I sure wish I could get your mother to do my laundry!"

I gave her that look that says, *In your dreams!*

The same thing was true on Sunday for Sunday school. The night before, Mama would wash our hair, straighten it with a straightening comb heated over the stove in the kitchen, and curl it in Shirley Temple curls for the next day. We wore black patent leather shoes (Mary Janes, they were called) that Mama would polish with Vaseline (yes, Vaseline). We wore them with snow-white ankle socks with lace around them. What a sight to see—starched dresses that stood out about three feet, with little skinny legs coming out of them, with white ankle socks.

Like many black families in the South, we spent Sundays in Sunday school and church services, often followed by a trip to my Aunt Bernice's house, by streetcar, where my grandma lived. Grandma prepared, for all of us, a soul food dinner of fried chicken, collard greens, macaroni and cheese, homemade hot rolls, and sweet potato pie or chocolate cake for dessert. When money was tight, our aunt Bernice, who was in charge (superintendent) of our Sunday school, would make her famous Jell-O mold with fruit cocktail in it. But when money was good, she would send us to the *Highs* store or the *DGS* to get vanilla ice cream to go with Grandma's cakes and/or pies.

During the week, Vee and I obeyed Mama's rules so that we could enjoy the freedoms she gave us. Some kids weren't even able to do what we could do. We came straight home from school and did our homework plus all of our chores.

Sometimes, when Mama would work overtime, on weekends, she would give us money to catch the bus, free-range, to see the Motown Revue and other shows at the now-infamous Howard Theatre—but we were only allowed to go to the matinee. Mama occasionally went to the evening or midnight shows on a hot date, so that was definitely out for us. I particularly enjoyed going to the Saturday matinees to see the Motown Revue, featuring such stars as the Temptations, the Supremes, Mary Wells, Marvin Gaye, Stevie Wonder, and the Commodores, who were all under the Motown label. Sometimes we would also catch James Brown, Aretha Franklin, Gladys Knight and the Pips, and other famous stars of the 1960s at the Howard.

The ticket prices were three to five dollars for the matinee—not bad compared to concert ticket prices today. And what a concert you got! To see my absolute favorite, the Motown Revue, with all those stars, all at the same time, for five dollars, was like dying and going to Motown Heaven.

When Mama would come home tired from working all that overtime, we would cheer her up by giving her our own version of the Motown Revue. She would sit in a chair in the living room or dining room, and Vee and I would sing and mimic such tunes as "Stop! In the Name of Love" and "Where Did Our Love Go," by the Supremes. We knew all the words and all of their moves. We even had our own little singing group called the Valettes, with two of our cousins, and we would sing outside of our aunt's house on Benning Road, trying to get discovered. I had lead roles on two of my favorite songs: "I Met Him on Sunday," and "Mama Said," both sung by the Shirelles. People walking by must have thought we were crazy or something!

When the Howard Theatre was dark, we were allowed to go roller-skating Uptown to Kalorama Road, in an area of town that is now called Adams Morgan. We were also allowed to stop off at the famous black eateries of the time, such as Ben's Chili Bowl, Eddie Leonard's, or

Florida Avenue Grill on the way home for a bite to eat. What we didn't eat, we took home as a snack for later.

My mother ran a tight ship, though. We weren't allowed to hang out in the street after dark and had to be in the house before the streetlights came on. And we were not allowed to act like groupies and hang around the stage door at the Howard Theatre to meet the stars and ask for autographs or do other forbidden things, such as going out with or going off with any of the stars. A lot of girls did that, and that's how some of them got "knocked up" (pregnant).

I literally watched the Washington Stadium being built and could see the lights from our bedroom window. It was originally the home of the Washington Senators baseball team. My friends and I were issued something called a *knothole card*, which allowed the neighborhood kids to enter the stadium after the sixth inning to see the end of the baseball games. Five to six of us (both boys and girls) from my neighborhood would occasionally go and check out the Senators. It was something to do during Washington's hot summer evenings.

We formed a little club called the Knothole Card Club. That was the first social organization I belonged to, and I was one of the ringleaders, even though I was a girl. I even made outfits for us to wear to the games and other outings. I guess you could say that our club was our little gang—a gang about fun, not violence. It certainly beat the other kind of gangs we knew about.

We eventually extended our club activities outside of baseball games and were bold enough to venture out of our neighborhood to engage in other activities, such as going to a movie, on a boat ride, to a local beach, or to an amusement park. We actually organized a trip where we took public transportation (a two-hour bus ride) from the inner city to the rural suburbs of Maryland to go to a newly desegregated amusement park named Glen Echo, where blacks had once been banned. Some nerve!

We were totally oblivious to the fact that we were engaging in a civil rights activity. We were all of about nine or ten years old. White folk stared us down, but we didn't care. All we knew was that we wanted to do what other children in our region did to have fun during the summer. The long bus ride was worth it, and we had a lot of fun.

In 1961, the Washington Redskins (now the Washington Commanders) moved into the stadium during the fall and early winter months. You could hear the roar of the crowd when the Redskins made a touchdown, and we would have to guess or ask fans leaving the stadium who won the game, because the home games were blacked out on TV during those days.

"Hey, lady, did the Skins win? What was the score?" Sometimes we got an answer and sometimes we didn't. Some people were stuck up and snooty, and some people weren't. I do remember that most of the patrons were white. Some of the women even wore fur coats to the games.

Washington and its surrounding "Redskins Territory" loved their Skins, and the Ford girls—all three of us, Mama included—grew to love the team too, though we called them the Burgundy and Gold. On game days, our neighborhood was full of cars, some parked illegally on our block and in the alley. We didn't care. We didn't have a car to have to worry about a parking space.

Mama, Vee, and I were as close to being a team as three females could get. As with any team, there were disagreements and arguments (three females living under the same roof, LOL), but our objective was always the same: to win at this thing called Life. Mama was the quarterback, and we were her rookies. You talk about Beast Mode! Mama was Beast Mode and Survivor Mode. She was a survivor long before Beyonce was even born.

Mama, the quarterback, made it quite clear that we'd better not drop or fumble the ball, if you get my drift. She didn't push too hard, like some parents, about school, however. She knew that could be a turnoff. I think we did well in school just to please her, not wanting to disappoint her.

My sister and I had chores, and lots of them. We had to work for what we wanted by running errands, babysitting, and doing odd jobs. Mama, the quarterback, told us what to do. My sister, being the oldest, was the wide receiver; she caught all of the responsibilities of being a big sister. Her number-one job was to look out for her little sister, a job that she sometimes found difficult. Who wants a little sister always tagging along everywhere? However, she did that job and did it well.

My sister made sure I got to and from school, that I did my homework, and that I didn't look at too much television. That last one was the hardest. I loved staying up late looking at TV. My favorite shows were the doctor shows: *Ben Casey* and *Marcus Welby, MD*. Early on, I wanted to be a medical doctor.

On our all-female family team, I was the running back. I ran to the store for my mother, my sister, and a lot of the neighbors, sometimes up to three times in one day. The closest grocery store was about six blocks away, and I knew all the shortcuts. It was on one of my runs to the store that darkness caught me one evening. I was almost raped.

A teenage boy I had never seen before, who was much older and stronger than I was, grabbed me from behind, putting me in a headlock around the throat with one hand and putting his other hand over my mouth. He said, "Don't you know better than being out after dark? Bad things can happen." He pulled me backward closer to him and started to drag me toward some bushes. When he took his hand off of my mouth, while pulling me backward to do God knows what, petrified and shaking, I said, "I was just going to the store for my mother. Please don't hurt me." I started to pray out loud. "Help me, Jesus!"

That strange boy must have felt sorry for me or something. He pushed me forward and let me go. As he ran away into the darkness, he said, "Don't get caught out here after dark, or something bad can happen to you!"

I must have talked or prayed my way out of that one. Holding my throat, I ran all the way home. I told my family and neighbors about the incident, and I never went to the store after dark again. We chalked it up that I had dodged a bullet that night, and that was that: no big deal.

Although I didn't get a good look at the guy, when out with family and friends, I was always on the lookout for him, hoping we could get some "street justice," especially my mother, who said if we ever saw him, she would "ring his neck." I never saw him again. However, even to this day, I rarely go out at night alone, especially to the grocery store.

A TURNING POINT: THE INAUGURATION OF PRESIDENT JOHN F. KENNEDY

Just as 1956 was the year that changed my family's composition forever with the separation of my mom and dad, the one year in the 1960s that had the greatest impact on me and my little family was probably 1961. That was the year John F. Kennedy was inaugurated and became president of the United States. Although it took her a while, that inauguration helped my mother move from very tough times, barely making ends meet, toward the lower middle class and closer to achieving her and my American dream.

Living in DC, adults and children are exposed to national politics daily. Unlike most Americans, especially those in the Deep South or on the West Coast, we get a daily dose of national news and politics. Often, in DC, our local news is national news. National figures and politicians are household names and feel like members of the family. The date in 1961 that I hold near and dear to my heart is January 19, 1961, the day before the inauguration of President John F. Kennedy.

It is a custom that the DC public school system, the DC government, and the federal government are closed on Inauguration Day every four years, as our city hosts the festivities. The day before, in 1961, DC was abuzz with the upcoming inauguration of young John F. Kennedy and the hope that he would bring change to our nation and to our city. Frank Sinatra and his buddies were throwing a fabulous pre-inauguration party for the Kennedys at the DC Armory, which was located just two blocks from where we lived, directly across the street from the new DC stadium. Everyone in our neighborhood was talking about that party, wishing they had an invitation. But something else happened on January 19, 1961. A nor'easter snowstorm hit Washington, DC that morning, dropping eight inches of snow on the nation's capital and threatening the cancelation of President Kennedy's inauguration parade and other festivities. That is a lot of snow for DC, given its narrow streets and public transit system, which was without a subway at that time.

A task force was put in place to clear the snow from the streets and get the parade route ready for after the inauguration the next day. DC public schools were closed (we got the news by TV not to report to school), and the federal government closed early. That meant that my mother, who worked at the Bureau of Engraving, which is located at 14th and C Streets, SW, near the parade route, was let go early, around noon. It was snowing like crazy at the time, about one to two inches an hour—known as a *whiteout*. For some reason, she did not have "her ride" that day. When she got outside, she knew a bus would be long in coming, and she wanted to get home to her girls. So, she hailed a cab. "Taxi, taxi!"

Mama jumped into a cab, and it headed down Independence Avenue for the short ride to our apartment. Traffic was heavy with cars and buses, since all the Feds were let out at the same time, yet the snow was still coming down at a heavy clip. All of a sudden, the cab began to skid and—bam!—collided into the back of a bus. The cab door that my mother was sitting next to flung open, and she was thrown from the cab onto the street and onto her back.

Although she refused to go to the hospital—she wanted to get home to her girls—she suffered a back injury that led to medical treatments and eventually back surgery. Lengthy lawsuits followed with the cab company and the bus company, and although it took several years, she would finally get a settlement. Eventually, we were able to move out of that one-bedroom apartment and on to a better life in the lower middle class that so many black federal government workers in DC were able to achieve. During those years before and after Mama's settlement, several major events took place in my life, both good and bad, that helped shape me, mold me, and motivate me to aspire to and acquire the status in life that I enjoy today.

President Kennedy's Inauguration. Photo taken by US Army Signal Corp

TWO
BULLIED FOR BEING SMART

FROM 1956 TO 1961, I attended Henry T. Blow Elementary School, located on the corner of 19th and Benning Road, NE, within the public school system of Washington, DC. To me, it was a wonderful place, not for its structure (the typical old red brick schoolhouse) but because of the teaching, learning, and love I received inside. I had wonderful, loving, and nurturing teachers who cared about their students and wanted them to learn. My teachers were surrogate mothers, and I wanted to please them by doing well.

Things were wonderful from kindergarten through the fourth grade. The students could have cared less that the school was majority black. We just learned all we could. All of my teachers were black, and we were all equal in their eyes. That was black Washington, DC, back then—segregated Washington. Even though it was after Brown v. Board of Education (1954), which desegregated public schools, DC students went to the schools in their neighborhood, and mine was mostly black.

We walked to school. There was no school busing yet. If your neighborhood was mostly black, your school was mostly black. True integration hadn't taken place because of the segregated housing and neighborhoods.

When I started kindergarten, my sister helped me with all of my schoolwork. She drilled me in math and in spelling, and we both often got straight As. It was never a competition, though, since we were three years apart. We were just known as "those smart Ford girls."

We came straight home from school and did our homework and then some. Because we didn't have a lot of store-bought games, we often made games out of learning. Vee would play the teacher, and I would be the student. I was always two to three years ahead of my classmates in math, and my math test scores were through the roof. To the delight of all my teachers, I placed in the ninetieth percentile or higher in math compared to my peers—"near genius," as some people would say. My IQ, as a result, was also very high.

SUMMERS IN DC

During the summers, before we were old enough to work, we were not allowed to hang out in the street other than going to Vacation Bible School at our church, to the local recreation center to swim, or to a specific show at the Howard Theatre. During the day, we would practice spelling, read books, and do math problems. Our childhood friends often called us bookworms, but we didn't care.

Early on, some of our favorite toys were paper dolls. Many of them we made ourselves. We collected hundreds of dresses from pattern books given to us by a fabric-store owner in our neighborhood. We made our paper dolls homes out of telephone books, decorating the rooms with pictures of furniture that we cut out of Sears catalogs. Later on, our Aunt Bernice taught us how to sew, so we turned our love for paper doll clothes into making our own clothes with a sewing machine that our mother was able to purchase for us.

Thus began our love of clothes and fine furnishings, which would play a major role in our lives later on and provide great motivation for us to achieve. For me, daydreaming was my way of visualizing what my life could be. I often say that I daydreamed my way out of the ghetto.

We also danced and listened to music on a new, modern-day stereo with portable speakers that Mama bought with over-time money. That stereo was a feminine, early version of a portable component set, in that it was salmon and white and stood on a metal stand. We would listen to Mama's jazz albums by Ramsey Louis, Ahmad Jamal, Nancy Wilson, Gloria Lynn, and Dakota Staton. Some of my favorite smooth jazz tunes were "In Crowd," by Ramsey Lewis, "Poinciana," by Ahmad Jamal, "I'm Glad There is You," by Gloria Lynn and "The Very Thought of You," by Nancy Wilson. Vee and I would dance to a nice little collection of 45s by our favorite Motown and other R&B stars that we were able to purchase from Waxie Maxie's Record Store with our baby-sitting money.

One day when no one was home, someone broke into our apartment and stole Mama's then new stereo set, but left the records. We have always believed that the thief was someone we knew, someone who knew of Mama's new acquisition. So, what did Mama do? She went out and bought another stereo set just like it and changed the locks on the front door with stronger ones. Our life in the ghetto was no cake walk.

My sister and I would also borrow a typewriter and practice book from a neighbor we admired who lived across the street. Her name was Shirley. She was young and beautiful (*hip and fly*, we would say). She got a good federal government job as a secretary after graduating from high school. She was a great role model for the young girls in the neighborhood. She got married and moved away, but she left her typewriter with her mother, who continued to allow us to borrow it. We thought we could get jobs as typists someday, and that was a big deal to us back then.

One summer night, we heard Shirley's mother screaming and sobbing. We ran to the front window to see what all the noise was about. We saw some of our neighbors come outside and go into Shirley's mother's house. My mother put on shoes and also ran across the street to see what was going on, telling us to stay in the house. She returned with tears streaming down her face, telling us to get out of the window and go to our bedroom.

Everyone was wondering what was happening. Neighbors in our building came to our apartment to talk to my mother, and we overheard them saying that Shirley was dead. She died trying to give herself an abortion because she and her husband weren't financially ready to have a baby. The neighborhood was devastated. A young, beautiful woman was gone too soon. Although she was married, she took drastic steps to end a pregnancy. Abortions were illegal back then, and unfortunately, some women did stupid things to end a pregnancy.

When Shirley died, my mother had a serious talk with Valeria and me about the birds and the bees, about not having sex too early, not getting pregnant until we were married, and about life's choices. For us, unfortunately, we had a real-life example to relate to. Shirley was gone at the age of twenty-four.

Later that week, my mother and many of our neighbors who knew her went to Shirley's funeral and the repast at her mother's apartment. When my mother returned, she told us that Shirley's mother wanted us to keep Shirley's typewriter. She did not want it returned, as it would be a painful reminder of what had happened to her daughter. Instead, she wanted us to keep it and use it to sharpen our typing skills, which would help us become marketable in the workplace. That act of kindness really paid off for us, later.

DEALING WITH BULLIES

My sister and I finally separated educationally when she graduated from elementary school and moved on to Eliot Junior High School just a couple of blocks away from where we lived. The principal and teachers there were excellent. But that's when serious trouble began. You see, back then, the DC public schools had a track system. Based on test scores, in junior high if not earlier, students were placed in basic, regular, college prep, or honors tracks. The tracking system was controversial and wasn't popular with a lot of parents, because your child's destiny was often based on where they were placed.

My sister was placed on the honors track in junior high, and that did not sit well with some of the other children who were not. That is when the bullying began. She and her peers in honors were often targeted for bullying. I remember one incident where graffiti was placed on the sidewalk outside the school, poking fun at several honors students and my sister and her friends in particular. There was talk about fighting and "ass-whipping."

My mother went up to the school with a baseball bat to talk to the principal, Mrs. Dotson (the bullies called her Turkey-Leg Dotson), about getting it to stop. Mama and a couple of the other parents made it quite clear that they weren't having it (the bullying), and word got out, especially about Mama and the baseball bat. I think that some of the bullying stopped because some of the kids doing the bullying were afraid that my mother and the other moms were going to take matters into their own hands and hand out some ass-whippings of their own.

As for me, my troubles started in fifth grade. Henry T. Blow Elementary School was closed down, to be demolished and rebuilt, and my knothole card buddies and I were transferred to another elementary school, even farther from where I lived, in a neighborhood that was much worse than the one we lived in closer to the stadium.

Of all my friends, I lived the farthest from the school, at least a mile and a quarter away. We would often walk home from school together until each of us would reach our home, and I would walk the last four blocks or so alone. One of my male friends, Darren, whom I had known since kindergarten, became a patrol boy, and we passed by his corner each day.

Mrs. Wilson was my fifth-grade teacher. She was wonderful. She was strikingly beautiful and very smart. She had beautiful chocolate brown skin that looked flawless and dark brown shoulder-length hair that she wore tightly waved and curled. She had beautiful clothes that

I admired. Most of the boys swooned over her. She encouraged us to do our best and mentored those of us who wanted to learn. But we also had some knuckleheads who didn't want to learn anything and were disrespectful to her and disruptive in class.

The fifth grade was an important one. I remember having a lot of homework, assessments, and standardized tests that year. I was doing very well, especially in math and spelling. One day in the late springtime, Mrs. Wilson explained to us that our standardized tests were back. She explained that she would talk to each of our parents as to how we did at the last PTA meeting.

At the end of the school day, Mrs. Wilson asked me to stay after school. I wondered what I had done bad that day, but she told me that I hadn't done anything wrong. Then she let the rest of the class go home. She sat me down close to her desk and asked me questions about what I thought about the test—and then straight-up asked me how I had come up with my answers. Most of her questions focused on the math section. She seemed to be intrigued by my results.

At first, I thought she felt that I had cheated or something. I answered all of her questions honestly. Back then, on the math portion, we didn't have, nor could we have used, calculators. We were given blank paper to work our math problems out on, and we turned our worksheets in with the test when we were done. How in the world could we cheat?

During our meeting, Mrs. Wilson pulled out my worksheets and had me go over them with her. I showed her how I got my answers. The test questions were multiple-choice. I had learned how to check my answers. With all that practicing during the summer months, I had also learned how to work really fast. I was able to finish the math test and then go back and check many of my answers by doing the problems backward, such as checking the subtraction problems by adding the answer to the bottom number to get the top number and vice versa for adding, and checking division problems by multiplying.

I had also learned how to do some math problems that were on the test that most children my age didn't know how to do yet, and that we hadn't learned in school yet, such as difficult fractions and a little algebra, so I knew I had done well. Mrs. Wilson told me that I had done an *excellent* job and had only missed a few of the questions in math on that standardized test. She said that was *fantastic*. To me, it was no big deal, although I was proud of myself.

"That is very rare," she said. "Almost unheard of in a school in DC." She told me how proud she was of me and said, "Can I give you a hug?" She hugged me and said that the principal would be in touch with me. *For what?* I asked myself. She told me not to talk to anyone about what we talked about. I happily gathered up my books and left.

When I got outside, to my surprise, about twenty-five students, and several from my class, were waiting for me. I knew I was in trouble. They began to surround me. Sheila, the tallest, biggest, and oldest girl in our class, appeared to be the ringleader.

"What did you and Mrs. Wilson talk about, huh? You think you the teacher's pet, don't you? You think you're cute, don't you?"

Most African Americans know what happens after that. They surrounded me; other children started to gather around, and the pushing started. I decided to just hold on to my books. I felt someone push me from behind toward Sheila, and someone pushed her toward me, and of course there were those dreaded words: "Fight, fight." Kids came from out of nowhere. It was like a mob scene.

I held on to my books and just started walking. I didn't know what to do: I had no cell phone and few friends. Every few blocks, the pushing and shoving would continue. Other students would join in and drop off, join in and drop off. Sheila would push, and I would just back up. She would push me, and someone would push me from behind toward her.

At one point, someone pushed me so hard, I fell to the ground on my knees. Blood started dripping out of my knees, and my books went flying. While on the ground, I felt a foot stomp me on the back, and I felt a kick to my side. I got into a fetal position to gather myself while lying on the ground. Then I picked up my books, got to my feet, and started walking again. I didn't know what else to do. I figured if I just kept walking, somehow, I would make it home.

I remembered what I learned in Sunday School and from Martin Luther King Jr.: "Turn the other cheek." I decided not to fight back. I just started to pray to myself, *Lord, please help me!*

Finally, one of my knothole card friends, Candy Proctor, came out of a corner store and joined me. She walked part of the way with me. "Why don't y'all leave her alone?" she asked the others. "What has she done to you?"

We finally came upon Darren's street corner, where he was the patrol boy. He stopped the crowd at the corner. "What's going on here?" he asked.

I walked up close to him, and he said, "I see you're in trouble."

I said, "Please call my sister!"

He said, "I'll try to hold them back."

He let Candy and I go across the street first, and we walked quickly ahead.

Candy said, "I'll call Valeria," and she dropped out of the crowd when we got to the block where she lived. Somehow, I made it a couple more blocks alone. The pushing and shoving had become less frequent, and the crowd was down to about fifteen kids. By then, I was a couple of blocks from home and close to my sister's school. I wasn't about to fight Sheila! She was twice my size.

Then, lo and behold, around the corner from our apartment building came Valeria. She seemed bigger than life to me at that moment, and to those kids. She walked up to the crowd and said, "What's going on here?" She said to Sheila, "You are twice her size, young lady. If you want to fight somebody, fight me!"

Valeria proceeded to take off her glasses, give them to me, and put up her fists to fight Sheila. The crowd took off running, including Sheila, and Vee and I took off running in the opposite direction, all the way home. We started laughing when we turned the corner and I asked how she knew I was in trouble.

She said she had come straight home from school and had gotten two calls, one from Candy Proctor and one from Darren, my friends since kindergarten, saying that I was in big trouble and to please come help. I will always be grateful to Vee for getting me out of a jam that day. My big sister came through for me, and I will always be thankful to her for that. I cleaned up my knees and waited for Mama to come home.

Candy, Darren, and I, on that day, became friends for life. Candy and I wound up going to the same high school. Darren and I, although we went to different high schools, became like brother and sister. We even went out to a few dances together while in high school, platonically. Candy is now a retired schoolteacher, and Darren's family is in the undertaking business in Atlanta. How fitting!

We told Mama what happened when she got home from work. She blew a gasket. She immediately called my father and asked him to take care of the matter. She knew that my father would be more diplomatic and that she would probably go to that school and go postal on somebody. "I am sick of those hoodlums messing with my children. Lord, don't let me have to hurt someone else's child!" she said.

Since Mama had never notified the school system that she and my dad were separated and had insisted that my sister and I never mention their separation to the teachers and administrators, she turned to my dad. For this situation, she knew she could depend on him, so she asked him to step up and step in.

The next morning, which was a Friday, Daddy took off from his job, picked me up in his car, and drove me to school. My mother had called ahead to tell them we were coming, and by the time we got there, the gossip mill was at work and everyone knew what had transpired. Although we went to my classroom first, Mrs. Wilson to us directly to the principal's office. I don't remember seeing Sheila in class that day when Daddy and I arrived. While escorting us to the principal's office, Mrs. Wilson apologized on behalf of my class by saying how sorry she was about what had happened and that things would be worked out.

Mrs. Demond, the principal, ushered us into her office as soon as we arrived. She also apologized for what had happened to me the day before. My father, though polite, was quite stern about not wanting me to be in an unsafe, dangerous, and abusive environment, with bullies who didn't respect themselves, much less others, especially since I had to walk so far alone to get home from school.

Mrs. Demond agreed and said she had a solution, something she had been thinking about since the test scores had come out. She told Daddy that if he and Mama would agree, she would recommend that the school system send me to the gifted and talented honors program at River Terrace Elementary, way across the Anacostia River, further out Benning Road, which would be a bus ride away. However, she said, that could not happen until sixth grade. Mrs. Demond insisted that I go straight home that Friday and think about it. The commitment from me would involve succeeding in an honors environment, with children who had been in honors since the third grade, and to the bus ride by public transportation that it would take for me to get to and from school. That made for a tough decision.

It didn't take my family long to make that decision, however. Daddy and I talked all the way home, and Mama and I talked at length over the weekend. When I returned to school that Monday, my mother and I notified Mrs. Wilson and Mrs. Demond that I wanted to be transferred to River Terrace Elementary School's honors program for sixth grade. Mom insisted that I stay in Mrs. Wilson's fifth grade until the end of the school year, which was just a few weeks away.

Sheila was disciplined for the bullying incident and suspended for a week but stayed in the class as well, which was quite awkward. I ignored her and the others for the rest of the school year. To me, she didn't exist, and I finished the school year and continued to do well, getting straight A's at the end of the term.

To this day, I have no idea whatever became of Sheila. I don't know what they said or did to her during her suspension, but somehow, I made it through to the end of the school year without another major bullying incident. Somebody was looking out for me: Mrs. Wilson,

Mrs. Demond, Darren, my dad, my mom, the Good Lord, or perhaps all of them.

So, what did I learn about life from that experience? I learned that no matter how smart you are or how hard you try to do the right thing, you *will* get knocked down and life *will* kick you around. When that happens, you have to pick yourself up, brush yourself off, and keep on walking. I would later learn the French term: *"C'est la vie!* That's life!"

THREE
THE TRANSITION TO HONORS: RIVER TERRACE TO ELIOT

MY RIVER TERRACE EXPERIENCE

IN THE FALL of 1962, I was transferred to River Terrace Elementary School. I joined the sixth-grade honors class as the new kid in the program. Although I quickly made friends with some of the girls and boys, deep down, I never felt as though I was a fully accepted member of the class. Many of them, having been identified as gifted and placed in the program as early as the third grade, had made strong bonds long before I arrived, and I believed that the teacher, Ms. Coney, felt put upon to accept a new girl. I felt that, subconsciously, she took it out on my grades, especially in the subjective subjects, such as English and creative writing. She already knew and/or had taught many of her students before.

Ms. Coney called me "girly," as if she didn't want to learn my name. I would tell her all the time, "My name is Gwynette Ford: Gwynette, G-W-Y-N-E-T-T-E." In addition, she seemed to favor the boys in the class. She pushed certain ones of them and gave them special attention, especially in math.

Even though we were in the sixth grade, we were smart enough to know that, back then, our society valued the worth of a man more than a woman, and that a race was often judged by the accomplishments of its men. Even the Civil Rights Movement, which was raging at the time, was led by black men; women were relegated to administrative and support roles, such as providing entertainment, performing secretarial duties, and preparing meals for the speakers and the marchers. Women did not hold high leadership positions in the movement. I understood and accepted that, but that didn't mean I liked it.

I knew, from that honors class in particular, that I was just as smart as some of those pickle-headed boys and smarter than many of the girls. In addition, some of the real smart boys were so stuck on themselves and so arrogant, I knew even back then that they would have a hard time getting along in life. Several of the girls were cool, and I hung out with two of them in particular outside the classroom: Gail Gray and Sheila Mabry. We three became good friends.

I was determined to graduate from that program, and I did excel—especially in, you guessed it, math. I will always love math because there is one correct answer, no one can deny that you got it right, and right is right. A lot of the kids in that class, especially one boy, Kendrick, always turned to me for help in math, often even copying off my paper. He wouldn't stop copying off my paper, so one time I gave him the wrong answers, then quickly changed my answers to the right ones. That stopped that practice.

I must admit, even at that young age, I got great delight and joy when I got my math papers back with all the answers marked correct. You should have seen the look on that teacher's face. Sometimes you could buy that look for a penny. When you are smart in subjects like that, no one can take that away from you. Learning this at an early age would come in handy for the rest of my life. Knowledge does not discriminate.

I couldn't wait to graduate. However, I did make a few new friends, had some good experiences, had many more good days than bad days, and best of all, there were no bullies.

ON TO JUNIOR HIGH SCHOOL

Although several of my new friends went on to a junior high school that was considered the best honors program in DC, Jefferson Junior High, which was located in the Southwest section of DC, Ms. Coney did not give me a recommendation to go there. You had to apply to that program if you were out of zone, and you had to have a recommendation from your sixth-grade teacher. Naturally, Ms. Coney gave the students she knew best her recommendations—those she'd had since third grade.

Therefore, I returned to my neighborhood school and went to Eliot Junior High, which was two blocks from where we lived, and where my sister had gone and excelled. Eliot had a great honors program in its own right. I was placed in the honors section, where there were twelve girls and twelve boys with high IQs. It became quite a case study in honors education, which was quite controversial at that time as to whether it helped smart children more, to be singled out and separated from the other kids and whether it helped or hurt "average" students not to be exposed to smart students.

For me, I couldn't have cared less. There were no more buses to catch or rushing and running into class so as not to be late. The five-minute walk to school was great. I was very happy. It would turn out to be one of the best things to happen to me in my life.

THE MARCH ON WASHINGTON ASSIGNMENT

I started at Eliot Junior High School in September of 1963, not long after the March on Washington, a major event during the civil rights movement that had taken place in August of that year. DC was full of excitement and tension during the summer of 1963, from Capitol Hill to all the neighborhoods across the city and region, and from the White House to every house in DC. History was in the making, and no one knew how it was going to play out.

On August 28, 1963, more than a quarter of a million Americans of all races, religions, ethnic, and cultural backgrounds gathered in Washington, DC on the National Mall for a political rally known as the March on Washington for Jobs and Freedom. Organized by a number of civil rights and religious groups, the event was designed to shed light on the political and social challenges and injustices that African Americans and other minorities faced across the country. The march, which became a key moment in the growing struggle for civil rights by minorities in the United States, ended with Martin Luther King Jr.'s famous "I Have a Dream" speech—a spirited call for racial justice and equality.

Noted as one of the largest political rallies for human rights in US history, the march was successful in pressuring the administrations of presidents John F. Kennedy and Lyndon B. Johnson to initiate strong federal civil rights bills that went before Congress. The March on Washington is credited with helping to pass the Civil Rights Act of 1964 and preceded the "Selma to Montgomery" voting rights marches, which led to the passage of the Voting Rights Act of 1965.

Everyone in Washington, especially the adults, (natives and non-natives, politicians and non-politicians), had an opinion about the civil rights movement. Our teachers and parents were no exception. Mr. Charles Dobbs, our homeroom and algebra teacher, was very involved in the movement, as were many other teachers and administrators in our school, including our principal, Mrs. Dotson.

One of our first assignments in homeroom when school started in 1963—an icebreaker designed to get us acquainted with one another—was for each of us to write about what we had done over the summer and then stand up, introduce ourselves, and tell our classmates about it. The discussion was to include the days and activities surrounding the March on Washington.

When it was my turn, I got up and discussed how I kept up with the news, helped my mother make sandwiches for the marchers and the tent city that followed, and watched the march and all of the speeches on TV, looking for my mother in the crowd. (My mother didn't allow me to march; she felt that I was too young, and besides, many people believed that there was going to be violence). I talked about how Dr. King's speech moved me and motivated me to be a better person and to be the best student I could be, and that I felt education was the key to equality. I still believe that to be true today. I said that I thought August 28, 1963, was a beautiful day, that the march was peaceful and impactful, and a great lesson was taught to our generation about dignity and equality.

One boy, who sat behind me, got up and talked about how moved he was by the events taking place on the National Mall. He and another classmate rode their bikes from Capitol Hill, where they lived, down to the National Mall and the Lincoln Memorial to hear the speeches. He talked about the sea of people and the positive vibe of the crowd, and described how they got off their bikes and walked around to take it all in. He said that when the speeches were over, they ran right into Dr. Martin Luther King and Julian Bond as they were leaving and got to shake their hands.

Our class began to bond after that assignment, and many of us became admirers of Dr. King and his message of nonviolence, love, peace, and equality for all. We were intellectually compatible and enjoyed matching wits with one another. Mr. Dobbs took a liking to us and got several of us involved in his civil rights activities.

March on Washington. Photo taken by Leffler, Warren K.

THE ASSASSINATION OF JOHN F. KENNEDY

Another major event happened my first year in junior high school. Just as we were settling into the first semester, John Fitzgerald Kennedy, the thirty-fifth president of the United States, was assassinated over the Thanksgiving holiday of 1963. We were out of school that day, as always on the Wednesday before Thanksgiving, as Capitol Hill took a break and federal workers from around the region began to leave the city, in masse, to go to destinations near and far for the holiday.

Happy to have a day off, the schoolchildren of Washington, DC, usually engaged in various activities the Wednesday before Thanksgiving, such as riding bikes, going shopping for a Thanksgiving outfit, or playing football in a park or sandlot. Like most people of our generation, I remember exactly what I was doing when I heard the news that President Kennedy had been shot. Mama had gone to work that day, and my sister and I were content with sleeping late, having a slow morning, and catching up with our favorite CBS soap opera, *As the World Turns*, at lunchtime. While we were watching the show—and most people remember this well—CBS broke into the broadcast with a special report, and news anchor Walter Cronkite made the famous confirming announcement that President Kennedy had been shot and killed in Dallas, Texas.

Washington, DC, in particular, along with the rest of the nation, went into deep mourning in the days leading up to and concluding with Kennedy's funeral and burial, with full military honors, at Arlington National Cemetery. In our city, where politicians and particularly the president are household names and often viewed as if they were family members, I remember the emotion of deep sadness that shrouded our city, families, and friends. I remember crying and crying uncontrollably and taking in every moment—from the horse-drawn caisson that carried Kennedy's body from the Capitol Rotunda to his funeral mass, through the burial and little John John's salute to his father—as if Kennedy was a close family member. My mother told everyone that I cried for three days. It was the saddest and most solemn Thanksgiving that I have experienced, or probably will ever experience in my lifetime.

We finally returned to school when the mourning period was over. Our honors class tried to get back to normal, although emotions were still running high. Mr. Dobbs allowed us to talk openly about what we were feeling in homeroom. The girls were sad, and the boys appeared to be angry that this could happen in our country. A spirited debate broke out about politics, the Russian connection, and the conspiracy theory surrounding the assassination.

As voices rose and the debate became more heated, I broke down in tears again and couldn't stop crying, along with some of the other girls in our class. One of the boys in our class, the one who sat behind me, jumped up and said, "Stop, stop, just stop all of this!" He gave an impassioned statement about moving on, getting educated, and getting involved in making this country a better place—a stronger America. He gave me a handkerchief from his pocket, as I cried and cried. He said to me, "Just stop all that crying, Gwynette! We are going to make a difference in this world, a world where this will never happen again."

That first day back to school was tough, but we got through it. Kennedy's death brought us closer as a class, and quite a class we would become-one of high achievers.

A FLY BLOCK GIRL

Although the honors program was very competitive, I was not disliked and bullied as much as I had been in elementary school. In fact, I was very popular. I intentionally created an image for myself that I liked. What type of image? That of being a fly block girl. What was a *fly block girl*? Well, in DC, that's the equivalent to being "Jenny from the Block" in JLo's (Jennifer Lopez's) New York or one of L.L. Cool J's "Around the Way Girls" in California.

A fly block girl looks good at all times, with the latest style of clothes and hair—one who looks and acts cool and knows the latest dances. That came naturally to me. I loved clothes and would babysit or run errands to make money to buy them, or I would make them on my sewing machine, creating things no one else would have. I loved these shoes called Nineteens, and I had them in several colors. The real ones (not knock-offs) cost $19.99, which was a lot money back then. They were made of soft leather or suede.

I also loved to dance. In fact, everyone on my mother's side of the family loved to dance, including my mother. One of our male neighbors, who we called Junior, taught my sister and I the DC Hand Dance and other popular dances, and he could really move.

I once went with my mother to a local beach party and put on an impromptu performance of the latest dance craze. People (mainly men) came up afterward and gave me money for that expert rendition. From that experience, I learned that people were willing to pay for a job well done. My mother allowed me to accept the money. She even told everyone in the family that I got enough money to buy lunch for a week and that I had enough left, along with babysitting money, to buy a new pair of Nineteens—a red pair. That was like buying a pair of Jordan's today.

All of this made me very popular, with the boys in particular—a lot of boys, not just the ones in my honors classes but throughout the school. I went to all the school dances and neighborhood parties and would "turn them out," as the saying goes, with my dance moves, fancy clothes, and hairdos. I guess you could say that I was "Nettie from the Block" or "Block Girl Nettie," and I owned it, with no shame.

As a result, a lot of the boys at school became my so-called friends. I was always more comfortable with the boys, in class and out, and I felt safe with them, as if no harm would come to me if they were around. And I must say, there was no serious bullying from the girls, just the normal girl bullshit: "She think she's cute! Where does she get her clothes from?" They knew that the boys had my back. I knew it too. I was the fly block girl in the honors program.

In DC, we had our own black version of *American Bandstand* called *Teenarama*, a dance show that came on after school. It was DC's version of *Soul Train* long before there was *Soul Train*. On occasion, some of the popular older male dancers at our school, who were able to get tickets to be on *Teenarama*, would invite me to go with them as their dance partner. They only took a girl who could really dance and dressed nice (a fly girl) with them, so it was an honor for me to oblige. I loved being on the show, and the guys I went with loved taking me.

Once, I broke my mother's rule and went on the show without her permission instead of going straight home after school. In my excitement of being asked to go, albeit at the last minute, I forgot that I had the house key. As a result, my sister was locked out of the house and had to stay at one of our neighbor's apartment until the show was over and I came home. She knew where I was when she saw me dance across the TV screen. Boy was I in trouble when I got home, but not for long: it was *Teenarama*, where I got to showcase our family's reputation of being good dancers.

GROWTH BEYOND MEASURE

At Eliot, I continued to flourish not just in math, which was still my best subject, but also in the sciences. I won first place in the school's science fair, thanks to the mentoring of my biology teacher, Mrs. Ball, who had quite a reputation for being mean and hard on her students. For some reason, she took a liking to me, and I to her. My science project on how to grow bigger, better vegetables was put on display at the DC Armory, and my family was really proud of that. To live in the city and win a science contest on how to grow better vegetables—that was really cool, or so I thought.

The teachers at Eliot seemed to really care and took pride in seeing their students succeed. They went out of their way to give us great experiences, such as taking us to movie premieres and local events. For example, our music teacher, Mrs. Liebowitz, taught us all of the songs to *The Sound of Music* and then took us to the Uptown Theatre to see the movie. Since we knew the storyline and all the songs, our class was able to better understand and appreciate that powerful movie about a widower who falls in love with a nun while she is caring for his children during the early days of Germany's occupation of Austria during World War II. That was a great outing. We learned a lot of WWII history and a lot about the power of love.

Mrs. Liebowitz also organized and produced extravagant talent shows that showcased our abilities. Our senior year was the beginning of the psychedelic era, so our last talent show highlighted boy and girl groups singing the latest hits, dressed in bell bottoms and all. One of the boys in our honors class was the MC and took on the role of a popular character of those times named Soul Finger.

I decided to do something different. I shredded my fly girl image and choreographed and performed "Second Hand Rose," the Barbara Streisand version from the movie *Funny Girl*. Second Hand Rose represented my alter ego, going back to the days when I wore secondhand clothes and hand-me-downs. Our show was a big hit. It was hilarious, and Mrs. Liebowitz was so proud of her star pupils, she cried.

Other teachers also went out of their way to do special things for us. They even took us to New York City for a weekend, where we went to Radio City, the Statue of Liberty, the Empire State Building, and the New York World's Fair of 1964–65, with its wonderful international exhibits and amusement park, which was literally out of this world for its time. We learned so much from those experiences and had a lot of fun also.

My English teacher, Mrs. Elridge, also took a liking to me and several other honors students. During the summer of 1965, she sent three of us to Howard University to take creative-writing classes for gifted students our age, designed to help us with our writing. That was the beginning of my love affair with Howard University. I had no idea that she was preparing us for professional writing and public speaking roles and little did I know that I would return to Howard and take it by storm one day.

At that Howard program, Ms. Toni Morrison, who became a famous writer, would come in from time to time to give us a master class in writing. She was fantastic and had a great impact on us.

My classmates and I would hang out on the Howard campus after class and often stop by the Wonder Bread Bakery, which was on the fringe of Howard's campus. The aroma that came from that bakery drew us to its discount store to buy day-old baked goods to snack on and take home to our families.

Our math teachers, who were extraordinary men in their own right, seemed to like me too, although I was a girl. The common stereotype of a male math teacher in an honors program is that he favors his male student protégés. However, my algebra and geometry teachers seemed to really like my math aptitude and wanted me to achieve. They pushed and challenged me. They called on me a lot and had me go to the board to solve difficult problems all the time so that my fellow classmates could see the steps involved, and I didn't disappoint.

One of my favorite teachers was Mrs. Regina Jervay, who taught French. All of her students loved sweet, beautiful Mrs. Jervay, especially the boys. Through her, I fell in love with the French language and all things French. I would study French and the French culture through my freshman year of college, for a total of seven years. Little did I know that as an adult, my first trip to Europe would be to France and that I would visit the City of Lights, Paris, on the first of several visits to France.

At Eliot, I felt safe and secure. My teachers motivated me to no end, and I achieved. I felt that there was nothing I couldn't do or be. Eliot had a major influence on me and on what I would become. For that, I will be forever grateful.

It was also at Eliot that I had my first crush, my first real boyfriend, and of course, that infamous first kiss. A fellow honors student, my crush was everything a girl could dream of in a first love. He was smart as a whip and quite handsome, with a great personality and good sense of humor to match. He was tender and kind, and he held my hand when he walked me home from school, while carrying my books with the other hand. We talked on the phone for hours. We were intellectually compatible, which drew us close to one another.

Together, we were "young, gifted, and black." My crush had good home training and displayed good manners and politeness, yet he was quite the athlete and had muscles as products of his athletic training. He had the charm and swag of Sidney Poitier and Denzel Washington and a smile that would melt my heart.

He was the boy who sat behind me in class and was so nice to me. He said that he liked my hairstyles and my hair bows, and that I smelled "so good" every morning. It must have been the soap I used, because I didn't wear perfume. I was his "Sugar Baby," and he was my "Hershey's Kiss." Mama liked my beau and called what we had puppy love. As for me, it was innocent and sweet, and I felt loved and protected. With him, I felt comfortable and safe.

However, our romance was eventually seen as a problem at school and at home. Our young and innocent love and all the emotions that went with it was getting a lot of attention from our fellow classmates and our teachers. We were seen as the class lovebirds (Romeo and Juliet) and soon became the objects of a lot of silly gossip. Mr. Dobbs, our homeroom and algebra teacher, and others encouraged us not to continue the romance because it was a distraction for the two of us and the rest of the class, thus keeping all of us from achieving our greatest potential as honors students. As a result, our romance fizzled, as most first loves do, and we eventually drifted apart.

AND THE VALEDICTORIAN WAS ...

I had the normal junior high school experiences at Eliot. I enjoyed going to school and was having fun. The big difference, however, was that I was the girl who often got straight As and could possibly become the valedictorian of the class, which was a big deal to many. All twenty-four of us in honors were very smart and any one of us could have been the valedictorian. Back then, for the most part, it all came down to your GPA.

Eliot Junior High School served middle-school-age children living in the inner city east of the US Capitol Building, the seat of the US Congress, representing the legislative branch of the US federal government. Eliot's territory ran north and south between East Capitol Street and Benning Road, and east and west from Lincoln Park to RFK Stadium. Until 1954 and the Brown v. Board of Education Supreme Court decision that desegregated the public schools in the United States and DC, that neighborhood and the surrounding schools were mostly white; it was a short distance to Capitol Hill for federal workers and Capitol Hill staffers. But after that decision, as in many inner city neighborhoods, there was white flight to the suburbs.

During the 1960s, when we lived there, the neighborhoods were mostly black, with only a few whites and Asian Americans; those who couldn't afford to leave the neighborhood or needed to stay for one reason or the other, such as owning businesses there and living in or near those businesses. In almost every honors class, there were at least one or two Asian American students, and our class was no exception. In my class, one such Asian American girl was Susen Yen, and we became both good friends and friendly competitors. Susen had two siblings, who had preceded her at Eliot. They were both the valedictorians of their respective classes.

There were also two Asian American sisters, but non-twins, in our class: the Liu sisters. The Liu sisters were very quiet and sat in the back of the class. They had difficulty with English and math, but eventually mastered both. Most of us in the class, found it hard to get close to the Liu sisters as friends. They had each other and stayed to themselves. They rarely participated in class and said very little to anyone.

Most of the black students stayed away from Susen and the Liu sisters, either out of ignorance, prejudice, jealousy, or a combination of the three. But my upbringing, my Sunday school teachings, and my own experiences taught me better than that. Susen and I became close, and she was a female friend I could relate to in several specific classes, especially in math.

We studied together often. She was friendly, funny, and, I thought, very attractive, with long black hair and a nice shape. She was a little shy, though, and some of the black students mistook that as being stuck-up, aloof, and arrogant. A fly block girl Susen was not, but she seemed to delight in the fact that I was. We got along very well and were intellectually well matched. I enjoyed being her friend.

Although we were friends and had each other's back, Susen and I competed furiously every term to see who would get the better grades - who would get all As, etc. In a way, we pushed each other. The overwhelming majority of the time, it would be me. Susen had a harder time in math and English than I did. She had the burden of a slight language barrier, in that English was not her family's first language. However, she got good grades in both subjects. She got stumped in math class at times and would call me on the phone and we would tackle difficult math problems together, often turning to a sibling for help. I clearly had a higher grade point average (GPA) at the end of most terms, although it was usually very close, by less than a percentage point some of the time. Susen and I did the math, so we know exactly where we stood with each other.

My junior year was a banner year for me. I was very active outside of the classroom. I served as vice president of the Student Council and our platform was to improve citizenship, promote school spirit, and improve student-teacher relationships. The council organized a student legal aid program to provide training for our future lawyers and improved communications between the council and the student body. To set an example, I did not miss one day of school and received a Perfect Attendance Award as a result. And going to school every day paid off, big time. I got straight A's every advisory that year. I also served as a nurse's aide to the school nurse, who gave me an award for my help.

At Eliot, the Senior Class Awards Ceremony was like the Olympics of achievement. Our honors class cleaned up. The awards flowed like fine champagne. In the individual subject category, I received an outstanding award in math (of course), and I was surprised when I got an award in English, which wasn't my favorite subject. In addition, different prestigious organizations in DC also gave out awards. Having served as Vice President of the Student Council with its lofty goals, I received awards from the American Legion and the DC Women's Bar Association. In science, I received awards from the Research Club of Washington, DC and the Washington Junior Academy of Sciences. On the social end, I was recognized as being popular in the *senior alphabet* and rewarded for my creativity and sewing by being voted for as the *best dressed girl* for the senior class Who's Who list that appeared in our *Eliot Teen Times* school newspaper.

So, when our graduation came around, I thought I was a shoe-in for valedictorian, and so did my family. I thought that I would be the valedictorian and that Susen would be the salutatorian. However, there was a big surprise in store for us. One morning, I got called to the principal's office, and that is never good. The principal, my homeroom teacher, Mr. Dobbs, who was also my math teacher; and Mrs. Elridge, my English teacher, were all there, with the graduation committee of teachers. They explained to me that yes, I had the highest GPA in the graduating class, but that my GPA, one of the Liu sisters', and Susen's were very close, in that order. They said that they wanted to honor all three of us at the graduation ceremony. They explained to me that they had decided to have two co-valedictorians and a salutatorian that year and that Amy and I would be co-valedictorians and Susen would be the salutatorian.

They admitted that my GPA was just a little higher than Amy's by less than a percentage point, and that Susen's GPA was just a little below both of ours. Susen and I had done the math, but we had no idea what Amy's grades were like. What Susen and I didn't know was that Amy Liu's GPA had dropped Susen to third place, and out as valedictorian and salutatorian.

They explained to me that for Susen not to be either could be devastating for her and maybe problematic for her and her family, given how smart she was; maybe even bringing shame upon them and her, given their culture. In addition, her older sister had been the valedictorian of her class, and who knows what kind of competition they had going on in their family. They felt that the emotional toll of not being either might bother Susen emotionally, and that they didn't want her to get depressed or worse. One teacher said, "You never know what goes on in families, and especially Chinese families, behind closed doors."

They said they knew I would understand and could handle their decision. They said that by me sharing the valedictorian title with Amy would give Susen the honor of being the salutatorian. They said they needed me to agree that there would be a tie between me and Amy and for my family to go along with that, too. I said that I was cool with that, although deep down I wasn't.

So, I would not have the honor of being *number one* all by myself, after working so hard for it. I felt let down, but I didn't show it. I knew that I was the best and so did lot of other people, including some of my fellow classmates, some of my teachers, and the principal. I made it seem like it was no big deal. Deep down inside, though, I was disappointed, but I got over it quickly.

They thanked me and said that Mrs. Elridge would help me with my speech, which would be last, and that they knew it would be the best. I said that it would be about civil rights, equal rights, rights for women, and how our class would make a difference in the world. I knew that the creative-writing class I had taken at Howard University would help me a lot in making my speech a great one. Later, when the GPA list was posted, it showed that Amy and I were tied and that Susen was next and that settled the issue.

And so it was. I shared the number-one ranking with an Asian American girl, and another Asian American girl who was a close friend that I liked, would get to be the salutatorian. I promised not to discuss the situation with anyone. However, several of my classmates figured out what happened. There was some gossip about it, and a few comments were made to me about being robbed, but we all took it in stride to save face for Susen. Who knows, they probably rounded the GPAs up or down.

Even at that young age, we were learning about empathy. I learned about compromise and compassion during that ordeal, as did my family, who went along to get along and did not make a fuss. We also learned a little about organizational politics, political compromise, and the kind of backroom deals that happen in the real world, especially in Washington, DC. In the end, we took it for what I learned in French class to be *"C'est la vie,"* meaning, "That's life!"

TWO GRADUATIONS

Our little family celebrated two graduations in June of 1966. It was an exciting, yet stressful time for my family. Two graduations can be tough economically for any family, so you can imagine what it was like for mine, one of little means. I graduated from Eliot as a co-valedictorian, and my sister from McKinley Technical High School from its honors track. As a family, we got through them both. Mama's accident settlement came in that year just in time to help pay for graduation expenses. My sister and I made beautiful white dresses to wear to our respective graduations.

Mom and Dad got through our graduations too, although there was a little tension between the two of them. After all that time, they had just gotten legally divorced after Mama's settlement. Daddy remarried within days of the divorce. To say the least, you could cut the tension with a knife, and hardly a word was said between the two.

Graduation Day came and went without incident. It was a happy occasion for all of us, and my speech was great, as everyone knew it would be. Everyone, especially Susen's family, was happy. My family was too, and so was I.

Eliot Junior High was where I found my sea legs, where I found confidence and accepted my God-given gifts: intelligence, compassion and empathy. I realized that those gifts could be used to define and design my destiny. I learned that a black girl from DC could be smart, intelligent, and fly at the same time. Yes, you can walk with your head held high and chew gum at the same time.

FOUR
ON MCKINLEY, ON MCKINLEY, VICTORY IS OUR AIM

THE SUMMER BEFORE I started high school was one of great transition for our family, for the Ford women would move into a new apartment and one of the Ford girls would move on to a new phase in her life: that of a college student. My sister applied to go to college and was accepted to Hampton Institute, as it was called at the time, a well-known HBCU (historically black colleges and universities) located in Hampton, Virginia. She was very excited about going off to college and being on her own.

After her lawsuit was settled from her accident, my mother decided to move us to a newer, nicer two-bedroom apartment. It was in the Southeast section of Washington on a newly developed portion of a street named Good Hope Road, in the area of SE called Anacostia, named after the Anacostia River that separates that part of Southeast from the rest of the city of Washington, DC. Little did we know what was to come!

We moved into an expensive, super-modern high-rise building called Mulberry Plaza. It had twelve stories, a circular driveway entrance, and a doorman named Charles. It also had a beautiful lobby and an exquisite party room, which quickly became the "it" place for wedding receptions and formal parties. It was also known as home to several numbers runners, high-priced call girls, and women of the night. Most of our neighbors, though, were hard-working residents who just ignored the illegal activity and went about their daily lives of going to work, making a living, and paying the bills for the luxury of living in Mulberry Plaza.

My mother was no exception. Given all of that luxury, the rent at Mulberry Plaza was not cheap. With Mama's rent, utilities, and other bills, even with her legal settlement and child support payments, things were still tough for her financially. She was still working just as hard as before and getting as much overtime as possible to pay the bills, keep a roof over our heads, and food in the refrigerator.

In the fall of 1966, I enrolled in McKinley Technical High School, where my sister had attended, located at 2nd and T Streets in Northeast Washington, a rock's throw from North Capitol Street, the street leading north away from the Capitol Building that separates the city's NE and NW sections. In fact, there were several cheers about our school's location that the students quickly learned, such as:

> *Every morning at 2nd and T: (Techites)*
> *Many people you will see! (Techites)*
> *Techites, are out of sight!*
> *Techites, are out of sight!*

Named after the twenty-fifth president of the United States, William McKinley, Tech (the pet name for the school) was one of the most popular high schools in the city at the time. It would be considered a magnet or Blue Ribbon school today. At that time, it was known for its college prep curriculum and college placement rate, which was very high. DC residents who wanted their children to go to college clamored to get their teens in, although the neighborhood that the school was located in was a relatively small residential neighborhood, surrounded by industrial buildings to the south and railroad tracks leading out of the city from Union Station to the northeast.

Structurally, McKinley Tech sat on top of one the highest elevations in the city. With several tasteful renovations, modernizations, and wings added over the years, it looked like a small Southern college campus, with a plaza and football stadium with breathtaking views of Washington's city landscape. It was known as the "School Up on the Hill." Another cheer we sang about our location, with the melody of a famous song, was as follows:

> *There's a School Up on a Hill*
> *Let's go, let's go, let's go. (Repeated several times.)*

During the 1960s, Tech's popularity and growth prompted administrative decisions that changed it from a ninth-through-twelfth to a tenth-through-twelfth-grade high school. In addition, students from outside the school's natural residential neighborhood boundaries had to apply to attend the school as out-of-zone students. Out-of-zone students had to have good grades (a 3.0 GPA or better) and come from the college prep or honors tracks of their junior high school. You also needed two recommendations from teachers from your junior high school.

Since I was a co-valedictorian of Eliot, my teachers there made sure I was accepted. McKinley was my high school of choice, and I was determined to go there. With my grades and glowing letters of recommendation, I had my letter of acceptance long before I graduated from Eliot.

THE LONG WALK

That fall, I was back to riding the public city bus to and from school with the use of "school tickets," which was how students got around town at that time. It was a long bus ride of about an hour and then a long walk up Eckington Place, past some industrial buildings and then up a set of steep steps on the backside of a hill leading up to the school. To get there on time, I would have to catch the 7:30 a.m. bus in front of Mulberry Plaza, but I felt it was worth the bus ride.

At first, I felt so alone. I hardly knew anybody from McKinley's neighborhood, and there were only three McKinley students living in the Plaza. Only a few students from Eliot went on to McKinley from my class, and I didn't have a boyfriend to hang out with. I was on my own to navigate the waters of that 2,400-student high school alone.

My strategy was to really concentrate on getting very good grades during my sophomore year so I wouldn't have to struggle and worry about pulling any grades up during my last two years. I knew that good grades and the school's reputation could get me into college, with an academic scholarship to pay for it. However, unlike junior high, I decided not to compete so hard to be number one and set myself up for the heartbreak I encountered when it was time to name a valedictorian. I decided to do my very best, of course, but to let my ranking just happen and not fret or worry about it. I also decided to have fun, to enjoy myself, and to experience all that high school had to offer.

Of course, I was placed in the honors track again, but we didn't have honors homerooms. They mixed the honors students in with all the other students for homerooms so that both groups would have exposure to what the real world was like, everyone all mixed in together. Although I guess I understood that strategy, I missed honors homeroom, where, for the most part, everyone was intellectually compatible and could relate to each other well. We had a mixed bag in my homeroom: some real smart people, a lot of college prep students, some fly girls, some not-so-fly girls, some athletes, and several dudes who acted like and probably were thugs. I stayed away from the thugs;

they scared me. But truly, we all learned a thing or two from one another, so I guess it was a good idea.

They placed the honors students in some classes together, such as honors English and biology, honors math, etc. But in some classes, like civics and history, you would have a mixed bag in terms of students. The mixed classes tended to be very large, with sometimes thirty to forty students in them. That arrangement allowed me to get to know some of the students outside of honors, especially the college prep students. I enjoyed all my classes at Tech.

In my struggle to find my way, I decided to make an effort to make new friends and try to fit in. All of the McKinley out-of-zone students who lived in my part of town quickly got to know one another. We rode some of the same buses just about every day and took that long walk up Eckington Place together to the school each morning.

One of my favorite aunts, my aunt Audrey—my mother's brother Lawrence's wife—put me in contact with one her nieces, who lived farther up the hill from me, off of Alabama Avenue. Antonia (we called her Toni for short) was two years ahead of me at Tech, and we became fast friends. She was a very popular cheerleader and one of the coolest girls in the school. She introduced me around as her cousin and showed me the ropes. We purposely tried to time our departure for school each day and were usually on the same bus. She took me under her wing, and she quickly became my new big sister.

I decided to take on my fly girl persona again: the fly girl in honors. It was harder this time around, however. For one, I had to drop the block girl part. That wasn't cool or popular at Tech. Most McKinley students looked down on block girls, so anything that was seen as "block" had to go, including my Nineteens. Everyone wore college prep or career girl clothes, so I had my work cut out for me. On top of that, there were so many fly girls at McKinley, there was plenty of competition. Tech had a citywide reputation for its fine women. Toni set a good example of college prep dressing, and she was fly at it.

I used my sewing machine to make new clothes and took on

babysitting jobs to buy shoes and clothes that I couldn't make. I had quite the wardrobe. I quickly became known as the girl with the fly clothes, and I had plenty of competition. One guy, a senior named Donny, called me *Hots* because I would wear the school's colors a lot, which were burgundy and grey, especially on game days. He particularly liked this light burgundy dress that I made to wear to one of the football games. He must have liked the color, thus giving me the name *Hots* long before that term was popular. He still calls me *Hots* to this day, over my strong objection.

I eventually got a part-time seasonal after-school and weekend job for extra spending money. It was my first retail job, at a sporting goods store named *Olympics*, located at 7th and G Streets, NW, not too far from McKinley. They sold gym clothes and tennis shoes to all the high school students in the city in their school colors. I learned how to use a cash register and further sharpened certain math skills. I also got to meet a lot of guys from Tech and other high schools who came to shop there and flirted with the "cute girls from Tech" who worked there.

Toni and I went everywhere and did everything together, especially when it came to sporting events, school dances, and house parties on weekends. We enjoyed shopping at a store named *"7 and 9"* for party dresses for petite girls. I went to every football and basketball game she cheered in, which was every game on the schedule (she never missed a game), so that she would never have to go into Southeast alone after dark.

Southeast in general, and Anacostia in particular, had a reputation of being kind of rough, with black-on-black crime (a lot of robbing and stealing). It just wasn't safe for girls to be out alone after dark. One day, we were on the bus, and Toni felt this guy put his hand into her duffel bag where she kept her wallet. She called him out and yelled, "Get your hand out of my bag!" The guy jumped off the bus and ran away.

Most of the time, we had a ride home after the games. Toni and another girl, Veronica (we called her Roni), who also lived in Mulberry Plaza and was a majorette at Tech, had boyfriends who were best friends. They both were out of school and had cars. Tommy Carter and George Lacy were their names. George (Lacy is what everyone called him) drove a fast, souped-up burgundy GTO that he called the GOAT (greatest of all time), and Tommy drove his dad's foreign car. On most game days, they both would attend, and one of them would drive us home, especially from away games.

Whatever the case, the five of us would be together after the games most of the time. We often stopped at the Hot Shoppe (by Marriott) after the games for a bite to eat, and we went to a lot of house parties together on weekends. With no boyfriend, I was always the fifth wheel, but they didn't seem to mind. In fact, they were always trying to fix me up with someone they knew. I would always tell them thanks but no thanks, but they wouldn't listen.

One day, however, one of our game-day plans blew up. It was an away-game day, late in the fall of 1966, when McKinley played Anacostia High in football at Anacostia. Usually for away games, McKinley provided school bus transportation to and from the game for athletes, cheerleaders, majorettes, the band, and students, and this game was no exception. However, because we lived in Anacostia, Toni, Roni, and I decided that although we would take the bus transport to the game, we would stay in Southeast after the game, rather than go all the way back to McKinley.

Roni arranged for Lacy and Tommy to pick us up in Lacy's GTO after the game to take us home. Toni and Roni gave me their book bags, purses, and coats to keep for them in the stands so that they wouldn't have to get back on the bus to retrieve them. I sat near the front of the stadium on Tech's side and put their belongings under the bleachers behind me. All the three of us would have to do was hang back after the game and wait for the guys. At least, that was the plan. But sometimes, plans fall apart.

The game went well. Tech was on a winning streak and did not disappoint. We won the game big time, and the band, majorettes, and cheerleaders showed out. But things went south from there. The

Anacostia students got angry and began to rush toward McKinley's side of the stadium like a stampede. Everyone started running, and all mayhem broke out. Rocks and bottles started flying.

The McKinley students started running to get on the buses. I didn't know what to do. Toni and Veronica had left their coats, book bags, and purses with me, which I had stashed under the bleachers. So, I ducked under the bleachers and waited for them to get off the field. By the time we gathered our things, we had fallen behind the other Tech students.

As the three of us approached our bus, we saw that the Anacostia students had beaten us to it. They were surrounding it and trying to push the bus over. Seeing that, we decided to walk away from the buses. We didn't see Lacy or Tommy in the crowd, so we decided to make a beeline toward Good Hope Road, on foot. At first, we decided to just try to blend in as if we were Anacostia students, hiding all clothing items that said we were from Tech under our coats, which covered up most of the evidence. I had left my Tech pom-poms under the bleachers.

We started to make our way out of the parking lot. We just started walking fast at first, as if we were part of the Anacostia crowd. Suddenly, some of the Anacostia students recognized that Toni's cheerleading shoes and Roni's majorette boots were not like Anacostia's. Some girls started yelling, "Tech, Tech!"

We took off running. It became a track race. It was on. Thank goodness we were athletic. We ran through the streets and through traffic, dodging cars. We ran through people's yards. Then it became a hurdle race. We started jumping over shrubs and hurdling over bushes. We even helped each other climb a lady's fence to lose some of the chasers. We finally made it to Good Hope Road and started sprinting toward a bus stop. However, there was no bus coming.

Lo and behold, around the corner came Lacy's burgundy GTO. It was Lacy and Tommy to the rescue. The car screeched ahead of us and stopped. Tommy jumped out to open the back door. Roni, Toni, and I jumped in, headfirst, like you see on TV. The GTO took off like a rocket. The Anacostia students picked up more rocks and bottles and hurled them at the GTO, but none of them hit the car. Lacy was too fast on the stick.

The guys apologized for not being in the bleachers. They said that when they got to Anacostia and saw the scoreboard, they knew there was going to be trouble, so they waited in the car outside the stadium, hoping we would think to come out and find them as we had planned. But when the mayhem and rock-throwing started, with people running everywhere, they decided to drive around, hoping to find us on the move. (There were no cell phones back then—they weren't invented yet!) Lacy figured that we would try to make it to Good Hope Road, so that's the route he took. They just drove around until they spotted us. Smart minds think alike.

Finally rescued, up the hill to Mulberry Plaza the five of us went, singing our favorite little personal cheer:

> *Ah, Tommy*
> *Ah, Toni*
> *Ah, Roni*
> *Ah, Lacy*
> *Ah, Nettie*

We sang it over and over until we got to Roni's apartment. We didn't stop for food. Instead, we decided to order pizza in. There was no going out to a party that night. The five of us stayed in and watched old movies on TV. As usual, I was the fifth wheel, but I didn't mind.

When I got home that night, my mother asked, "How did things go today?"

I said, "Fine."

Then she asked, "Who won the game?'

I said, "We did."

And that was the end of that.

PLEDGING, CHEERING, AND DATING

The rest of my sophomore year went without incident for the most part. I worked hard at getting good grades and made the honor roll each quarter. I got to know more people and got involved in school activities. I joined Toni's sorority, which was a lot of fun.

Yes, our high school had sororities and fraternities, or versions thereof, just like those in college. We had Kappas, Qs (QKD Fraternity), and other clubs for the boys. Our club was called the Des Fielles. Many of my big sisters went on to college and to pledge a sorority. Most pledged Alpha Kappa Alpha, the nation's first and oldest black sorority, and some pledged other sororities. Our high school club gave parties, went to parties together, and had sleepovers where we talked and giggled, mostly about school and boys.

The pledging process was funny to me. I didn't let the silly pranks such as swallowing a raw egg and mild hazing get to me. It also gave me the opportunity to meet other girls, some older, outside of the classroom, and alumni who would come back to talk to us about college life and other things.

I also went out for cheerleading, and of course, I made it. Toni had taught me all of the cheers throughout the year, and by going to all the football and basketball games, I had learned all the cheers by heart and all the steps, gymnastics, moves, and mannerisms that a cheerleader should have, long before the tryouts. Some people thought I made it because I was Toni's cousin, but deep in my heart, I believed I made it because I knew the cheers and would make a good—no, a *great*—cheerleader, which I proved to be over and over again once I made it.

As one of the shortest girls and lighter in weight, I was tasked with climbing to the top of the human pyramid, but I wasn't afraid. I never fell. Also because of my height, my cheering position was on one end, where I could really showcase my moves. I preferred to be on people's left-side view from the front so that they would have to look left to the end to see me. My nickname, Nettie, was engraved on my bullhorn.

Finally, after the winter break of my tenth-grade year, I met and dated a guy I liked from Tommy and Lacy's fraternity. His name was Frank, but everyone called him Franky. He was from a large family of six children. For some reason, early in my dating years, I was attracted to guys from large working-class families. I think it was my hidden desire for more siblings, especially for at least one brother, or a desire to have a lot of children myself, I guess, having come from a small family.

Franky was a senior, as were Toni and Roni. He had an older sister, a brother in my sophomore class at Tech, and three younger siblings, who took to me and I to them, especially his younger brothers. Franky's mother liked me a lot, but his father didn't seem to. I felt that his dad thought of me as some fast-tailed girl who would distract his son from the goals he had set or something. Nothing could be further from the truth, but that's the impression I got about his father. I was supportive of Franky and his goals and checked his math homework and writing assignments. I even helped him with his college application essays and proofread all of them.

Franky took me to his senior prom—my first prom experience. It was great to get all dressed up like Cinderella going to the ball. We had a great time going out to dinner before, dancing the night away at the prom, going to a breakfast party afterward, and getting home when the sun was coming up. That was the typical prom experience in Washington, DC. We felt all grown up, and our parents let us stay out all night. Most of all, I got to go to Toni's and Roni's prom to help them celebrate their upcoming graduation from high school. We all had a ball.

My relationship with Franky lasted through what would be a delightful summer romance. We did all the things that young couples do during DC's hot summers: cookouts, day trips to the beach, amusement parks, and summer parties. However, I knew I was taking a risk with Franky in terms of a long-term relationship, in that he was going off to college when the summer was over. I knew that most long-distance relationships that young don't last for long after the older person goes off to college, and, in our case, I was right. Not being able to survive the long distance, our relationship ended after my club had a Christmas *Red and White Ball* during his freshman Christmas break. Once again, it was a matter of *"C'est la vie!* That's life."

JUNIOR YEAR

The year of 1968 turned out to be another year that helped shape my future. I spent my weekdays living the life of a typical high-school cheerleader: up super-early, getting to school early to practice, especially on days when we had a game, and coming home late after practice or a game.

Fridays were the best, though hectic. I would get up early, study for whatever tests we had that day, get to school early for a run-though of the cheers we would perform at Friday's game, go to class, take whatever tests we had that day, cheer at the game, go home, relax, take a hot bath, get dressed in party attire, and go out with friends, club sisters, and fellow cheerleaders to the Friday night parties. We usually won our Friday games, so that made for a long, hectic, but fun day.

Sleep-deprived, I usually slept in on Saturdays, getting up later than I did during the week. I did my Saturday chores, went to the library if I needed to, and came back home to go out to Saturday-night parties. That was my normal week: school, studying, cheerleading, and partying. I guess that made me a party girl, but I got my schoolwork done and even found time to go to church on Sunday and teach kindergarten children in Sunday school at Mount Carmel Baptist Church once a month as a substitute teacher.

I needed to keep a 3.0 (B) average or better to keep cheering, but I set my goal much higher than that. I didn't intend to cut it that close and deal with all the tears and drama that came if you got thrown off the squad for bad grades. How embarrassing would that have been! My goal was to get at least a 3.5 (B+) or better GPA to not only keep cheering, but to get into college with an academic scholarship. I knew what I had to do to make it into college, and nothing and no one was going to stop me, not even the guys I dated (mostly athletes) that year. I really didn't have time for a serious relationship.

As I had in junior high, I surrounded myself with respectful, smart guys—college prep guys mostly—whom I called my brothers. They were usually in our brother fraternity, the Qs (QKD Fraternity). There were four guys that I was really close to: Kenny Hodge, Michael Bradley, Greg Robinson, and George Lacy, the guy with the infamous burgundy GTO. I ate lunch with my in-school brothers and danced with all of them at school dances and private parties. We had a lot of fun together. Most importantly, they told me what guys to look out for and what guys not to date because they had bad reputations. They protected me and my reputation. They told me that a couple of football players I dated were no good and to stay away from them.

The basketball season got underway in earnest after Christmas. Our basketball team was one of the best in the city. In the winter of 1968, they won the Inter-High Public High School East Division Championship, having beat all of the Northeast and Southeast high schools, such as Eastern, Spingarn, and Anacostia. For the city-wide public school championship, Tech had to play the top high school with the best record of the public high schools from the West, which was Dunbar High, located not far from McKinley but on the west side of North Capitol Street. Having the best record of the two schools, Tech had home-court advantage and played Dunbar on a Friday evening in Tech's gym.

That championship game drew a large crowd. McKinley had a large following within our huge school, and from alumni and other schools from the East, and so did Dunbar from the West. I recall how packed the gymnasium was—so packed that the cheerleaders had to sit on the floor of the sidelines rather than on the first row of the bleachers where we usually sat. There were college scouts, sports reporters, and even some of our former cheerleaders at that game. You could feel the tension in the air: two great rivals, East and West, going at it on the court.

Under the leadership of their coach, ironically named McKinley Armstrong, our budding team, made up mostly of juniors from my class, beat Dunbar decisively. Well, of course, that didn't sit well with the Dunbar fans. They were hot under the collar. Thankfully, in his infinite wisdom, our principal had called the Metropolitan Police at halftime, and they showed up in good numbers to secure the players, the sidelines, and the McKinley students to avoid fighting inside the gym.

The principal came on the loudspeaker and asked all of the Dunbar fans to leave. The police urged the Dunbar fans to leave the gym without incident, and even had to escort some of them out. Some were giving us the finger, using profanity, and saying, "You may have won the game, but you won't win the fight. Just step outside!"

Fear took me over. *Aw, hell,* I said to myself. *What am I going to do? They are outside, and we are inside. How am I going to get home, way across town?*

Just then, the principal came back on the loudspeaker and announced, "All McKinley students, stay in your seats." He had the security guards lock the doors, locking us inside. Then he said, "Get out your ID and a dance partner, and get ready to dance."

Dance music came on, and the lights were dimmed. The music started cranking, and the students started dancing. We did the Jerk and the Boogaloo to no end.

It seemed like a good strategy at the time. Mr. Rhodes, our great principal, was buying time while he figured out how to get a thousand students home safely and while the police tried to clear the immediate area of Dunbar fans. As time went on, it got darker and darker outside, and I got more worried. How in the hell was I going to get to Southeast safely?

Then a slow record came on by Billy Stewart ("Sitting in the Park"). George Lacy, one of my play brothers, walked up to me and asked me to dance. He was always a trusted brother/friend when I needed one. He said, "Would you like to bop?" (That was a popular slow dance in DC that had waltz-like moves with a few holding-your-partner-type moves, like in *Dancing with the Stars* today, and not the bump-and-grind type slow-dance moves. To bop, your partner needed to know what he was doing to not step on your toes. Lacy knew I could bop, so we got going.

While holding me close, he said, "Nettie, you're shaking. Are you nervous? What's the matter?"

I said, "Yeah, I don't know what I'm going to do when we get out of here."

Always the jokester, he said, "Oh, I thought I was making you tremble with my charm!"

I said, "No, I know you, my brother. I'm not trembling over you. It's just that I don't know how I'm going to get home without riding the bus into Dunbar territory at my transfer point to get to Southeast. And it's dark out there."

He used a popular phrase and asked, "So, are you flying solo?" That meant was I alone that night but could double for was I seeing anyone. I said, "Yeah, I'm flying solo every night these days!"

He then asked me, "What happened to that football player I was seeing you with?"

I answered, "That was over before it began, really!"

So, like a Shakespearean actor, he said, "Well, let me take you home in my chariot, my lady."

I said, "Oh, thanks, Lacy, I would really appreciate that!"

After a few more fast dances, we saw the guards go to the doors and unlock them. We were then released to go home. It was after eight o'clock and pitch black outside. Lacy grabbed my books and grabbed me by the hand and rushed me to his car—that Burgundy GTO that had been my ride home so many times when I was in the tenth grade. But this time, it felt different. It was just Lacy and me. It felt like he alone was taking me home *after the dance*, just the two of us.

On the way home, I asked about him and Veronica. I had heard rumors about a breakup, but I wanted to get it from the horse's mouth. He explained to me that in fact they had broken up—the summer right after she graduated. He told me she had gotten back together with a guy named Jeff that she had been dating before Lacy came along. Jeff had come back to DC after serving in Vietnam.

Lacy said that he knew that he was never first with Veronica—that Jeff was the love of her life. He knew she would go back to Jeff when he got out of the service. He said that he and Veronica had a casual thing going on back then, nothing serious. Lacy said that Veronica and Jeff had gotten married as soon as he got back from Vietnam, after she graduated. It was no big deal as far as Lacy was concerned.

I had heard some of those rumors but had lost touch with Veronica after she graduated and moved out of Mulberry Plaza. I said, "Man, that's messed up."

Always one to lighten the mood, Lacy said, "Naw, she's the one that messed up, and I'm not messed up about it. Besides, look who I'm taking home tonight—one of the best cheerleaders on the planet."

He then changed the subject, and we rapped about various and sundry things for the rest of the ride home. He told me about the junior college he attended in the mornings while working full-time at the post office in the afternoons and evenings, collecting the mail from office buildings downtown and neighborhood boxes (called PM collection). He said that he also made time to come to all of McKinley's games after school. He said that his social life still centered around McKinley and its Northeast neighborhoods, seeing old friends and teachers, and meeting new students, like me. Back then, we called that "robbing the cradle," when older guys go back to their high school to check out the younger girls.

I asked him why everyone called him Lacy, and he said because his first name was George, and that was a lame first name. Everyone in high school called him "Lacy" or "Lace," which was cooler. I said, "Oh, I see. So, I'll call you Lacy then."

The song on the radio was "I'm Gonna Make You Love Me" by the Temptations and the Supremes. Lacy pulled right up to the lobby door to let me out. Charles, the doorman, came running up to the car door before Lacy could get my books to come around to my side.

Charles, who was openly gay, asked me, "Why are you getting here so late tonight, young lady? Your mother called down to the lobby asking if I had seen you."

I explained that there had been trouble after the game and that we had gotten locked into the gymnasium until the coast was clear. I told him that I would explain everything to my mother when I got upstairs.

Charles said, "Then you'd better get your little self on upstairs, rather than lollygagging with this dude."

By then, Lacy had made it around to my side of the car with my books. Giving them to me, he said to Charles, "Excuse me, sir, I haven't finished with her yet."

Charles said, "And what are you doing with her? Didn't I see you here with that Veronica girl a couple of years ago? Isn't this one a little young for you?"

I said, "Charles, mind ya!" That means *mind your business* in ghetto-eze. He looked at me, rolling his eyes. So, I said, "Yeah, mind ya business!" Charles rolled his eyes back at me again and went inside the lobby door, still watching us.

Then Lacy said, "As I was about to say when we were so rudely interrupted, are you busy tomorrow night?"

I said, "No, I don't think so."

Lacy replied, "So why don't we catch a movie? I hear that there is a new James Bond flick out."

I said, "Sure, why not?" Then I added, "Lacy, are you asking me out on a date?"

He said, "Yeah, I guess I am," and we both laughed. Then Lacy said, "So I will pick you up around 6 p.m., and we'll grab a bite to eat before the movie." Then he pecked me on the cheek with his lips and walked away toward his car.

When I passed the desk, Charles yelled, "Ah, I saw that. I'm gonna tell your mama. Letting that boy kiss you like that."

I heard Lacy yell back, "That wasn't a kiss. That was a peck. You wouldn't know the difference between the two if you saw it, least more experienced it!"

I went on up to our apartment and told Mama everything that had happened, including my ride home with Lacy and the invitation to go to a movie.

She said, "Isn't that Lacy a little old for you? How old is he? Isn't he out of high school?"

I said, "I think he is nineteen or twenty."

She said, "Then you are jailbait at sixteen! Both of you better watch yourselves, and you know what I mean, because I won't hesitate to come down on his old ass if he takes advantage of you!"

I said, "Aw, Ma! He's a nice guy!" and retired to my room.

Our first date was real sweet. Lacy picked me up right on time. We stopped to have burgers, fries, and milkshakes at the Hot Shoppe (by Marriott), and then we went to see the James Bond flick *You Only Live Twice*. It didn't disappoint and was action-packed. We really enjoyed it.

I was home by midnight, which was early for both of us. I think Lacy was trying to be respectful and not overstep any boundaries on our first date, and I appreciated that. I thought I knew him, and I was right. He was really a nice guy, and I liked him. I said to myself, *I hope he asks me out on a second date.*

When I got home to our apartment, my mother asked me, "How was the movie? I see you are home before curfew!"

I said, "Great." And I went straight to bed. There was church, studying, chores, more studying, and preparing for the next week of school to be done on Sunday.

Lacy called on Sunday evening to ask me out on another date the following weekend. And that ritual went on and on and on. We went out every weekend, sometimes on both Friday night and Saturday night. We were becoming an item. We went to movies, to parties, out to concerts, and on all the normal dates that young people were into in DC at the time. For a young man his age, Lacy had a good job, working full-time at the postal service. In his own words, he liked "fine cars, fine women, fine food, and fine wine." He never was cheap and always picked up the tab, not allowing me to pay for anything.

He loved good food, so we went out to eat often, to some of the most popular restaurants among people our age, such as Gusty's, an Italian restaurant, and Blackie's House of Beef. Lacy took me out to Blackie's on my seventeenth birthday. That was the first time in my life I was able to order a T-bone steak at a restaurant. It was a magical evening. Talk about being wined and dined—without the wine, of course. I wasn't into underage drinking at that time.

I soon found myself falling in love with this guy. He was nothing like his reputation. He was funny, sweet, and kind, and he loved spoiling me. Most of all, he made me laugh, and I needed that in my life. He called me every night and would pick me up from school anytime I asked, and even if I didn't.

If I had practice or some other activity that kept me at school until dark, he was always there. He would turn in his postal truck and drive a short distance to pick me up from Tech and take me to Southeast. I knew he was going way out of his way to do so much with and for me, but he said he didn't mind, and I enjoyed all of the attention.

He even introduced me to his mother on one of our early dates. Who does that? He said that they were very close and that he wanted me to meet the only other woman in his life. He said he wanted us to meet and get to know one another. Lacy was winning my heart, and I was falling in love with him, hard.

Winter quickly melted into the spring of 1968. Again, several national and local events would take place that would touch my life and further shape the person I would become. They would also have a significant impact on my relationship with Lacy.

THE ASSASSINATION OF MARTIN LUTHER KING JR.

During the spring of 1968, after the basketball season was over, it was time for me to buckle down to some serious schoolwork. My goal was to get really good grades for the last two quarters to keep my GPA around a 3.5 or higher, so I could get inducted into the National Honor Society, a sure bet for getting into college.

On Thursday, April 4, 1968, Dr. Martin Luther King Jr., the revered American clergyman and civil rights leader, was fatally shot while standing on a balcony of the Lorraine Motel in Memphis, Tennessee, where he was staying. The prominent leader of the civil rights movement and Nobel Peace Prize laureate, who was known for his use of nonviolence and civil disobedience, was in Memphis to support African American sanitation workers there who were striking due to low wages and poor working conditions.[1]

A Baptist minister and founder of the Southern Christian Leadership Conference (SCLC), King had led the civil rights movement since the mid-1950s, using a combination of powerful words and nonviolent tactics such as sit-ins, boycotts, and protest marches—including the massive March on Washington in 1963—to fight discrimination and achieve significant civil and voting rights for African Americans.

However, during the spring of 1968, King was under significant criticism from some young African American activists who favored a more confrontational approach to seeking the goals of the civil rights movement, such as Stokely Carmichael, H. Rap Brown, and their followers. These young radicals were attracted more closely to the ideals of black nationalist leader Malcolm X, who was assassinated in 1965 and had condemned King's advocacy of nonviolence as not being able to deal with the continuing oppression of African Americans. Therefore, during that spring, King was strategically seeking to widen his appeal beyond his own race by speaking out publicly against the Vietnam War and working to form a coalition on behalf of all poor Americans, both black and white, to address such issues as poverty and unemployment. Dr. King was planning another march on Washington, DC, to lobby

---

[1] Lotus, "House Divided," 1968.

Congress on behalf of the poor when he and other SCLC leaders were called to Memphis, Tennessee, to help the sanitation workers.[2]

On April 3, the night before he was killed, King spoke at the Mason Temple Church in Memphis, where he gave the now famous "I've Been to the Mountaintop" speech that seemed to foreshadow his untimely death. The next evening, just after six o'clock, as he was waiting to go to dinner with his colleagues, Dr. King was shot while standing on a balcony of the Lorraine Motel, where he was known to stay when he came to Memphis. It is believed that a single bullet struck King from a Remington model 760 hunting rifle. The bullet entered through King's right cheek, breaking his jawbone and several vertebrae as it traveled down his spinal cord, severing his jugular vein and major arteries in the process, before lodging in his shoulder.[3]

King fell violently backward onto the balcony floor, unconscious. Ralph Abernathy, King's right-hand man, and Andrew Young, another colleague from SCLS, ran to King's aide and found that he still had a pulse. He was rushed to Saint Joseph's Hospital, but he never regained consciousness and was pronounced dead about an hour later, at the age of thirty-nine. Shortly after the shot was fired, witnesses saw a white male, later identified as a small-time criminal named James Earle Ray, a fugitive from the Missouri State Penitentiary, running from a boardinghouse near the Lorraine Motel, carrying a bundle that was later found on the sidewalk beside the rooming house. Authorities later concluded that Ray, who was staying at the rooming house, fired the fatal bullet from a common bathroom there. His fingerprints were found on the rifle used to kill King, as well as a scope and a pair of binoculars.[4]

Eerily, King's assassination seemed very similar to the assassination of President John F. Kennedy. Both had the markings of a conspiracy

---

[2] Op cit.

[3] Posner, "Killing the Dream," 1998.

[4] Op. cit.

and a cover-up. These two murders would haunt our country and affect my life for years to come.

THE HOLY WEEK UPRISINGS

The days that followed seemed like a never-ending nightmare to me. As with the Kennedy assassination, the mourning period and burial of King happened over a holiday, this time during Easter Holy Week. For the second time in five years, I found myself in shock and dismay. Another one of my heroes, whom I loved and admired, had been struck down by an assassin's bullet. I kept asking myself, *How could a man who stood for nonviolence and peace meet such a violent death?*

Shock waves spread around the world with the news that King had been assassinated. As word of the assassination and a possible conspiracy spread, shock, distress, and anger over King's death incited riots in over a hundred cities all across the United States, including burning and looting, with DC, Chicago, and Baltimore being the cities most affected.

In Washington, DC, after King's assassination, crowds began to gather during the evening hours of April 4 at Fourteenth and U Streets, NW, in the Shaw neighborhood near Howard University. Lead by Stokely Carmichael, a Trinidad and Tobago–born activist who had parted with King in 1966 and been removed as head of the Student Nonviolent Coordinating Committee in 1967, members in the crowd demanded that store owners close in King's honor. Although polite at first, the crowd got out of control and began breaking windows. By eleven that night, a riot was in full bloom, and widespread looting and burning had begun, in DC and in other cities across the country.[5]

After King's funeral and the Easter break, DC students were allowed to return to school—however, under a dusk-to-dawn curfew. That meant we could only be on the streets during daylight hours,

---

[5] Pepper, "Orders to Kill," 1995.

which basically meant just going to school and coming straight home. I recall that it was also getting close to the end of the school year and at a crucial exam cycle.

One exam I had coming up was in a class called Lab Tech. Part of the class was similar to an anatomy class, where we had to learn all the systems of a mammal and all its parts. Our teacher used cat cadavers to do that. He even allowed us to take a dead cat home to study for our tests. We had an anatomy test scheduled for the Friday after we returned from Easter break.

Feeling that I had fallen behind in my studies during our days of mourning and the Easter break, I stayed after school that Thursday with some of my classmates to study the cat for the test. I still didn't think I was quite ready for the test, so I waited until my classmates were all done to sign the cat out, so I could take it home to study it that night. I told my teacher and fellow classmates goodbye and headed to the bus stop for my long bus ride home. There were only a few of my fellow students on my first bus, and I watched them all get off.

Once I got on my last bus for home, I began to get nervous. There were no Tech students on that bus. The sun was quickly going down, and it was beginning to get dark. I was afraid that it was going to be dark by the time I got to Southeast, and sure enough, by the time the bus got to Good Hope Road, in heavy rush-hour traffic, it was pitch black outside. I had let the time and the curfew slip away from me.

I began to pray. "God, please don't let me get caught." Surely, I thought I could make it from the bus stop across the street to Mulberry Plaza.

When the bus pulled up to my stop, I was the only one who got up to get off. I hopped off using the back door. The bus pulled off into the rush-hour traffic. As I stood there waiting for the traffic to clear so I could cross the street, sure enough, up rolled a military jeep with four young National Guardsmen in it: two black and two white. They jumped out and surrounded me.

One asked, "Young lady, do you know it's after curfew?"

I replied, "Yes, sir."

A second one asked, "Where are you coming from?"

I said, "School, sir."

A third one—a handsome young black soldier, I must add—said, "School was over a few hours ago. Explain yourself, ma'am!"

It was all I could do to keep from wetting in my pants. But in a soft voice, I said. "Well, sir, I attend McKinley Tech High School. I have an exam tomorrow. I stayed late to study with my teacher and fellow classmates, and time kind of got away from me, since I live way out here and all. I am so sorry. I am not trying to break the law or anything. I just want to do well on my test tomorrow."

The fourth guardsman, a white guy, said, "And you expect us to believe that? Where are your fellow classmates? I don't see any. What's in that bag? And what's that I smell?" He looked around and then at my bag.

I answered, "Yes, sir. I am one of the few students who lives this far out, so I was the last one on the bus tonight. This was our first week back at school, and the first day I stayed late since the curfew was put in place. I thought I could make it home before dark, but the bus got caught in rush-hour traffic."

I added, "What's in my bag? It's a dead cat. But don't worry, sir, it's a cadaver. This is what we were studying and had me on the bus so late. We have an anatomy test tomorrow, and I had to wait until everyone was finished with it so I could sign it out overnight to study it. Would you like to see it?"

All four of the guardsmen came close to look in the bag, and then they grabbed their noses and pulled back. One of the white guys started to gag. Two of them guarded me, and two of them caucused.

The handsome black guardsman came back, stood in front of me, and said, "Young lady, we are going to let you go. Let this be a lesson to you. Never disobey a directive of the United States government. We are going to escort you across the street. You go inside your residence and don't come out until tomorrow morning to go to school. And take that dead, stinky cat with you."

Two of the guardsmen stopped traffic and another escorted me across the street. They made an example of me. Drivers were rubbernecking in their cars. I was so embarrassed. Once across the street, I took off running into our apartment building. Of course, Charles, the doorman, with his radar eyes, had seen some of what had happened, and he said, "Ooh, girl, you gonna get it when you get upstairs."

I replied, "Mind your damn business, Charles," and proceeded to the elevator.

He replied, "No, she didn't just curse at me? You smarty-pants you!"

When I got upstairs to our apartment, my mother was beside herself. "Girl, where have you been? Didn't you know you weren't supposed to be on the street after dark? I've been worried sick, and Lacy has been calling every five minutes asking for you. He said he drove by the school looking for you, and they said you were gone so he went home so he wouldn't get caught on the street himself. Where have you been all this time?"

I responded, "Trying to get home." I broke down in tears. I told her what happened, that I stayed late studying and waited for that dumb cat. I didn't know that Lacy would come. I said that he was on curfew too and had to get off the street by dark. "Better me than him, a young black man! So, I caught the bus, and it got caught in rush-hour traffic."

Then Mama made a proclamation that surprised me. She said, "That's it. We are out of here." She meant out of Southeast. She was getting tired of living so far out. "This takes the cake. We are moving back to Northeast this summer. I'm going to start looking as soon as they lift this damn curfew. You are going to do your senior year a little closer to Tech."

I said, "Really, Mom? Oh, thank you." I gave my mom a big hug.

Then she said, "Now, go call Lacy. He is getting on my last nerve. *"Is she home yet?* What is he, your boyfriend or something? I ain't never had no man checking up on me like that. Y'all got it like that or something? He's about to give himself a heart attack."

I said, "Oh, Ma, cut Lacy some slack. He's one of the good guys."

The curfew was eventually lifted, and the rest of the school year went on without incident. Lacy and I grew even closer, and we spent all of our free time together, especially on the weekends.

ANOTHER PROM AND DC SUMMER

One of Lacy's best friends, David, had a girlfriend who was a senior at Tech and we double-dated with them a lot. David hadn't gone to Tech, so we went with them when he took his girlfriend to her prom so that David could be with people he knew. Knowing David's date and several of my cheerleader buddies who were also seniors, I was delighted to go to their prom. After the prom, we did the usual DC ritual, staying out all night, dancing the night away, and making the after-parties and breakfasts.

That night, George asked me to go steady with him, and of course I said yes. It was only a formality. In my eyes mind, and heart, we had been exclusive for weeks. The asking and acknowledgement just made it official. We were now an item. I was spoken for.

As soon as school was out, my mother and I moved back to far Northeast into an apartment complex named Fort Chaplin Park. These were garden apartments and more to my mother's liking. She got us a large two-bedroom place with a patio, and Vee and I had enough space to be comfortable when she came home from Hampton.

The summer of 1968 was quite delightful. Lacy and I did everything that young couples in DC like to do: hung out in Georgetown; went to the beach, concerts, and amusement parks; and of course, went to house parties and cook-outs where we would dance. That was the one thing we did well together, the one thing we had most in common that brought us close: dancing.

During the summer days, however, like other young people in

DC, Lacy and I both worked. That summer, I was able to land a job in a special program that the federal government set up for children of federal government employees. If your parents worked for the Feds, you could apply to the Summer Youth Employment Program, which was instituted after the riots to give young people something meaningful to do during the summer to keep them out of trouble. A similar program was later started within the DC government by a young politician by the name of Marion Barry.

I applied and was accepted to the federal government program by the Department of the Navy, since both my parents worked for the Feds at other agencies. I was hired as a civilian, as a GS-2 low-level clerical office worker, and I was granted a secret clearance after being investigated, which meant that I could handle secret documents. Basically, that meant I had no criminal record and had declared my loyalty to the United States, which was no big deal to most native Washingtonians who grew up being loyal to this country and pledging allegiance to the US flag every day at school. I was only seventeen years old, and though I knew nothing from nothing, I did know that I loved Washington, DC, and the United States. I would have no problem handling secret documents.

I worked at the Main Navy Building, which was at Navy Headquarters, located back then at 14th and Constitution Avenue in downtown DC, a good bus ride from our new apartment. I worked for a group of naval officers who were engineers. I was supervised by an Asian American female. We were an odd couple but got along very well, sort of like Susen and I had at Eliot. She liked me, and I liked her. She thought I was smart and vice versa.

My job was very simple and the typing skills that I learned with the use of my neighbor's typewriter when I was younger, came in handy. I typed memos and forms, answered phones, and ran errands, mainly carrying documents, some of them marked *secret*, to and from the Pentagon and the Navy Yard, which I caught a shuttle bus to and from. I liked the job a lot, and my mom, dad, and extended family were very proud of me. I was the only teenager in the family to land a job like that. Little did I know that many years later, the Navy wing of the Pentagon that I was in and out of, almost daily, would be hit by a plane used by terrorists on 9/11/2001.

I worked forty hours per week and got off promptly at five o'clock. Often, Lacy would pick me up from work when he was finished with his appointed rounds or on his break from the post office. My GS-2 pay was very little; it was at the bottom of the federal government pay scale, a few hundred dollars every two weeks, but for a seventeen-year-old, not that bad. I bought shoes, clothes, and fabric to make outfits for my senior year. I saved the rest for college and my upcoming senior-year expenses, such as senior pictures, class ring, applications to college, the senior-class trip, and of course, senior prom and graduation.

Those senior-year expenses seemed overwhelming. To top things off, my mother announced that she had run out of savings from her accident and would have no money for me to go to college. Her exact words were: "You're on your own, kid!" What a shock! I believed, for so long, that a college education would be my ticket to success. So, I knew I had to do two things. First and foremost, I had to work hard in school to get my GPA as high as possible to get a scholarship to go to college. Second of all, I had to work and save as much money as possible for my senior year and for college. These two goals would take *perseverance, hope, and determination* (PHD).

So that July, I started looking for a part-time job that would last through the school year. I got a tip from a club sister that department stores were hiring young black girls to work retail, also as a result of the riots. Retailers were reaching out to the black community, especially those that had only a handful of black employees. The bottom line was that maybe if they hired more young black people, they wouldn't become targets if there was further unrest.

I decided to try my luck with a department store named Woodward and Lothrop, an upscale store in downtown Washington not far from the Main Navy Building. I was told that I needed to be eighteen years old and to bring a copy my birth certificate. So, I did something desperate: I changed my birth year from 1951 to 1950 by changing the 1 to a 0, with no problem, and told no one about that.

With a reference from the navy department, I was hired right away, for two evenings during the week and all day on Saturday. I was placed in the candy department, selling fine candies and chocolates. I had to learn all the name brands and all the flavors. My favorite name brand was Russell Stover's.

They told me I could keep the part-time job when school started and, as long as I did well, even through college, during holidays and summers. That suited me and my plans for my future just fine. It would take *PHD*, but I knew I could pull it off.

I loved working at "Woodies," which was the nickname Washingtonians had for the store. I got a 20 percent discount on beautiful, well-made designer clothes and quickly learned where every clearance rack in the store was, especially in the Junior and Misses departments.

Woodward and Lothrop. Photo taken from National Photo Company Collection (Library of Congress).

SENIOR YEAR

My senior year in high school was quite memorable. It was everything I wished for. My class schedule was great, cheerleading couldn't be better, and I was in love with a man who gave me plenty of attention and was always there for me.

Lacy enrolled in Howard University in the fall of 1968, after attending Northern Virginia Community College for two years and serving in the Civil Air Patrol in lieu of the army during the Vietnam War. Although he was drafted by the army, due to a basketball injury and knee surgery, he received a 4F and didn't make it out of basic training, which was fine with him. He kept his job with the post office to pay for college, and he doted on me on date nights.

One day, he asked me to be his math tutor. I said to him, "I'm just starting the twelfth grade. You are in college. Are you crazy?"

He said to me, "Aren't you taking AP math classes?"

I said, "Yes."

Then he said, "What grade did you last get?"

I said, "An A."

Then he said, "Fine, then you are better at math than I am. I need you to be my tutor. I've only had basic math, for dummies like me, and I need to pass college algebra to stay in college, and it's also required for my major. So, I need you to tutor me. I know you can do it. I trust you, Nettie! You are smarter than me. Believe me! I need you!"

So, I became Lacy's math tutor. How could I say no? He would pick me up after cheerleading practice, and we would study at his house, my apartment, or the library. Most of the time we would go to the library so as not to get distracted. However, on Sunday, after church and cheerleading practice, we did some serious studying over at his house because his mother often worked on Sunday. He and his mother lived in a lovely Cape Cod detached house with a huge yard in a quiet neighborhood in NE Washington, called Brookland. They had lived there since Lacy was a toddler.

I didn't mind tutoring him. It brought us closer together as a couple, and it helped me sharpen my math skills and prepare for the SAT exam. However, on one warm Sunday afternoon that fall, after cheerleading practice, while we were studying at his house, a knock came to the front door.

Lacy's mother was nursing a patient that day, so she wasn't home. I was in the kitchen, taking a break and getting a cool drink, when I heard a commotion at the door. One of Lacy's old girlfriends, JoAnn Sales, had barged her way into the house and was asking, "Where is she? Where is that bitch?"

I came out of the kitchen and asked, "What's going on?"

JoAnn yelled, "Are you the new girlfriend?"

This chick was about two years older than me and appeared to have been drinking. She was sauced up, as they say. She seemed to be upset that Lacy had moved on with someone else. In fact, she was mad about it.

I proudly responded, with an attitude, "Yes, I am. And who wants to know?"

Then she turned to Lacy and said, "So that's your new girl I've heard so much about?"

Lacy responded, "JoAnn, it's been over between us for months. I told you that way back in December. Remember? I told you I was moving on."

JoAnn said, "So I'll show you what I think about you and her." She proceeded to go over to the fireplace mantel, pick up Lacy's mother's delicate ceramic pieces one by one, and throw them onto the hardwood floor, smashing them to bits.

Lacy ran over to her, grabbed her, spun her around, and held her in front of him, with her back to him and her arms pinned, so she couldn't get loose. His German shepherd, Star, came running toward her, barking and in attack mode. Lacy had to command the dog to sit. Star sat down, but continued to bark at her.

All of this was scaring me. I was scared for JoAnn and what Star would do to her. Each time Lacy would let her go, she would grab another item and throw it onto the wood floor. Neither one of us wanted to call the police on her, so Lacy kept trying to hold her back and calm her down.

He asked me to take Star, go around the corner to our friend Donny's house, and ask Donny to come give him a hand. He asked me, "Can you get home alone? Do you have money?"

I said, "Sure. I always carry mad money, you know that!" Then I said, "Later," and left.

Well, I had never gone anywhere with Star alone before, because I was halfway scared of her, but I complied with what I was asked to do. I took Star and walked around to Donny's house. I told him that JoAnn was at Lacy's house, tearing up the place. I asked him if I could use his phone to call a cab, and he said, "Sure."

When the cab came and I got in it to go home, Donny took Star and started walking toward Lacy's house. And that was that.

Well, I was mad as hell! Mad at JoAnn for coming over there, drunk as a skunk. Mad at Lacy for letting her in and allowing her to tear up his mother's house like that. Mad that neither of us wanted to call the police. And mad at myself for not having the guts to beat her ass. I should have wiped the floor up with her hair! Somebody could have gotten seriously hurt that day, though.

That was the second incident concerning one of Lacy's old girlfriends and me. The first was when an old girlfriend showed up at my church one Sunday to check me out. Her name was Carolyn Murray, and she was the daughter of a wealthy club owner in DC who owned a supper club near Howard University's campus. She drove a yellow convertible Corvette and used to take Lacy's mom shopping, do her hair, and run errands for her. She knew a girl I knew at my church and came by one Sunday to see who she thought her competition was, I guess.

I had done my homework on Miss Carolyn. When I saw her roll up in her Corvette after church, I knew exactly who she was. I was just glad that I was dressed to kill that Sunday, with a grey wool flannel walking suit that I had made with a floppy hat to match. I was looking good that Sunday, if I must say so myself.

Lacy had told me all about Miss Carolyn Murray and how she had tried to buy his affection, to no avail. So when Carolyn and my fellow church member were staring me down outside of the church, I walked right up to them and said, "Well, hello! You must be Carolyn Murray. I've heard about you and your antics from Lacy. So happy to make your acquaintance." I reached out to shake her hand and she obliged, reluctantly.

After a pleasant chat, she began to make a beeline toward her car. As she walked away, I said, "Why don't you stick around to say hello to Lacy? He'll be here to pick me up in a minute. I know he would be happy to see you here."

She said, "No, that's OK."

Then I said, "So sorry you have to leave so soon. I'll be sure to tell him you came to visit today."

She and my fellow church member appeared to be in shock. I don't think either of them knew that I knew who she was. Although they were a couple of years older than me, having done my homework on them, I knew that they had gone to high school together. I put two and two together, and I was good at doing that.

Of course, I told Lacy about Carolyn's visit, and it didn't sit well with him at all. I don't think he liked her boldness. I chalked that up as a win for me and a loss for Carolyn, I hoped.

While riding home in the cab after the JoAnn incident, I began to question my relationship with Lacy for the first time. Were we getting too serious? Was he too much for me to handle, with the age difference and all the baggage he was bringing into our relationship? Was our relationship taking too much time and attention away from my studies and my plans for my future? And how did Mrs. Lacy, his mother, feel about us? Did she prefer someone like Carolyn over me? The answers to all of those questions were no, no, and no.

When I got home, I grabbed some dinner and went straight to my room to study. To say the least, I got very little studying done. I didn't tell my mother about either incident. She probably would not have allowed me to go out with Lacy anymore. So, when he called, I played like nothing was wrong between us in front of my mother. The first time he called, I hung up on him, as if it was a wrong number. By the third time he called, begging me not to hang up on him anymore, my mother was getting suspicious that something was wrong, so I took his call and just listened.

He said, "Nettie, are you mad? Can I come over to get you and take you somewhere so we can talk about what happened?"

I agreed to see him because we needed to clear the air, and I didn't want him to come over and talk about what happened in front of my mother.

So, we went out to the Hot Shoppe to cool off and talk over ice cream sundaes. I admit, I had an attitude, big time, but I listened, somewhat, to what he had to say. He admitted that he didn't handle the incident correctly by letting JoAnn into the house. He told me that she was known for her violent actions toward brothers and would not have hesitated to slash the tires on his GTO or worse, and he didn't want that.

He begged my forgiveness and asked for a fresh start. I told him to clean up his past and that one more incident with a girl from his past would be a deal breaker for me. I reluctantly allowed him to kiss me as a gesture of good faith, knowing that I would be watching to see how he handled women from his past in the future. I was no fool, nor was I going to be a doormat. He was going to have to win my trust all over again, and he did. He showered me with attention, was always around, and barely let me out of his sight.

Some mornings, he came all the way out to far Northeast from Brookland, which was near McKinley, to take me to school. Most evenings after cheerleading practice or work, there he was, with his "chariot," waiting to take me home. He came to every game I cheered in to make sure I got home OK. I couldn't shake him if I wanted to. You would think we were married or living together. He knew most of the guys I knew at school, especially my "play brothers" and most of the athletes, and they all knew I was spoken for. I later found out that the message had been spread all over town, not just at McKinley.

I continued to tutor Lacy in math and helped him prepare for the math final he needed to pass in order to stay at Howard and move on in his business major. I told him I thought he was ready, based on all the math skills and tricks I had taught him that I had learned over the years, but I really wasn't sure.

A couple of days after the test, he picked me up in the GOAT and we rode up to Howard University. He was so nervous, he was sweating bullets. He took me by the hand, and we went to the wall where all of the grades were posted. He looked for his ID number and there it was: he had gotten an 82 on the final and a C in the class. He had passed.

He picked me up and swung me around and around, yelling, "We did it. We did it."

I kept saying, "No, you did it. You did it." It had taken *PHD*, but I knew he could do it.

He said, "I wouldn't have made it without you, not without you!"

Then he said something very touching: "You have no idea what you've done for me. You have changed my life. I have never had a girlfriend really care about me and my well-being the way you do. I love you, Nettie. I will love you 'til my dying day!"

That type of declaration of love blew me away. I knew right then and there that Lacy was a keeper. I loved him back and was willing to hang in there with him. He needed me and I needed him to get through this thing we call life.

He then gave me a passionate kiss right there in the hallway. He took me to Blackie's for a steak dinner that weekend to celebrate. I had my first filet mignon ever, and of course, I couldn't eat it all. It was way too much for me. I was so embarrassed. So Lacy ate the rest for me. I knew right then and there that Lacy and I were meant to be together, maybe even for the rest of our lives.

WE'RE NUMBER ONE!

Sports-wise and cheerleading-wise, things couldn't have gone better for the Trainers, as our teams were called, during the 1968-69 academic year. In the fall of 1968, our football team won the East title with an unblemished 6–0 regular season record, beating all of the public high schools in Northeast and Southeast, including chief rivals Eastern and Ballou and our nemesis, Anacostia. However, the Trainers lost the citywide Inter-High Championship to the West champions, the Cardozo Purple Wave.

Although I was upset, I wasn't in tears like my fellow cheerleaders, because my kindergarten and fifth-grade hero, Darren, played defensive back for Cardozo. I kept hearing, "Tackle by Darren Tabbs." It seemed as if Darren was in on every tackle against the Trainers that day. Under my outward frown and displeasure, deep in my soul, was a little-bitty warm smile for my old friend and protector.

Darren and I had gone out together a couple of times when I was between boyfriends in the eleventh grade, but I had told him that we couldn't take our relationship any further than friendship. I told him that I saw him more like a brother than a boyfriend. I will always wonder if our relationship, or lack thereof, gave him the motivation to make all of those tackles that day. He was eventually named defensive high school player of the year in 1968 by the *Washington Post*. Hurray for Darren!

The Trainers did even better in basketball in 1969. The star players, known as the Magnificent Seven, won the Inter-High East by beating their rival, Anacostia; the citywide Inter-High Championship by beating the West champion—yes, it was the Cardozo Purple Wave, again. In addition, our basketball team won the city-wide Regional Championship by beating the Catholic school champion, Demantha. Demantha's star player was a guy named James Brown, who is now the famous sports commentator. McKinley's team gained recognition on a national scale, and the Trainers received a fourth-place rating in a noted national high school poll.

Yet, the *Washington Post* did not rank McKinley Tech as number one in the DC Metropolitan Area, instead giving their top ranking to our opponent, Dematha, the predominately white suburban Catholic school we had beaten for the city-wide championship. Using no apparent guidelines, this national newspaper had seemingly ignored the statistics and given Dematha its number-one ranking, which appeared to have racial overtones.

The Post had given Dematha its number-one ranking although Dematha had beaten McKinley only once out of three outings during the season, at the Knights of Columbus Tournament. But Tech came back to beat Dematha in the city-wide championship and had beaten them once in the early part of the season. No one understood the *Post's* logic!

This did not sit well with many of the teachers, administrators, and students at McKinley Tech. So, a "March on the *Washington Post*" was organized by the teachers and students to protest what we felt was a racist act. And of course, the cheerleaders were expected to be there, in uniform, leading the charge.

When I went home to tell my mother what was being planned, she blew a gasket, again. Again, I heard the party line of what-ifs. What if the wrong people saw me protesting? What if I were seen on TV or in the *Washington Post* protesting, for God's sake? What if college recruiters found out? What if people from her job saw me? What would people say? And what if it got back to her supervisor? Not wanting to risk losing her good government job, my mother forbade me to go to the march. She told me I'd better come straight home from school and to tell my teachers and cheerleading coach, "Thanks, but no thanks."

I'm sure you've gotten to know me by now. There was no way in hell I was going to be left out of that action. I was *determined* to march. So, on the morning of March 18, 1969, I put on my cheerleading uniform after my mother went to work, and I put enough money from my savings for cab fare home into my sock. My plan was to go to the march on the team bus, march for a little while, and then jump in a cab and beat Mama home. And my plan worked, almost.

Over two hundred students, with chaperones, went to the march right after school to protest what we thought was the *Washington Post*'s unfair treatment. We went by any means necessary: school bus, public transportation, private cars, and cabs. There was no subway back then. We picketed with signs and chants outside the *Post* building in downtown Washington.

"Not tomorrow, not today, we want action right away!" and "We're number one!" were some of the chants. Inside the building, a delegation of teachers and student leaders were discussing the seemingly racist action with the *Post*'s editors. They were presented with a petition, signed by 1,600 of McKinley Tech's students, faculty and supporters, many of whom were *Post* customers, protesting the *Post*'s decision to rank Dematha as number one. The protest was covered by all of the local TV stations and all of the newspapers—including some *Washington Post* reporters.

My plan went like clockwork. I went to the protest with my fellow cheerleaders and classmates on the team buses. We got to the *Post* building by three thirty. I protested at the front of the march with my fellow cheerleaders. After a while, I dropped out, hailed a cab, and got home just before my mother did. I pulled off my uniform and was in my room and into my books by the time Mama got home. I went to bed early that night as well, around ten o'clock, and I made sure the TV was turned off.

Sure enough, the protest was reported on the eleven o'clock news broadcasts and appeared in the local newspapers the next day. Evidently, some of my mothers' coworkers had seen me on TV that night and mentioned it to her the next day. Boy, did she let me have it. When she got home from work the next day, she said, "So-and-so saw you on TV last night. Didn't I tell you not to go to that protest march?"

Surprisingly, she just fussed at me. Evidently, she didn't get in trouble at work, and her friends probably backed our cause, which may have brought her around. She was mad that I disobeyed her more than anything else. She didn't punish me or anything else, though. She seemed to respect me for my *determination* to stand up for what I believed in.

After three days of talks, the *Washington Post* agreed to rank McKinley Tech as the number-one high school basketball team in the region. Did they understand that their ranking had economic implications for some of the boys on the team? Many of us did! At the end of the season and after all the protesting, all of the seniors on McKinley's team received college basketball scholarships.

The McKinley Tech Trainers also did well in baseball, tennis, and track during the 1968–69 school year. However, cheerleaders were not required to cheer at those sporting events. Personally, I went to a couple of baseball games and track meets because I had friends involved, and Lacy and I went to the Penn Relays in Philadelphia to see the McKinley and Howard track teams participate in track and field at that meet. That was a fun out-of-town date, watching McKinley and Howard compete, respectively.

The rest of school year went well for me also, without any other controversies. My senior activities went as planned. Spring of 1969 was packed with activities and decisions to be made. I got my SAT scores back, and they were very good. Most colleges at that time would consider students scoring above 600 in both math and English for financial aid. I got way over 600, closer to 700 in math, and close to 600 on the verbal section, which gave me well over 1,200 as a combined score. That was good enough to get some pretty good scholarship offers.

Also, that spring, the class rankings came out at the end of the third quarter. My class rank was number 9 of the top 10 out of 711 students, which put me in the top 2 percent of the graduating class and got me inducted into McKinley's Pharaoh's chapter of the National Honor Society and listed in "Who's Who." Not bad for a cheerleader who went to all of the required sporting events, every dance, and many of the parties; had an active social life; and had a fly, mature, college boyfriend. My class rank also looked good on my college applications, along with being a cheerleader, believe it or not. Cheerleading showed recruiters that you had good leadership skills, that you could multitask (handle more than one responsibility at the same time), and that you were extroverted and well-rounded, which were all useful for succeeding in college.

Number 10 in our class was this cool guy named Leon Williams, who gave the best house parties in the school, so I was in good company. We called ourselves No. 9 and No. 10, the Cool Ones. We were inducted into the National Honor Society together, and both of us made the "Who's Who" list. We were examples that at McKinley, it was OK to be smart, cool, and fly, too.

OUR CLASS TRIP, PROM, AND GRADUATION

Next came the senior-class trip to Montreal, Canada. We had a blast, sightseeing by day and partying by night. Many of us, including me, had never been outside of the United States, so that was a first and a real treat for me. Though I was there without my boyfriend, I had a ball. Because it was four girls to a room, I spent most of my evenings covering up for and playing lookout for my roommates while they broke curfew to hang out with various boys, mainly the basketball players, since three of us were cheerleaders.

I didn't mind playing den mother. I had sworn off all athletes. I had learned that many of them didn't mean you any good. They could give you a bad reputation or worse. I tried to tell the girls that, but did they listen? No.

The prom and graduation were icing on the cake. The prom was a dream date come true. I made a beautiful yellow-gold gown to wear, with a gold metallic bodice and a yellow-gold crepe bottom. Lacy wore a gold-tone tuxedo dinner jacket with black tuxedo pants and shoes. We were quite the pair.

Our prom was held at the luxurious, prestigious Sheraton Park

Hotel in the uptown Cleveland Park section of Northwest Washington on Woodley Road, near the National Zoo and Rock Creek Park. The hotel is one of the oldest and most beautifully appointed in the city. The ballroom where we had our prom is one of the largest in the city, with a beautiful spiral staircase as an entrance. All eyes were on the staircase as couples made their entrance. I felt like a fairy-tale princess as we arrived in Lacy's burgundy GTO and as we made our way down that staircase. However, with all eyes on you, you had to be careful not to trip on the stairs.

The evening was beautiful. The dinner was lovely, and we danced the night away. And the after-parties and the breakfasts were "the bomb".

Graduation was a great event also. Our graduation was held at Washington's DAR (Daughters of the American Revolution) Constitution Hall, where major concerts and events are held, as were graduations for most of the large public high schools in DC at that time. Constitution Hall was large enough to hold all of the graduates and their family members—much larger than the average high school auditorium, although most of them were a good size. It was very prestigious to have your graduation held there. We had not forgotten that there was a time when blacks were not allowed to appear or attend events at Constitution Hall during the Jim Crow era, including opera star Marion Anderson, who was denied the opportunity to sing there. So, to have your high school graduation held there was quite a feat.

So, Washington's teens were exposed to the best venues and attractions early in life back then. For some, it was the only time in life they would have a chance to experience venues like the Sheraton Park Hotel and/or Constitution Hall. For others of the middle class, it would become a lifestyle, a standard to live by: only the best.

Our graduating class had a baccalaureate—a prayer service—at McKinley the Sunday before graduation, to bless us and send us on our way. The next day was graduation. I made a beautiful white-eyelet two-piece dress and pants set for the two-day event from fabric I purchased at Woodies. I wore the one-piece mini coatdress to the baccalaureate and the two-piece pantsuit under my gown on graduation day. My family members and friends came to both events. I was able to sit on the stage of Constitution Hall as number nine of the graduating class and as a member of the National Honor Society and "Who's Who" on graduation day. That was really cool. I felt like a celebrity.

After the ceremony, we took pictures on the steps of Constitution Hall with friends and family. I was on top of the world. I had graduated from a high school that I absolutely loved, which was once segregated, and celebrated my graduation sitting on the stage in a venue that once did not allow black people to perform there—not even opera singer Marion Anderson. How poignant was that? That was not lost on many of us.

McKinley Tech had helped me transition from a young block girl from Southeast into a college-bound young lady. I owe Tech and its teachers and administrators a lot for helping me, the great-great-great-granddaughter of a slave named Sookey Jubeter, to become the person I am today. They taught me how to do things the "McKinley Way," our motto that stands for *excellence and integrity*. I will never forget the invaluable lessons I learned at McKinley Tech and will always cherish the days I spent at the "School Up on the Hill."

FIVE
HAIL, HAIL, LINCOLN!

THE DAYS AND years that immediately followed high school were filled with wonder and intrigue for me. I often say that Lincoln University found me and that I found myself at Lincoln, for I entered Lincoln as a teenage girl and graduated as a college-educated woman. I will never forget the days and years that I spent living, learning, and loving at Lincoln. Lincoln University had a great impact on my life.

My summer of 1969, before I started at Lincoln, fit the theme "work hard and play hard." I went back to the Department of the Navy full-time to my previous job and continued to work part-time at Woodies. My supervisor at Navy announced when I returned that she had recommended me for a top-secret clearance, which meant another investigation, and she told me it would carry with it a promotion to a GS-3 on the federal pay scale and a slight increase in pay.

About two weeks later, after Sunday school, one of my old Sunday school teachers and mentors caught up with me after church. She asked me, "What did you do?"

I looked at her and said, "What?"

She said, "The FBI was here asking questions about you."

Then I said, "Oh, that." I had to explain to her the clearance process and that the investigation was for my job at Navy. She understood, but for someone over eighty years old, it was somewhat unsettling. They had asked if I was loyal to the United States or did I have a beef with the USA.

I did get the top-secret clearance, which allowed me to handle top-secret documents, which was no big deal to me. To be honest, I never paid much attention to the documents I carried around. The engineers I worked for never sealed the envelopes they gave me either. They trusted me that much. All I knew was that they were working on battleships of some sort.

They even had me pick up their paychecks from the Pentagon every two weeks. Payroll would just give me the paychecks in a stack, and I would sort them by name, put them in individual envelopes, and pass them out to the officers when I returned to the office. Doing that, I got to see what they were making: four to five times more than I was. So, I knew I needed to go to college to live the way they did. Getting a college degree was my ticket to success.

A TOUGH DECISION

I knew that it would take *perseverance, hope, and determination* (PHD) to make it to and through college, so I worked my two jobs and tried to make time for Lacy to have a little fun, which was a tall order. He would pick me up from work several times a week, especially on the nights when I worked at Woodies. I worked my butt off and saved as much money as I could until it was time to go off to college.

During my senior year of high school, I applied to a number of colleges. Unlike a lot of my friends who decided to go to southern HBCUs (historically black colleges and universities) like Hampton, Virginia State, and Spelman, I decided I wanted to go north. The experience I had on the train when I was five years old had left a terrible taste in my mouth about the South, I think, plus I tended to do things differently from other people.

All of the schools I applied to were north of DC. I can't even remember them all, but I do remember the ones that offered me scholarships: Boston University, Rutgers in New Jersey, Temple in Philadelphia, Central State in Ohio, Lincoln University in Pennsylvania, and Morgan State in Baltimore. It was tough making a decision among them, but here was my logic:

Boston University—a majority white school that my idol, Martin Luther King Jr., had attended, was the farthest away and the most prestigious. It had the major I wanted, physical therapy, but it was very expensive, and the financial-aid package was full of loans and other contingencies. In addition, Lacy said it was too far away and he was doubtful as to how often he would be able to come see me. So reluctantly, I crossed Boston off the list. I knew that Boston would kill my relationship with my boyfriend.

Central State also came off the list. An old boyfriend of mine was there on a football scholarship. I didn't want to be bothered by him.

That left Rutgers, Temple, Lincoln, and Morgan—two majority white schools and two HBCUs. Though it was close by, I didn't think I would like living in Baltimore, so I scratched Morgan State off the list. Morgan was too close to DC, and I would probably run home too much, which would keep me from studying.

I didn't know anybody in New Jersey, so that eliminated Rutgers. That left my two favorites in Pennsylvania: Temple and Lincoln.

Lincoln was the oldest degree-granting HBCU in the country. Founded in 1854, it had been an all-male school and only started taking girls in good numbers in the mid-1960s. It had offered me the best scholarship: full tuition, no loans, and work-study for spending money and expenses. All I had to do was come up with room and board money.

Lincoln was located in rural Chester County, Pennsylvania. From its brochure, I could tell that it was a beautiful oasis in the middle of the rolling hills of Pennsylvania. Some of the famous men who had graduated from Lincoln included Roscoe Lee Brown, the famous actor; Langston Hughes, the famous poet; Thurgood Marshall, the first black man to serve on the US Supreme Court; and Horace Mann Bond, the father of Julian Bond and the first African American president of Lincoln. From 1854 to 1954, its first one hundred years, Lincoln produced about 20 percent of the black physicians and over 10 percent of the black lawyers in the United States.

Though that sounded appealing and ideal for studying, Lincoln was very isolated and only accessible by an occasional bus or by car, which would make me dependent upon the bus, my dad, or Lacy for transportation. I didn't have a car, and the bus situation was questionable. However, a few Tech alums were there, and they told me you could always get a ride home for a couple of dollars.

By contrast, Temple, a majority white school, was in the heart of Philadelphia. It had the major I wanted, physical therapy, and was easily accessible by train, bus, and car. So, at first, I chose Temple, which was familiar to everyone because Bill Cosby was an alumnus and had run track there. I told the guidance counselor at Tech that I was going to Temple. However, that would eventually change.

In early July, I reported to Temple for orientation. I caught the train up to see what it would be like as a major mode of transportation that could get me to and from. I was given my course load for physical therapy and finally met with a financial-aid counselor about my scholarship offer. To my surprise, the financial-aid package was not at all what I thought it would be. It was packed with loans and other fees and was very expensive. On the train ride home, I worried as to how I would make it through financially. The numbers just didn't add up.

In addition, Temple was in "the hood" in Philly, and you weren't allowed to leave the dorm at night without permission. I had a real problem with that, having been able to come and go as I pleased all through high school. Yet here you had Temple, a predominantly white school in the middle of the black ghetto, and even the black students weren't free to come and go as they pleased. I said to myself, "What kind of shit is this?"

One night, they held a "white students only" meeting, and they told the black students we could meet together on our own if we wanted to. So, a bunch of us held a meet and greet. There we found out that the "whites only" meeting was to teach the white students how to survive in the hood. I said to myself, *I could have taught that class!*

When I returned to DC, I moped around for a couple of days. When my mother asked me what was wrong, I told her I didn't think I could afford to go to Temple. She suggested that I call Lincoln to see if I could still come, with a scholarship of course. I called and was told that they would check to see if the tuition scholarship was still available, but that I would have to wait for someone not to show up to get a room; the freshman dorm rooms were all spoken for. I told them how badly I wanted to attend Lincoln, and would they please see what they could do.

When I discussed my plan with Lacy, our conversation got a little tense. After all, I was about to leave him and go off on my own to get the education that I thought I needed in order to be successful in life—at a predominantly male school to boot. One day, he asked me why I hadn't considered Howard. I told him that Howard was too expensive and offered very few scholarships and a lot of loans to folk from DC. They preferred students from other cities and states and international students to keep their national/international status. Lacy knew that this was true.

He offered to marry me and suggested that we could work our way through college as he was doing—something I knew I could not do and do well in school. Although I was blown away by the offer, I thought that we were too young to get married and that it would put a strain on our relationship, and I didn't want to start a marriage like that. To be working, going to school, and probably starting a family all at the same time was often a formula for failure. I had seen it for myself or heard about it too many times, and we had both promised one other that if we married, it would be forever. No separation, no divorce.

I knew that eventually the love I had for Lacy would lead to "baby makes three," and neither of us was ready for that type of responsibility either. So, marriage, a family, and housekeeping would have to wait. To get where we wanted to go in life would take *PHD* on both our parts, not marriage at our young age.

Meanwhile, Lincoln called and told me I still had a tuition scholarship. I knew that going to Lincoln was the best thing for me. With a hug and kiss, I got Lacy to agree. So, come fall of 1969, off to Lincoln University I would go.

LINCOLN-BOUND

I started packing as soon as Lincoln University informed me that my scholarship was still valid and that all I needed to pay for were my books, small fees, and room and board. That was the best offer of them all: no loans, no package deal, and no additional big bills. They also told me to report to the work-study office; I had a paying job waiting for me that would help with my day-to-day expenses.

I was elated and over the moon with joy. I couldn't ask for anything more than that. I had saved every dollar I could to make sure I had enough for my room and board, because you had to pay for that each semester, in full, by cash or check, or be sent home. There was no installment plan or credit card payments allowed, and there was no meal plan or dining dollars like they have on college campuses nowadays, where you pay as you go. It was pay or go home.

By August of 1969, I was packed and ready to go. I gave the required two weeks' notice to the Navy Department and to my part-time job at Woodward and Lothrop. The naval office I worked for gave me a little going-away party with cake and ice cream. The officers/engineers even gave me several going-off-to-college gifts that their wives or our office manager had probably helped them pick out. They seemed genuinely happy for me. Leaving the Department of the Navy was bittersweet for me, but they assured me that a job was there for me during my summers and even full-time if things didn't work out for me in college.

My last day of work at Woodies was on a Saturday. I went to the personnel office to finalize my departure, clean out my locker, and turn in my keys. Then I went back to the candy department to work out my shift. A young man from the shipping department came by and bought some loose candy, about a quarter pound. He took a piece out of the bag and began to eat it. He appeared to be on his fifteen-minute break.

Then he said, "I was just by the personnel office to turn in my keys and badge, and they told me there was a young lady in the candy department who was going to Lincoln University."

I responded, "Yes, that would be me."

He said, "So when I asked them who you were, they told me. I've seen you around, but I had no idea you were going to Lincoln. You are always so well dressed. I thought you were a professional working girl. You know what I mean—full-time somewhere else by day, and here part-time on evenings and weekends. You don't look like a freshman to me!"

I asked, "Oh? So, what does a freshman look like?"

He responded, "Oh, pardon my manners. Allow me to introduce myself. My name is Walter Mason, and I am going into my sophomore year at Lincoln." Walter had graduated from Roosevelt High School, home of the Rough Riders, in Northwest DC.

He proceeded to tell me all about Lincoln: how beautiful the campus was and how different it was from DC. He put a lot of my worries to rest. He told me that it was a friendly campus, with a fair amount of students from the DC area, and that I would have no problem making friends and getting back and forth to DC on weekends and holidays, or to anywhere on the East Coast, for that matter. Someone with a car was always going somewhere and always taking on passengers for gas money and tolls. He said he had a car, so just to ask.

He told me that I would probably be living in the new women's dorm where his girlfriend lived. Yes, he quickly let me know that he was spoken for, so there was no flirtation going on there. But he did say that I would have no problem making friends, given the way I looked.

I asked him what he meant. He said, "You'll see!"

Then he said, "I've got to go. It's past my break time, but you'll be fine. Although Lincoln is 70 percent male, you won't have any problems. Believe me, you'll see!"

I asked once more, as he walked away, "And what does a freshman look like?"

He said, "Not like you! I mean, they don't dress like you. They wear jeans and T-shirts, and they are wearing Afros now. Keep that in mind if you want to fit in," he said as he walked away.

Well, I had just met a male guardian angel. I didn't know it then, but Walter would look out for me, from a distance, and protect me and my reputation for the years he had left at Lincoln, just as the boys had done for me at Eliot and McKinley. We would become lifelong friends, even to this day. And you know, there's one thing about guardian angels: you don't have to see them to know that they are there.

MOVE-IN WEEKEND

That next weekend was move-in weekend for all freshmen at Lincoln. I needed someone with a car to take me and my stuff. My dad was taking my sister back to Hampton, so he was unavailable. So, with my mother's permission, I asked my boyfriend, Lacy, to take me and my mother up to Lincoln to drop me off. What an unusual request—almost unheard of for most freshmen, to be dropped off to college by your boyfriend, a guy who didn't even want you to leave him in the first place.

He said of course he would take me! That is my George Lacy, quite a guy! He knew how much going to college meant to me, and he knew it was something I had to do to be fulfilled.

So, on the second Saturday of August of 1969, we packed up the GTO and off to Lincoln we went, with Mama in the back seat. I went to Lincoln sight unseen, due to my last-minute decision to go there, so I took in every mile of our journey, especially after we got off the main highway to the side roads that took us to the school.

I looked for the Mason-Dixon Line that I had heard so much about, for when a slave crossed that dividing line between Maryland and Pennsylvania, separating North from South, supposedly, that meant they were free. I looked and looked for it, and suddenly, there it was - this tiny little sign that said, "Mason-Dixon Line." I could only imagine how a slave on the Underground Railroad must have felt to be free of bondage. In a way, I too became free that day: free to become anything I wanted to be.

Once we were in Pennsylvania, there were country roads, rolling hills, and miles and miles of small Pennsylvania farms, growing mostly corn but other small crops also, all along the way. It was like seeing something out of a picture book about farming and old farmhouse architecture. As we got closer to the campus, we began to smell something. My mother said, "What's that I smell? What is that stinking?"

Looking out the window, I said, "Look! It's a fertilizer plant! Fertie the Bull!"

Then Lacy said, "No wonder your tuition is so cheap! Can you imagine smelling that all day, when the wind is blowing toward the campus? Pew-wee!"

That smell would become all too familiar, from time to time, when the wind blew in the direction of Lincoln. We finally got to Lincoln around midday. We drove through this beautiful arch, done in stone and iron masonry, that had Lincoln University written in ironwork across the top. The Lincoln Memorial Arch was erected in honor of the Lincoln men who served in World War I and was dedicated by US President Warren G. Harding in 1921, to the nation's first degree granting HBCU.

We stopped at the administration building, where we were welcomed. I picked up the key to my temporary dorm room there. I also paid my room and board for the first semester—the largest check I had ever written up to that time in my life.

I was assigned to a temporary room in Ashman Hall, a dorm for female upper-classmen. Because upper-class girls were not due to arrive until the next week, I had a room all to myself, with only one other freshman on that floor with me. She was in the same situation that I was in, waiting for a room in the freshman dorm to open up.

With the dorm key, I received a list of mandatory activities that I had to attend during Freshman Week. The first was a dinner that night. They made it clear that no parents would be allowed; it was a "freshmen only" event. I think it was to get all of the parents to go home.

I didn't unpack all my things, because hopefully, I would be moving into a freshman dorm in a couple of days. So, I unpacked enough clothing to last me during Freshman Week. I then said my goodbyes to Lacy and Mama, and they went on their way. For the first time in almost two years, my mother saw me kiss my boyfriend. I gave him a big kiss and hug.

After they left, I must say, I got a little homesick. I thought about how I would miss them both and how I would miss my life and lifestyle back in DC. But Lincoln didn't give me time to feel too blue. Before I knew it, it was time to freshen up and get ready for the freshmen welcome dinner. I put on a nice dress and headed to the student union building, a quick walk away.

As I entered the dining hall, I was approached by a tall, slender, and beautiful female with the biggest, neatest Afro I had ever seen. With a smile, she said, "Hello! Welcome to Lincoln University. My name is Paula, and I will serve as your Campus Pal this week." I gave her my name and told her I was from Washington, DC.

She said, "Oh, so you are Gwynette! We've been expecting you. I'm from DC too." She told me that she was from Southeast and had graduated from Anacostia High School, that dreaded school that used to beat up Tech students if we beat them in football or basketball. I told her that I had graduated from McKinley, and she said, "Oh, my boyfriend went to Tech." I told her that Lacy, my boyfriend, had too. That pronouncement softened my feelings about her having gone to a rival high school.

She then said that she went home often to see her beau and that she had a car on campus. If I needed a ride home, she said she would be happy to take me. We hit it off quite well.

She then asked me, "Do you have a nickname?"

I answered, "Yes, it's Nettie."

She responded. "Great, then I'll call you Nettie."

Paula was the first female upper-classman on campus to offer me a friendly gesture and a ride home, which I would accept many times over. Little did I know when I met her that she would become one of my closest and dearest friends, and a trusted confidante for life.

Since I had arrived for dinner early, Paula sat me at an empty table. I watched some of the other freshman women as they arrived. Paula brought two other freshman girls from DC over to my table—Katherine Ross (Kat) and Tonya Green (Tee). While talking, Tonya and I realized we had met before, in DC, once while in junior high school at a meeting of an organization we were a part of called American Teens Against Cancer, where we represented our respective schools, and once as cheerleaders, where we did the same thing. We were later joined by a New Yorker named Nona Booker, and by the only person I had ever met from Cape Cod, Massachusetts, Carolyn Coleman.

We were joined by other freshmen at our table that day, but these four women would become my best friends for life. Little did I know at the time that I had met the future bridesmaids at my wedding and the future godmothers of my children. We hit it off immediately and couldn't stop talking about our backgrounds, our families, and our experiences in high school. Three of us had been cheerleaders, one was a majorette, and one was accident-prone. All of us were smart. We had all graduated at the top of our graduating classes. We knew exactly why Lincoln had recruited us: we were smart, and we would be called "the chosen few." We were not only chosen to coeducate the school but to match wits with the boys and achieve in our own right and by our own merit. We were the new lioness cubs of Lincoln University, the name given to Lincoln women after Lincoln's mascot, the Lincoln Lion.

All four of my new friends had been assigned to the new dormitory for women—one so new that it didn't have a name yet. So, it was called the *new women's dorm*. I knew that's where I wanted to be, so I vowed that I would lobby, first thing that Monday morning, to be placed in the *new women's dorm* to be with them.

Back in my borrowed dorm room after dinner, after talking to Lacy on the phone after he got back to DC, I was so homesick, I cried myself to sleep. On Sunday, after mandatory chapel service, I began to select classes that would lead me to my goal of early graduation. My strategy was to study hard, keep a low profile, stay out of trouble, get my degree, and get back to my life in DC and to Lacy as soon as possible. However, things would change throughout the year.

UNEXPECTED ATTENTION

By that Wednesday, I had a room assignment in the new women's dorm, on the fourth (top) floor. Not to be seen, I started to move my suitcases that Wednesday night in the dark. It was raining, so I trudged across a field between the two dorms in the rain with those heavy suitcases. Exhausted and soaking wet, I stopped after my third trip and decided to move my shoes and other things that did not come in a suitcase the next day. Upper-classmen were also beginning to return each day in larger numbers. I figured I would just blend in and finish moving the rest of my things in while they were moving in. That was a big mistake.

In the light of day, you could be seen—and I was seen, all right. I had twenty to twenty-five pairs of shoes, and of course I dropped a couple of boxes that I had to pick up while moving across the field and up four flights of stairs. No big deal, or so I thought. But by the time the story got out around the campus that week, I was the freshman who came to Lincoln with a lot of clothes and fifty or more pair of shoes that I kept dropping everywhere. I was hot gossip. Everyone wanted to know who I was: "the freshman with all those shoes."

I found it a little embarrassing. I got a little unexpected attention from that incident, but at least it wasn't bad attention. I just shrugged it off and forgot about it. The gossip eventually died off.

Unexpected attention number two involved my work-study assignment on the front desk of my dorm in the evenings from seven to midnight. Being on the front desk meant that I received the formal phone calls coming into the dorm's general number, and I had to lock the front doors at curfew time, which was midnight. That job allowed me to get to know all the girls who lived in my dorm, but it also meant that I knew a lot about their personal lives, on and off campus: whose family was always calling for them, who was dating whom, and who was hanging out past curfew.

Of course, I made friends because I was lenient with the curfew rules and always let the girls slip in a few minutes late, by at least fifteen minutes past midnight, or to get that last kiss at the door. Their boyfriends were also grateful, and my homeboy from DC, Walter, was the biggest violator of all. He always brought his girlfriend back to the dorm late, so he always owed me a favor in return. Down the road, Walter would find himself looking out for his homegirl, and he always came through.

Unexpected attention number three was the attention that all the girls on Lincoln's campus got in general, and the freshman girls in particular, from the male students on campus. Lincoln, an all-male school when it was founded in 1854, didn't admit female students in earnest until after its centennial in 1954. Most of them had to live off campus or with a faculty member's family until the mid-1960s, when the first female dorm was opened. When I arrived, there were only two major female dorms, and one of them was the new dorm that I was able to get into.

At best, Lincoln was about 70 percent male and 30 percent female, and they were still getting used to having girls on campus. That showed in the curricular offerings, extracurricular activities, and bad behavior of some of the male students on campus. There was a lot of whistling, catcalling, and *"joning"* (critiquing), as it was called back then, out of the windows of the male dorms as girls walked by. Some of the boys weren't used to having girls around.

In order to get to the cafeteria, many female students had to walk past several male dorms and a park bench called the *rabble bench* where male students would gather to shoot the breeze or as they called it, *rabble* (what we call rap or just plain gossip), and to check out the young ladies. It was hard to avoid walking past it, but I tried.

During Freshman Week, a lot of male upperclassmen were already on campus for various reasons. One day, I was approached by a group of them who told me that they were *Scrollers*—members of the pledge club of Kappa Alpha Psi Fraternity, Inc. They were perfect gentlemen and gave me lots of compliments about my looks. They asked if I would accept an invitation to join their Scroller Court, a female support group. I must say, I was caught off guard.

Although I was familiar with the African American Greek letter fraternities and sororities, called the Devine Nine, I had a lot of questions. What would I have to do? How time-consuming would it be? Would anything sexual be involved? I was worried about how Lacy would take me being on a fraternity court.

My homeboy, Walter, was a Scroller at the time and answered all my questions satisfactorily. Basically, it involved coming to help host their social activities and just show up looking pretty, which I thought wouldn't take up too much of my time. So reluctantly, I said I would accept their invitation, since Walter said it would be OK and he would make sure nothing bad or unsavory happened to me. I agreed and thought it would be an OK experience. I hoped that Lacy would be OK with my decision.

That was the beginning of my participation in black Greek life on campus, which was somewhat controversial at the time. A lot of African American students during that time were embracing the more Afrocentric culture of the times rather than black Greek life. However, I found the experience pleasant enough that when those Scrollers crossed over and became Kappas, they asked me onto the Kappa Alpha Psi court, and I agreed to serve.

FIRST SEMESTER

My first semester was filled with studying and the typical college activities. I took the maximum freshman academic load that was allowed. I felt well prepared for my college courses, having attended McKinley Tech in DC. As a result of the honors courses I took in junior and senior high school, I was able to test out of or not take some of the basic freshman courses. That allowed me to accelerate into some of the upper-level courses I needed to graduate, skipping over some of the lower-level classes.

For example, since I had six years of French coming in, I only needed two semesters (one year instead of two) of French in college. Since I'd had a lot of algebra classes in high school, I only needed college algebra/trigonometry and calculus (one year of math). Therefore, I was able to knock one year of foreign language and one year of math off of my requirements toward graduation.

One day, while I was at the front desk in my dorm, someone pointed out a senior to me and told me that she was graduating in just three years. She was quiet and strikingly beautiful. I introduced myself and made it a point to get to know her. Every time she passed the desk when I was on duty, I would casually ask her questions about how she managed to get to the point where she was graduating in just three years, and she shared her strategy with me.

I said to myself, *If she can do it, I can do it*. My very first semester, I made up my mind that I would finish undergraduate school in three years. Like her, I had already started to knock off courses by not needing to take some of those basic courses that, in essence, I had already had in honors in high school.

The easiest class I had my first semester was biology, thanks to Eliot and McKinley Tech. The class was like an anatomy class, and the instructor was a brother (a black man) from DC. Thanks to all those tests and late nights studying that cat in high school, I knew all the anatomy systems of a mammal. All I had to do was transfer that knowledge to the human body.

It got out that I was getting As on my exams and lab work, so I quickly became popular amongst my classmates. Everyone wanted to be my friend and study with me, especially several pre-med and non-pre-med "get-over" students. I knew that game and I knew how to play it, or not to play it, in my favor.

For example, my hardest class that semester was college algebra/trigonometry, believe or not. I was even shocked myself. I had gotten rusty in math, or it had gotten more difficult or something. My dorm mates and I were getting worried about that class. So, I asked this brother named Gary who I knew from Tech—who Lincoln had recruited on a math scholarship—to tutor my dorm mates and me in math. In exchange, I would tutor him, and anyone who wanted to join us, in biology and teach them the systems of the body.

We spent many a late-night session exchanging knowledge. We would find an empty classroom (Lincoln never locked the classrooms) and go to work studying. He would get up to the board and teach us the math, and then I would get up and go over the parts of the body. And it worked. We were all learning from each other, and our grades would show it.

You see, unlike some colleges that are very competitive, where the motto is "I've got mine, and you got yours to get," at Lincoln, our motto was "If I know it, you know it!" In other words, if I know it, I'll teach it to you. That strategy worked for a lot of us—if the students were serious and put in the effort. If you weren't serious, shame on you! To me, everyone at Lincoln was smart, like my honors classmates at Eliot and McKinley. To me, at Lincoln, everyone was "young, gifted, and black." As Lincoln Lions, we roar.

EXTRACURRICULAR ACTIVITIES

In order to get some of the freshman women involved in campus life, our gym teacher, Mrs. White—the wife of a State Department diplomat who was taking a sabbatical to teach at Lincoln—decided to have a freshman cheerleading squad. She made the announcement in our freshman gym class. Since one of Lincoln's recruitment strategies was to recruit cheerleaders from inner-city high schools, there were a lot of former high school cheerleaders in our freshman class. Several of us got together, and a group of us joined Mrs. White's cheerleading squad.

As our experience would have it, Mrs. White's entire freshman cheerleading squad was made up of former high school cheerleaders, and I must say, we were *the bomb* and the talk of the campus, especially among the male population. We made it very easy on ourselves. We took the best cheers from each of our high schools and taught them to one another. We couldn't tell if people were coming to the games to see the team, which was the junior varsity basketball team, or to see the dynamite cheerleaders—especially all of those Lincoln Lion men, and they could roar.

Our uniforms were great: cute little pleated skirts in our school colors of blue and orange, with cute little tops or warm sweaters, depending on the weather. And when we stomped, our soft, well-groomed Afros would sway with every move.

Now, that was attention that was intended. We were there to support the team. It was fun and one way to stay in shape and avoid gaining those fifteen pounds, the so-called "freshman fifteen" that a lot of freshman girls gain from eating college cafeteria food after high school. I didn't gain one pound. Cheerleading and other extracurricular activities, both physical and mental, made my first semester at Lincoln a lot of fun.

Like the years before it, music was an important aspect of our college years. We enjoyed playing, dancing, and making love to the music of our times. We arrived on campus to such songs as "Hot Fun in the Summertime" and "Can't Get Next to You." And we mellowed out to "Going in Circles," "Just My Imagination," and "Didn't I Blow Your Mind This Time." We partied to music by R&B royalty such as James Brown, the Temptations, the Jackson 5, Aretha Franklin, Smokey Robinson and the Miracles, Roberta Flack, Donnie Hathaway, Isaac Hayes, and newer groups like the Fifth Dimension, the Friends of Distinction, the Stylistics, the Delfonics, and of course, Earth, Wind, and Fire, one of my favorites.

During my freshman year, I went home at least once or twice a month to see Lacy, thanks to rides from Paula. She and I became very close, and our rides back and forth were filled with heart-to-heart talks. Although she was just a year ahead of me at Lincoln, Paula was wise beyond her years. Maybe that was because she was the youngest of three and had a sister and a brother who were older and worldly. We would talk about life and love, and she would always give me good advice, especially about things she had experienced and learned the year before, including how to hold on to a long-distance boyfriend. One of those things was to go home often, which we were doing.

Paula and Joe, her boyfriend, had been in separate singing groups, so she went home often to see him in concert. We rode up and down the highway to and from DC in her little blue Volkswagen Bug, with music blasting on her radio. Those were good times—except for one snowy night, when we skidded off the road into a snowbank, but we weren't hurt.

My freshman class was known as the Party Hardy Class, and we lived up to the motto: "When we party, we party hardy." We could party with the best of them. There were mixers and dances in the student union, dorm parties, and parties off campus in cities like Philadelphia, New York, and DC.

Some of the male students at Lincoln were downright crazy, in a funny way. They engaged all kinds of shenanigans and silly pranks. The most frequent ones were panty raids and serenades at the girls' dorms. During my freshmen year, the girls rarely locked their bedroom doors, so groups of boys would run through the dorms, especially when girls were at dinner, a night game or dance, and steal panties from their dresser drawers for bragging rights for those who were able to grab the most panties. It got so bad, girls started to lock their doors to stop the raids. And the fraternities would come out at various times during the night and sing their songs outside of the dorm windows. Most of the time the girls would peek out of their windows to hear the three-part harmony, but at 2 'clock in the morning, that could be annoying if you had to get up early for class the next day.

All kinds of crazy games and pranks would go on at the male dormitory parties, especially games with alcohol, like *spin the bottle* and *99 bottles on the wall*. Once a group of boys wrote on my friend Carolyn's face with black magic marker. Because she had a fair complexion, she couldn't wash it off, so she tried to steam it off because she needed to go home, and she wound up burning her face, but not seriously. As time went on, those silly pranks stopped, because college students during that era became more mature and sophisticated due to the world events around us. More specifically, the females at Lincoln decided that they'd had enough of the pranks against them and took action (complaints and confrontations) to get them to stop.

MUSIC AND AWARENESS

There were concerts at Mary Dod Brown Chapel, in the student union, and off campus with artists such as Kool & the Gang out of Philadelphia, the Moments, and Gil Scott-Heron, who was a student at Lincoln at the time, along with a couple of his band members. Gil was already popular on and off campus when our freshmen class entered. He was a couple of years ahead of us and already had a major record deal. He had already written "The Revolution Will Not Be Televised," and "In the Bottle," which we heard time and time again at every talent show and concert.

Although he had a musician's flair and a New York air about him, Gil was cordial and friendly to everyone. He called me and my girlfriends from DC the "little bousie girls from DC," meaning that we were conservative, sophisticated, and traditionally college-prep-like in the way we looked, dressed, and acted. We took no offense to the title and did not take that as an insult, for in a way, it was true.

Our girl group became more culturally aware and Afrocentric during our years at Lincoln. We tried to get with the times. I, for one, "bushed out" my hair and dropped my nickname. Gil and other students didn't like my nickname, *Nettie*. They told me it was a slave name and to drop it and I did while I was at Lincoln. Only a few close friends at Lincoln and my family back home would call me Nettie from then on.

My first homecoming experience was mind-blowing: one straight week of something going on every night, from poetry readings, a gospel concert, a theatrical presentation, and the Miss Lincoln pageant to a musical concert and, of course, dances and parties. The music concert featured Kool & the Gang, local talent, campus talent, and finally Gil Scott-Heron and his group. That was the formula for many concerts to come. And your act better be good, or you got pennies or acorns thrown your way. I was really shocked the first time I saw that happen. *How rude!* I thought.

A RESTLESS GENERATION

We were a restless, revolutionary generation. Our weapons of choice were the powerful use of protests, boycotts, and sit-ins. We would use these weapons to bring about change on campus and to advocate for change off campus for our communities, our cities, our country, and the world. Our generation was a standard-bearer for truth, freedom, and justice. We were instrumental in challenging the establishment to be more inclusive and to embrace all people, young and old, rich and poor, and of every race, color and religion.

During my first semester alone, we protested against or for any and everything, from our refusal to wear freshman beanies (little hats to distinguish us as freshmen) to better food in the cafeteria, twenty-four-hour visitation (meaning free love) in the dorms, and better health services at the student health center. The last two affected me most.

Before my first homecoming experience, the entire campus won the right to twenty-four-hour visitation in the dorms and the respect that we were responsible adults over eighteen. That put an end to my job as a receptionist and doorkeeper at my dorm. Although I was well liked, my services were no longer needed.

So, I reported to the work-study office to get a new job assignment. I was assigned to the library and reluctantly accepted. The receptionist job was right where I lived and was so convenient, I could even wear my robe and slippers downstairs to lock the door. Working at the library would mean having to bundle up during the winter months to walk across campus to the library and walk home in the dark after work. However, even with the inconveniences, I took the job because I needed the spending money.

Then, not long after my first homecoming experience at Lincoln, tragedy struck. One of Gil Scott-Heron's band members died on campus for reasons that are still unknown to this day. For one thing, there appeared to be a link between his death and alleged inadequate medical facilities at the health center that plagued Lincoln at the time. Like the sudden death of many musicians of our times, rumors were flying about a drug overdose. Other reasons that were also circulating was that there was an asthma attack, inadequate staff on duty at the health center late at night, and that the paramedics weren't called in time to save the victim. These rumors sparked massive protests and pickets on campus that led to major changes to the medical facilities and protocols. That incident shook me to my core—that someone had to die before something was done to correct the facilities problem.

That incident dominated the conversation at Lincoln until Thanksgiving. I went home for the Thanksgiving break upset and disappointed. When I returned, I couldn't wait to take my final exams and go home for winter break.

My grades at the end of my first semester at Lincoln were as follows: I got an A in biology, a B in Intermediate French, and a C+ in college algebra and trigonometry—the lowest grade in math, or any subject for that matter, that I had gotten in school, ever. Lincoln gave out pluses and minuses to either boost or lessen your GPA, and I needed a 3.0 grade-point average to keep my scholarship. I got a 3.3 GPA overall and barely made the dean's list my first semester, and I vowed to do better. That was cutting it close, so I knew I needed to study a little harder.

Surprisingly, I got an A– in humanities, which shocked me. My instructor for that class chose a very Afrocentric girl from New York City as my partner. I wasn't sure how the partnership would work out, for we were so very different in several ways. My partner was an English major from the mean streets of Harlem and much more mature and worldly than I was. To me, she seemed much older and wiser, with more life experiences than I had and a tougher demeanor. She pushed me beyond my limit in that class, farther than I had ever gone culturally before: to read more, to write more, and to appreciate and use the English language more. She even taught how to rhyme more.

Our oral presentations received rave reviews from our classmates and from our instructor. I dug deep, back into that creative-writing class I had taken at Howard University in junior high, and thanks to my teammate, I got an A- in that class.

I also got an A in physical education. Mrs. White taught us how to play and score as many sports as she could fit into a semester: gymnastics, tennis, soccer, volleyball, lacrosse and bowling. I think she did that to teach us how to be knowledgeable, sophisticated, and well-rounded women of the world. She certainly made me the huge Olympics fan that I am today. She taught us how to be fearless Lincoln Lionesses, like our Lincoln Lion mascot, while at the same time teaching us to be reserved and refined young ladies.

At the end of the semester, as we passed Ferdie the Bull on our way to DC, holding my nose, I reflected on those first few months on campus. My first semester at Lincoln was quite a learning experience, to say the least. Not only did I learn a lot in the classrooms, I also learned a lot more about life and love than I knew when I arrived. I became more mature, culturally aware, and more sophisticated. I also learned that life isn't going to give you anything. You have to roll up your sleeves and work for what you want out of life.

A MUCH NEEDED WINTER BREAK

Winter breaks at Lincoln University were long ones. Because of the harsh winters in Pennsylvania, the break lasted from early December, right after finals, through the Christmas and New Year holidays and until February 1st, when we had to return to the campus. The holidays were wonderful. Paula had a great Christmas party at her parents' beautiful home in Anacostia. Almost all of the Lincoln students from DC and a lot of our fellow Lincoln Lions from Philly to New York came down. In addition, I got to meet Paula's parents, her brother and sister, and a lot of her friends from high school. It was the best party of the holiday season.

We had all of January off for a graded class called *January Break* to do an academic project off campus for credit for a pass-or-fail grade; and to also work for money; or to do nothing other than our project, if we wanted to. I chose to work at Woodies, assisting with end-of-the-year inventory, which involved math and balance sheets and doubled as an opportunity to make some extra cash. So, my January paper was about business administration and centered around retailing and marketing. In my spare time, I made some heavy winter clothes out of woolens and corduroys for those cold winter days I would have to endure when we returned to Lincoln. And of course, I was able to see more of my beau, Lacy.

SPRING 1970

As had been the case before on my life's journey, several events and life choices occurred at Lincoln my first year that would affect me in a profound way. First, my roommate, who was one of the few white girls on campus, did not return for a second semester. Although I enjoyed a week or so of having a room to myself, I knew that the administration would soon attempt to fill its vacancies, so I took matters into my own hands. To avoid getting some random person I did not know or did not want, I began to look for a new roommate.

Circumstances would have it that Kat, from the freshman welcome dinner, was also without a roommate. So, we marched over to student affairs and asked if we could be roommates and got official permission. We were so happy to be given the choice rather than be assigned some random person. We couldn't wait to tell the rest of our friends and to move in together. That was to be the beginning of a lifelong friendship, one of the strongest bonds I would make in my life. Kat would become my ace, my walking partner, a future bridesmaid and godmother to my future child, and my sister by another mother. That's what Kat would become to me.

Second semester plugged along. During the first six weeks, it was so cold, you barely wanted to go outside. We hardly ever went to the cafeteria for breakfast, it was so cold. Since we didn't have a fridge, we would bring milk, juice, and soda back from dinner, store them in jars, and hang them out of the back window in a plastic bag so we could have cold milk and juice in the morning before we went to class.

We would go to our first class at nine or ten in the morning, when the sun was up, and go to the cafeteria for lunch and dinner. Kat and I both worked at the library, so we would work there between classes and until the day staff went home, and then we would go to dinner together. After dinner, I would go back to the library to study every night, Monday through Thursday, until it closed at ten o'clock.

I found it difficult to study in the dorm or in our room (too many distractions). Kat was OK studying in the room without me. We would compare notes and homework when I came in from the library. That was my routine, unless I had a game to cheer at, which was one night during the week (usually Tuesday night) and once on the weekend (usually Saturday).

Come spring, when the cold weather gave way to warmer temperatures, students couldn't wait to hang out outside, and the guys would gather around the rabble bench. Spring was in the air, and you could hear songs such as "Grazing in the Grass" and "Rock Creek Park" blasting from the open windows of the male dorms. One thing that stood out about most of the students at Lincoln was that just about every student was "into" something: music, dance, poetry, the movement, Afros and dashikis, a fraternity or sorority, social awareness or activism, or yes, even drugs.

For me, in the spring of 1970, that "something" would be a sorority. Spring ushered in sorority rushes and fraternity smokers for recruiting potential new members. I only went to one rush, for there was only one sorority I was interested in joining. That would be Alpha Kappa Alpha, the first and oldest African American sorority, founded in 1908 on the campus of Howard University. My sister had pledged AKA the year before and was already a member, as was Toni at Virginia State and a lot of my friends and club sisters from McKinley in DC. There was only one choice for me, and that was AKA, as one of our sayings goes: *there is only one way, and that's AKA*. I would later pen a song as a take on Eddie Kendrick's famous Temptations' hit, "Just My Imagination", *"It was just an inspiration, to pledge AKA!"*

I had no problem getting accepted as a pledgee (my grades and reputation were good, and I had other AKAs as references). But little did I know what I was getting myself into. Sixteen of us were accepted. After paying our fees and searching our hearts as to whether AKA was really what we wanted, a dozen of us made it to the pledge line, called "Ivies", named after the ivy vine: it grows and clings.

At Lincoln, again, things were different. Instead of pledging eight weeks straight, Greek lines at Lincoln pledged four weeks in the spring and four weeks in the fall. What agony! It would be like pledging a whole academic year, with a summer break, which really wasn't a break. At Lincoln, the AKAs and the Deltas, the two largest black sororities in the country and staunch rivals, had only gotten their charters in December 1969, just minutes apart—with the AKAs being first, by luck and tradition. So, both sororities' spring 1970 lines were their first lines to actually pledge on Lincoln's campus. Lincoln's AKA founding line and charter line, as they were called, all pledged under the graduate chapter in Philadelphia. So let me just say that the AKAs and Deltas had something to prove; that they were forces to be reckoned with on Lincoln's campus. That was not a good thing for us pledgees.

You see, at Lincoln, the three oldest and largest black fraternities in the US—the Alphas, the Kappas, and the Ques—were known as being part of the "Bloody Triangle," made up of the Lincoln, Morgan State, and Cheney State fraternities. They pledged hard and were known to haze. So, the sororities felt that they needed to be tough too. To say the least, we pledged hard—without any violence, though. There were a lot of errands to run, late nights, sleep deprivation, and in-your-face confrontation. However, it was important to the sorority that since we were the first line on campus, everything was legal, just shy of hazing.

I thought all of it was funny. I never let on that I knew they were bluffing, and I never let them unnerve me. I remained cool. Being from the hood in DC, when a big sister would get in my face, I would say to myself, *I wish you would! If you do, it is on!* But that never happened; they were just bluffing. I maintained my cool at all times and made it past the first four weeks.

During that time, we lost several pledgees, one of whom was a fellow cheerleader and dear friend from DC, Tee. She didn't like the tactics of the big sisters, so she dropped off line. "I was about to hurt somebody," is what she always said. She said she didn't want her Southeast DC background to come out on any of the big sisters, so she quit.

We had one weekend off line during that time. That was Penn Relay weekend. The Penn Relays are a major track meet held in Philadelphia the last weekend of April every year, usually around my birthday, which is April 26th. College and some high school track teams come from all over the country to compete. It was a major weekend for Lincoln students. Hundreds of Lincoln students flocked to Philly to attend the relays and to party. A lot of other HBCUs and their students came there too. It was like a mini spring break in the North. All of the fraternities and sororities either gave or attended major parties throughout the weekend.

That year, our dean of pledgees, Rita, planned to go to the relays along with several of our big sisters, so she officially let us off line for the weekend to assure that nothing would happen between the pledgees and other big sisters while she was gone. She put us on lockdown and told us to stay in our rooms, lock our doors, and not to come out. However, since I was on the Kappa Court, I was supposed to be in Philly for their major affair—a Penn Relay cabaret. So, I broke the lockdown rule and went to Philly that Saturday night to attend the Kappa affair, taking two of my line sisters, Dorcas and Sharon, with me. The Kappas made sure we had a ride to and from. They called their brother "our chauffeur for the night." He was very polite and a good driver.

Why did I think we wouldn't run into any of our big sisters at the Kappa Cabaret? Sure enough, we ran smack dab into our dean of pledgees and several big sisters who were dating Kappas. We were polite and said hello and nothing more. I apologized to Rita for breaking her orders but told her that the Kappas expected me to be there to be introduced as one of their court members and that I didn't want to come to Philly alone. She appeared to understand, but our other big sisters did not. If looks could kill!

Still, everyone stayed cool. That's the AKA way: no drama in public. But we knew we would be in trouble once we got back to campus. So, I said the hell with it, and we partied and had a great time. I celebrated my nineteenth birthday with the Kappas while at the party. We got back to campus at daybreak Sunday morning and went straight to bed, with our doors locked. We did catch major shade from our big sisters when we got back, especially me, but we took it on the chin, because we only had a few more days before we had to get off line for final exams.

We got off line the last day of April, by university rules, but still had a lot to do: scrapbooks to make, service projects to complete, outfits to sew, and a lot still to learn about the sorority before we were done. Officially, we would not go back on line until the fall of 1970, but in the meantime, we would be busy.

One of the guiding principles of Alpha Kappa Alpha sorority is "Service to All Mankind." To that end, our pledge line, as a service project that spring, chose to tutor some of the young black children from the black village near our campus. The children were members of Hosanna AUMP Church. Built in 1843 by free blacks, Hosanna Church was a stop on the Underground Railroad and a social and spiritual center that played a crucial role in the founding of Ashman Institute, which later became our Lincoln University, the first HBCU to provide four-year baccalaureate degrees to black males. So, the relationship between Hosanna Church and Lincoln was very special.

Once a week, on Thursdays, I would skip lunch in the cafeteria to tutor the village children, in math of course, during my lunch hour. The sorority provided the funds for a light lunch for the children, who were in the fifth grade, a school year that meant so much to me, from my experiences back in DC at that age, and we would work on math problems while eating. It was quite an enjoyable activity for me. We would have a great time together, learning and laughing, while playing math games. After our session, I would walk the children back to their church, which was a short distance from Lincoln's chapel. It was a nice break from my heavy, heady routine

THE REVOLUTION WOULD NOT BE TELEVISED

In early May 1970, our campus was restless. You could feel the tension in the air. There was deep division throughout the nation over the Vietnam

War. Thousands of people in the United States were openly against the war, as were many students on Lincoln's campus. The ending of college deferments, which previously had exempted most college students from the draft and service in Vietnam, further contributed to campus distress among our mostly male student population.

On April 30, 1970, President Richard Nixon held a news conference to announce that the United States would invade Cambodia and that 150,000 more young American men would need to be drafted for an expansion of the Vietnam War effort. This provoked massive protests on college campuses across the country. These protests were usually peaceful and included such things as rallies, marches, and the burning of draft cards. To dodge the draft, some young men fled to Canada or to other countries in the Western hemisphere. College students made sure they remained enrolled to try to avoid getting drafted. One of the best known of these protests occurred at Kent State University in Ohio. On Friday, May 1, also known as May Day, Kent State students held an antiwar protest. That evening, several incidents occurred, including rocks and bottles being thrown at police officers and the lighting of bonfires. These incidents led to the closing of bars earlier than the normal closing time to reduce alcohol consumption. Eventually students, other antiwar activists, and non-student agitators began to break windows and loot stores.[6]

On May 2, the mayor of Kent declared a state of emergency and requested that the governor send Ohio National Guardsmen to Kent State to assist in maintaining order. When the guardsmen arrived, they found the ROTC building on the campus, which Kent State officials had previously boarded up and had planned to raze, in flames. Protesters celebrated the building's destruction, jeered the firefighters who were fighting the fire, and sliced the hoses that were being used to extinguish the flames. The National Guard members, in their attempt to restore order, resorted to tear gas to disperse the protesters.

---

[6] Backderf, "Kent State: Four Dead in Ohio," 2020.

On Monday, May 4, 1970, when classes resumed at Kent State after a weekend of unrest, antiwar protesters scheduled a rally for noon. Kent State officials attempted to ban the gathering but were unsuccessful. As the protest began, National Guardsmen fired tear gas at the demonstrators. Due to the wind, the tear gas proved ineffective. Some of the protestors threw the canisters, along with rocks, back at the guardsmen. Some of the demonstrators yelled slogans like "Pigs off campus!" Around seventy-five guardsmen advanced on the protestors with rifles and bayonets. During that altercation, approximately twenty-eight guardsmen, purportedly fearing for their lives, opened fire on the unarmed crowd, killing four students and wounding nine. It was reported that two of the students who died actually had not participated in the protests. Kent State was closed for the spring quarter immediately after the shootings on May 4. Other Ohio institutions followed suit. Rather than causing a decline in national protests, the Kent State shootings actually escalated protests on campuses throughout the country. These protests also helped to show the US public that the antiwar protesters were not just hippies, drug addicts, and promoters of free love. They included middle- and upper-class students, as well as educated people. [7]

The Vietnam War and the Kent State shootings dominated conversations at Lincoln in the dorms, at the dinner tables, and among campus leaders and antiwar activists across Lincoln's campus. Ten days later, on May 14, 1970, another incident occurred on the campus of Jackson State University, an HBCU in Jackson, Mississippi. During a student protest there, police and state troopers fired automatic weapons into a dormitory, killing two students and wounding nine others. It was reported that no warning was given and no evidence was found of student snipers being in the dorm that might have justified the shootings.[8]

---

[7] op. cit.
[8] Bristow. "Steeped in the Blood of Racism," 2020.

Unlike the Kent State incident, however, the Jackson State episode gained very little national attention, embittering black college students across the country who felt that the killing of black students was not taken as seriously as that of white students. The Jackson State incident prompted student leaders at Lincoln and other HBCUs throughout the nation to plan a response, not only to protest the Vietnam War but to also bring attention to the insensitivity shown to black student protesters. Large numbers of black soldiers were serving our country in Vietnam.

Word began to spread around Lincoln's campus that a protest march down Route 1 and into Oxford was being planned. Lincoln students were waiting for information as to which day and time and for instructions as I planned my last day of tutoring for my young students from Hosanna Church. Most of us thought that the Friday after our last day of classes for the year would be the right day for a protest.

RUNNING FROM THE KU KLUX KLAN

I will never forget the last Thursday of classes that May of 1970. That morning was just like all the other mornings in early May. I woke up at my normal time, around seven thirty. I knew that this was my last day to tutor my children, so I had planned something special. We would have a last-day celebration around noon, and I was going to give them goody bags for the summer. I had purchased and collected things in DC, around Oxford, and from the campus bookstore all semester to put in the little gift bags: cookies and candy, crayons, socks, notebooks, paper, pencils and pens, and Lincoln mugs, buttons, and paraphernalia. I made up my bed, pulled out the goody bags, and laid everything out on the bed while Kat was in the bathroom.

On my way to the shower, I heard the chapel bells ringing, which wasn't unusual for that time of the morning. Back in the day, with no cell phones and only one phone on each floor of the dorm, announcements and special assemblies were called by the ringing of the chapel bells. I figured that if it were something important, somebody would get the message and bring it back to the dorm after breakfast. That's usually how messages were passed along on our small campus, through word of mouth.

I passed Kat in the hallway as I was about to enter the bathroom. She had a nine o'clock class. We did a high five to acknowledge each other. I asked, "You heading out?"

Her response was, "Yeah, see you after lunch. You ready for your kids?"

I answered, "Last day. I'm ready for 'em. See you back here for our two o'clock class, OK?" Off I went to shower and get ready for my day.

I assembled my goody bags and put them all in two big shopping bags. I took them with me to class so I wouldn't have to come back to the dorm before my session with the kids.

When I got to class, which was an advanced quantitative class, the professor announced as I came in the door that we were having our last quiz—the fifth and final quiz before the final exam. That's how he checked to see if we had been studying. Out of five quizzes, he would take your highest four grades, or you could only take four and skip one, and he would use those four toward your final grade.

My strategy was to take all five quizzes and let him use the highest four toward my final grade. That was usually the best strategy for me to max out my average. So, I picked up the quiz from the professor's desk, sat down, and went right to work so I could get out of there a little early to set up for my tutoring session with my kids.

I looked up once and saw that only about four other classmates had sat down to take the quiz. I also saw out of the corner of my eye that a couple of classmates had peeked in and seen that a quiz was going on and didn't come in, choosing to pass on the last quiz. I guessed they didn't need that last quiz to get the grade they wanted. *Oh, well, that's on them*, I said to myself. I put my head back into my own quiz.

I got stuck on one of the problems, so it took a while to finish, but I figured out the answer and was done. I was the last one left in the room, which was usual for me. I had always stayed to the end of a test to double-check my answers since elementary school.

When I turned in my quiz, the professor, who drove in from Philadelphia for each class, said, "Where is everyone today?"

I replied, "Well, since this is the last quiz, I guess they passed on this one. I want you to use my highest four grades, so I took all of them. So, here's my fifth. I think I did well, but we'll see, huh? I'll see you at the final. Promise you won't be too hard on us!" With that, I left to set up for my tutoring class with my kids.

I went straight to the lower level of the student union to the room the AKAs had reserved for tutoring. I didn't notice anything out of the ordinary. Students were dashing about campus, mostly going toward their dorms after eating in the student union. I saw several cars leaving the campus with several passengers, and they waved as they passed.

When I got to the tutoring room, my young students were there already, having walked over from the church. They were on spring break from their elementary school, so they couldn't wait for our celebration to start. When I arrived, I noticed that the cafeteria workers hadn't brought our lunch in yet. I figured they were going to wait to the end of the class to make it more like a party.

So, I gave the kids their goody bags at the beginning of the session. I let them look inside to see all of the goodies that were in there, and as with most fifth graders, there were oohs and aahs, laughter and chatter, and of course they wanted to eat some of the candy rather than wait until after lunch.

As I was trying to get the kids to settle down, especially to put the candy back into the goody bags, I glanced at the window in the door, and there was my homeboy, Walter, looking in. I waved him off, but he wouldn't leave the window.

Then one of my young men said, "Miss Ford, someone is trying to get your attention," and the class began to giggle. Walter was beckoning me to come to the door. Reluctantly, I went to the door, opened it, and stepped out to see what he wanted.

Walter asked, "What are you doing?"

I told him I was tutoring my kids and to leave us alone. He then said, "Haven't you heard? The president has closed the school as of twelve noon because of that Jackson State mess. Lincoln is officially closed," he said, looking at his watch.

I said, "What? Holy shit!"

"Yes, Lincoln is now closed," Walter said. "We have until one o'clock to be off campus. I ran upstairs to grab something to eat before leaving." He showed me a bag of goodies with fruit and stuff in it that he had gotten from the cafeteria. "My ride is waiting outside. I didn't bring my car back after spring break. Everybody is just about gone. Where have you been all morning? Didn't you hear the church bells ringing? Get those kids back to the village and get off this campus. The Klan is on their way here to do God knows what! They are on their way. They have been seen marching up Route 1. Get outta here, girl. See if Paula is still here and catch a ride with her. I just saw her packing up her car. She asked me had I seen you. Glad I did. Good luck. Check in with me when you get back to DC, you hear? Gotta go!"

With that, he was gone.

I started to panic but calmed myself, went back in the room, and said, "OK, kids, no class today. Instead, we are going to have a race back to the church. Grab your goody bags and let's go!"

I grabbed my things, lined the kids up, and we took off running. Thank goodness, I had on tennis shoes that day. I chased them across the campus toward their church. To get there, we had to pass my dorm. As we approached, we saw cars zipping by. A couple of people yelled out of their rolled down windows, "Get off campus!"

One person yelled, "The Klan is coming! The Klan is coming!"

As we got closer to my dorm, I say Gil Scott-Heron standing there, as if he was guarding the door. He had bullets strapped across his chest and a rifle in his hands. I said to myself, *Oh my God, what is going on?*

Then I saw Paula bolt out of the front door of the dorm past him. She said, "Girl, where have you been? I have been asking about you all morning! If you want to ride with me, pack one bag and get down here, fast! I'm leaving in ten minutes."

I answered, "Don't leave me! I'll be right there!"

Then Gil said, "OK, DC ladies. Get it together! Get out of here! Hurry up, Gwynette!"

I chased the children to the edge of the campus. I looked both ways and didn't see anyone coming. Being able to see their church, I stopped but told them not to stop and to run straight to their church. Last one there would be a rotten egg. You should have seen their little legs going. When I knew they were almost safe, I flew back to the dorm.

Paula was at her car packing it up when I passed the parking lot. She said, "I'm leaving in five minutes, with or without you. I have room for you and one suitcase. Oh, and bring two scarves."

I said, "OK, I'll be right back. Don't leave me."

Gil was still at the door on guard. I asked him, "Why are you dressed like that?"

He said, "No one is gonna come in this dorm to touch our women, but through me! Gwynette, you got five minutes and I'm outta here too. You are the last one to go!"

We both said to each other, "The revolution will not be televised!"

I chuckled to myself and flew up the four flights of stairs, three steps at a time, to my room. Kat was already gone. She must have hitched a ride with someone. She left a note that said to keep my key, lock the door, and the university would let us know when it was safe to come back and get the rest of our things. I threw a few things into one small suitcase, mainly underwear, a couple of jeans, a few tops, a pair of my favorite casual shoes, and a pair of tennis shoes. I remembered that Paula had said to bring two scarves. So, I grabbed two from my dresser drawer and put them into my shoulder bag.

Then I flew down the stairs, out the door, toward Paula's car. Sure enough, she was waiting for me, with the car running, and off we went toward Oxford and Route 1—and right into trouble.

Paula filled me in as to what was going on as we drove toward

Oxford, pass Ferdie the Bull. She was one of the few people I knew who did the healthy thing and went to breakfast every morning. That's where she heard that the university had gotten word that the Klan were on their way to Oxford. They had found out that Lincoln was planning to stage an antiwar march and rally and were planning on a confrontation in Oxford or at Lincoln.

The president had decided to close down Lincoln at noon to prevent the Klan from coming and doing who knows what to the campus. He wanted all the students to be gone if they came to the gate. So, he gave the students four hours' notice, to get off the campus by bus, car, or "any means necessary."

The campus looked deserted when we were leaving. We said we never knew that college students could move so fast. Paula said that she heard that every Greyhound and Trailways bus coming through Route 1 going north and south was packed to the front doors, with students willing to stand all the way to all points north and south. She said some students who didn't have bus fare had taken the risk and were thumbing rides.

And where was I? I was clueless. I went to class, took my quiz, and went straight to tutor the village kids. I was so grateful that Walter had given me the heads up, I didn't know what to do, and I was so thankful that Paula had waited for me.

Here was our dilemma. In order to get to DC, we had to go through Oxford. And where was the Klan headed? To Oxford. We were praying all the way to Oxford that we would beat the Klan there, cut through town, by-pass Rt. 1, take the side roads, and head straight to 95 South to Baltimore and DC. The million-dollar question was: would we get through Oxford before the Klan got there?

As we drove down the Baltimore Pike, pass Ferdie the Bull, toward the town of Oxford, Paula said, "Did you bring those scarves I asked you to bring?"

I said, "Yeah!"

She then said, "Pull them out. We need to put them on. Let's tie these 'fros down!"

I went first. I pulled one out from my shoulder bag and tied down my 'fro by knotting the scarf at the nape of the back of my neck. Paula was a different story. She waited until she got to the stoplight at the edge of town. Her 'fro was so big, I gave her the larger scarf. She folded it as large as she could and tied her 'fro down by knotting the scarf under her chin.

When the light changed, Paula took off through Oxford via Route 1 as fast as she could through the town, without calling too much attention to us. While driving on Route 1, before we could turn off, we spotted a mob of Klansmen coming right toward us. Paula started to speed up to take a left turn to the hilly back roads she usually took to get to Route 95. Just as she turned, the Klan spotted us. They started to run after the car. She put her foot to the floor to speed as fast as her little Volkswagen would go. As she looked in the rearview mirror, she yelled, "Duck!"

I quickly looked behind me and saw two Klansmen standing in the road behind us with shotguns drawn. I ducked down, and I reached over and pulled Paula over toward me. She kept her hands firmly on the wheel. We heard three to five shots, as she drove about 50 feet without seeing the road. "Boom, boom, boom!"

When the shooting stopped, we both sat up. We started to feel our bodies to make sure we weren't shot. Then we turned around to see if the car was OK and if we were being followed. Everything was OK. We were OK, the car was OK, we had outrun the Klan, but our nerves were shot.

Paula asked, "Nettie, are you OK? Do you need me to stop?"

I said, "Hell no, don't stop. Girl, I'm fine. Don't stop until we get to the Chesapeake House. I gotta go to the bathroom, but we need to get the hell out of Klan territory! I can hold it!"

Thank God those Klansmen didn't know how to shoot their guns that well to hit their target. Did we laugh about that? Is the Pope Catholic?

So that was that. We were scared out of our wits. Paula's little blue Volkswagen flew over that hilly road and onto 95 South. We stopped at the Chesapeake House to go to the bathroom, to calm down with a cool drink, and to call home to tell our parents and boyfriends what had happened and that we were OK. We made it home to DC as fast as we could.

After we were home for about a week, the non-graduating Lincoln students received a letter from the president giving us until summer school started at the end of May to return to campus to collect the rest of our belongings and clear out of the dorms. We were also told that we would not have to take final exams and would receive the average of the grades that we had achieved up to the time that school closed. Those averages would be our final grades. I had achieved a 3.51 GPA that semester, which meant that I had made the dean's list, so I was very pleased. In essence, that was the end of my freshman year.

Lacy, his buddy Donny, and I drove up to Lincoln one sunny day in late May to collect the rest of my things. We made sure it was after the tensions in Oxford had died down, and during the day so we wouldn't get caught in Pennsylvania Klan country at night. When we got to "Ferdie the Bull" fertilizer plant, Donny said, "What's that I smell? Did someone fart?"

Lacy said, "No, man, that's Ferdie the Bull!"

Donny asked, "Who the hell is Ferdie the Bull?"

I responded, "No silly, Ferdie the Bull is the fertilizer plant we just passed."

Donny said, "Well, Ferdie the Bull is one stinky dude!"

The three of us cracked up!

After my experience with the Klan and the closing of the school, Lacy set me down and asked me again to consider transferring to Howard to be with him. My being at Lincoln was putting a strain on our relationship. After a couple of days and much thought, I worked out a strategy that I hoped would settle things once and for all.

I met with Lacy to reveal my plan to graduate early. I immediately signed up for summer school at the University of the District of Columbia. I decided to take six credit hours, two courses, in addition to working the two jobs I had worked the summer before: full time at the Navy Department and part-time at Woodward and Lothrop. Six hours would be equivalent to a half a semester. The credits would then be transferred back to Lincoln. Two years of that would be equivalent to one semester. In addition, taking an overload each semester of twenty-one credits would give me another extra semester, which would allow me to graduate a year early.

Lacy reluctantly agreed to my decision. We both knew it would be hard on me, both physically and mentally, and on both of us emotionally and as a couple. I said to him, "If we really love each other, we will make this work. Two more years, and I'll be back home to you, full-time."

I began to execute my plan that summer of 1970. It was a tight schedule, but on most days when I would leave my jobs or leave school at night, there was Lacy, in the burgundy GTO, waiting to pick me up. That was how we were able to spend time together during the week, and on most weekends, we relaxed and had fun when I didn't have to study. My plan was getting off to a good start.

YEAR TWO AT LINCOLN

I returned to Lincoln for year two determined to execute my plan to graduate in three years. I knew I needed to buckle down to accomplish that goal and that there were several things I needed to do. It would take *perseverance, hope, and determination* (PHD).

First, we were asked to finalize our choice of a major at the beginning of our second year in order to map out a plan of courses needed for graduation. I had thought about that during the summer and decided not to major in biology or any of the sciences because of all of the labs. I needed work-study to make ends meet financially, and labs took time away from work.

I decided to major in economics and business administration. I had taken an intro class in that department during my freshman year, and it was very interesting. I knew I would be able to do the math involved, but would I be able to understand the theory? I decided to load up on accounting classes, which were heavy in math and business, and let that be my concentration rather than theory, although I still had to take a fair share of economics classes.

I signed up for twenty-one credit hours that semester, including Introduction to Accounting and Macroeconomics. It was going to be tough going into a male-dominated field of study, but I knew I was up to the task and could do it with PHD. Of course, on top of that, I would still be pledging AKA that semester. As they say, "When the going gets tough, the tough get going!"

The second thing on my agenda was that in order to concentrate on my studies and graduate early, I needed to stop cheerleading. It was too time-consuming and physically taxing, especially going to the away games. It was hard giving up something I loved doing so much, but I decided to go to the office of sweet little Mrs. White to tell her, "I quit."

I wasn't alone in my decision to quit. My fellow Ivy line sister and good friend Dorcas had also decided to stop cheering, so we went to see Mrs. White together. We both had scholarships at stake and had to concentrate on keeping them. We had talked over the summer and knew that something had to go. That something needed to be cheerleading, and so it would be.

I thanked Mrs. White for being such a positive role model and example of what a loving wife, awesome mother, and working woman could be. When I explained to her my reasons for quitting, she understood. She wished me luck with my goal to graduate early and with my young man, Lacy. Dorcas and I left Mrs. White's office in tears, hugging each other, but knowing we had taken another step toward growing up and another step toward graduation.

The one thing we both just couldn't give up and knew we had to finish was our initiation into Alpha Kappa Alpha Sorority, Inc. Dorcas and I had met with Sharon, number one on our line because she was four foot ten, once in Philly and once in DC over the summer to select fabric and plan our outfits for "hell week" and our initiation activities. We were the seamstresses of our line, so we were charged with making clothes for all the girls. We had fun during the summer picking out fly patterns and beautiful pink and green fabric from Woodies where I worked and hanging out together to get better acquainted. We made most of the dresses, pantsuits, vests, and other items during the summer except for the final fittings, which we would do when we returned on line.

We were the first AKA line at Lincoln to pledge on campus. The charter line and founding line had pledged under the graduate chapter in Philadelphia. We were the first line that had not pledged under the graduate chapter, who were AKAs who had graduated from college already. So, the campus anxiously awaited our arrival that fall, including our Ivy sisters who had dropped off line and all my friends.

When we returned from summer break, there were nine of us left on the line. We were determined that all nine of us would make it through and that we would lose not one more. We would support and motivate one another come hell or high water. We called ourselves the *Ninth Dimension*, sort of after the singing group the Fifth Dimension, which was very popular back then. We practiced our songs and our stepping every night in the basement of one of the classroom buildings that wasn't being used by anyone else.

Sharon was number one, an important position, charged with getting the line going. I was number four, to keep things going from the middle, and Dorcas was number nine, the tallest, who brought up the rear. We three seamstresses were known as the in-crowd or the fly girls because we were the three bold ones who went off campus to the Penn Relay parties during the spring pledge period.

The sororities and fraternities who had initiates put them back on-line in September of 1970 for four more weeks—four more weeks of torture. From sunup to sundown, from breakfast to bedtime, with the exception of classes, we did everything together. We had to eat together, study together, learn to sing and step together, and yes, catch the raft of our big sisters together, until we could all break away to get some shut-eye, which wasn't much.

Three weeks went by quickly. Then came hell week. We had to look alike, walk in line everywhere together, and perform in public. It was an exciting yet frightening time. We had to prepare to be presented to the public as new initiates, which meant singing, stepping, and looking good.

Finally came Friday night—hell night—when we crossed the burning sands and professed our love for Alpha Kappa Alpha sorority. The next day, Saturday, October 10, 1970, we were initiated into the sorority in a formal, secret ceremony. I am not at liberty to discuss either of those two events, but I will say this: you would have probably been able to hear me shout "I love Alpha Kappa Alpha" a block away.

My sister came down to Lincoln from Penn State, where she had just started graduate school, to pin me. After singing with all of the AKAs who were on campus for our ceremony, I was able to go back to my dorm room. It was all decorated in pink and green, and I had loads of gifts and toys (pink and green stuffed animals, dolls, and clothes) all over my bed. We toasted my initiation with pink champagne and wine.

On Sunday, all of the AKAs on campus at the time got together to sing one more time, in front of the student union building. Afterward, I saw my sister off to Penn State and went back to my dorm room. All I wanted to do was sleep like there was no tomorrow. I just wanted to sleep and sleep and sleep.

Come Monday morning, it was back to class and back to normal. The one thing that was different was that I was an AKA for the rest of my life. Otherwise, it was back to classes, which I had been mostly sleeping through for four weeks; back to my work-study job, which I had been sleeping through for four weeks; and back to studying, which I hadn't been doing much of.

I was so behind in my studies, and midterm exams were right around the corner. I began to panic. Once I settled myself down, I knew what I had to do: study, study, and study some more. Just as with pledging, my plan went from sunup to sundown. Whenever I wasn't in class or working, I would be studying, and since I worked in the library, that would be easy to do. I only stopped to eat lunch and dinner. After dinner, it was back to the library until it closed. I would get sleepy and take little catnaps in the library, and sometimes I would leave the library a little early to catch the end of a night basketball game. I would squeeze in a little social life on the weekends, to be with my new sorority sisters and hang out with my friends.

I decided not to go home until Thanksgiving, which Lacy wasn't happy about. That would be the hardest thing I had to do and the longest stretch that I had stayed away from home. I said to myself that if I could just make it through midterms to Thanksgiving in one piece, I would be OK.

Kat was very helpful and supportive of me during my pledging days and after. She had chosen not to pledge a sorority when I did. She said she wanted to wait and see what it was like for other people before she tried it out. I used to call her Chicken Little, but it probably wasn't a bad strategy. I was determined to talk her into pledging AKA and on pinning her as my sorority sister before she graduated, and I made that my ultimate goal for her.

As friends, Kat and I became even closer that semester. After I pledged, we did everything together. We went to class together, worked at the library together, ate our meals together, studied a lot together, and yes, along with our DC crew, partied together. Some people would say Kat and I were connected at the hip. Today, we would be considered BFFs, *best friends forever.*

Because Kat was tall and fair and I was short and brown, some people called us Mutt and Jeff or Salt and Pepper, and others called us

Cheech and Chong or Frick and Frack. When we would hang out in the cafeteria, Kat could read lips to figure out what people were saying, and we would say that she could see around corners and had eyes in the back of her head. She would give us the latest scoop and the hottest gossip. Truly, those were good old days and the best of times.

Kat and I had the same major and took most of our classes together. If we needed help or got stuck on an accounting problem or something, we would compare notes after I got back to the room from the library. That worked out well for us. Together, it usually didn't take long for us to come up with the right answers for our out of class assignments.

Studying for midterm exams was like going through hell week all over again. I was so behind, I decided to start from the beginning of each class and teach myself the material as if the class was just starting, rather than relying on my notes, since I had dozed off in most of my classes while I was pledging. I went back to the first page of each book for every class and taught myself the material all over again. That was painful and time-consuming, especially in economics, but it worked.

Midterm exams came and went. Homecoming came and went. Lacy came up for homecoming with a couple of his friends, and they got to meet some of my new sorority sisters and hang out with my DC crew. A lot of fun was had by all.

Pretty soon, Thanksgiving rolled around, and I got to go home to a great home-cooked Thanksgiving meal. For me, the Thanksgiving break lasted about ten days. My classes were on Tuesdays and Thursdays. We were also allowed three cuts (absences without penalty) per semester. I would save my cuts and use two of them (the Thursday and Tuesday before Turkey Day) for my Thanksgiving break. I would leave campus with Paula on that Tuesday evening after classes, a week before the holiday, and come back the Sunday after. That gave me a long Thanksgiving break.

I used my Thanksgiving break of 1970 to catch up on some much-needed sleep and real rest, and to renew my body and spirit. I was exhausted physically and mentally. I took my books home, and while

Mama was at work, I continued to study to understand the semester's material. Lacy and I took in a few movies and a couple of parties. As always, he was loving, kind, and supportive, and we had fun hanging out together. His mother thought I was looking kind of thin, so she had me over to dinner a lot.

When I returned to Lincoln after Thanksgiving, it was time to study for final exams. I went back to the same study routine I had for midterms: study, study, and study some more. Before we knew it, finals were upon us.

My last final exam that semester would change the rest of my college career. That semester, Kat and I took a mandatory course in business law, which was required for all accounting, economics, and prelaw students. To say the least, the class was filled to capacity at Lincoln every semester, with mostly male students. Kat and I were two of the few females in the class.

The class was taught by our accounting professor, Mr. Washington. He was an excellent, practical professor who was a board-certified CPA out of Philadelphia. He was serious and no-nonsense and made us do our work in black ink, like in the real accounting world. We could not turn in any spreadsheets with erasure marks. That meant that if we made a mistake, we had to copy everything over again, in black ink.

Well, Mr. Washington decided that in order to prepare us for the CPA exam, he would give us old business law sections of the CPA exam as our midterm and final exams. So, the final exam was a taste as to what that section of the CPA exam would be like.

Kat and I were struggling in that class. It was my first taste of legal terminology and legal cases period, least more in business, examining things such as torts, legal liability, and malpractice. We studied and studied day and night for that class, and we had pulled an all-nighter for the final.

The final was scheduled for two hours, from ten o'clock to noon, so as usual, we went straight from the dorm to the classroom, with very little breakfast, only some cereal, milk, and juice that we had in our room. We got there before the test started and sat about two rows apart from one another near the front of the room. We knew the exam would be multiple-choice and standardized, with No. 2 pencils and all, and we were right. It was very intimidating. Our strategy was to read every case and every question, and to answer every question no matter what—to guess at the answer if we had to, but to answer it.

We watched as the classroom filled up with our classmates, many shaking their heads as if to say, *I'm not ready for this*. Professor Washington handed out the exam, the answer sheets, and the No. 2 pencils and told us to begin. Some people signed their name on the answer sheet, took one look at the exam, got up, turned it in blank, and left. That usually meant they hadn't studied, were unprepared, and were going to fail the class, only to have to come back another semester and take the class again.

Kat and I weren't having that. We looked at each other, shook our heads *no*, and went to work, carrying out our strategy. I read every question and every case, sometimes twice, and answered every question, whether I was sure of the answer or not.

An hour into the exam, people began to trickle out, one by one. By eleven thirty, three-fourths of the class was gone. Many people left muttering *"I give up"* or *"I can't take no more!"*

Around then, my stomach started to growl. But I said to myself, *Quit? Not me!* Kat and I kept going and going. I wasn't about to stop until I finished the whole thing.

A little before noon, I was finished. I sat there and looked over the exam. On some of the questions, I didn't have a clue as to whether my answers were right or wrong, but at least I tried. I looked at Kat, and she looked at me from across the room. We were the only two students left in the classroom. We shrugged our shoulders at each other, got up, and turned in our exams as the church bells rang signaling that it was noon. By then, I was starving.

Professor Washington, an older, distinguished, mixed gray-haired gentleman, took our exams and asked us to have a seat nearer to his desk. I said to myself, *Oh no, what did we do? Did he think we were cheating or something?* Kat and I sat back down holding our books, looking curiously at each other.

First, Professor Washington thanked us for staying to the end of the exam. He said, "See how the class reacted to this challenge? They all left, except you two. I have been watching you girls and checking up on you two."

Kat and I just looked at each other and shrugged our shoulders. I responded, "Professor Washington, I was *determined* to finish! I believe in finishing what you start!"

He went on to say, "I understand that you two are both from DC and that you are roommates, huh? Well, you're just what I've been looking for! I've been wanting to get you two alone. Don't get me wrong, it's for something honorable, and it's not about this class. It's about the accounting classes. I've been watching you two in our accounting classes for some time, and I just finished grading your accounting exams. Ms. Reese, you got an A, and Ms. Ford, you got an A– on the final. It is obvious that the two of you study together. Your homework is nice and neat and always correct, and your exams are the best in the class. What I want to ask you ladies is whether you would like to tutor the incoming students in the Accounting I class next semester, especially some the boys who are struggling? Some of them will be taking the class for the second time."

Professor Washington went on to say he had gotten grant money from NABA, the National Association of Black Accountants, to train more black accountants, and that organization would be paying our salaries. He explained that we would start right after January break, and that our job would be to work with the Accounting I students outside of class on their homework assignments and to help prepare them for their exams and their final.

If all went well the next semester, there was a possibility for us to continue with the job the next year, which would be my last year. The pay would be ten dollars an hour for up to twenty hours per week, with the possibility of more hours during the exam period. We would keep our own timesheets and could see students whenever we wanted, at the library, the classrooms, and/or in the dorms. Professor Washington said that we could think about the offer over the January break and let him know when we returned. If our answer was *no*, he would get someone else.

I thought about it for a couple of seconds. The offer was too good to turn down and didn't need to be thought about over the break. That was about $200 a week, more than we were making at the library and way less boring.

I said, "Professor, I don't need to think about it over the break. If it's OK with you, sir, I would like to accept the job offer right now, so I can study and prepare a work schedule for tutoring over the break."

Kat chimed in, "Me too, sir. I accept the offer too."

Professor Washington said, "OK, this matter is now settled. I will prepare the paperwork before I leave for the holidays and get it to the A-Building. You ladies check in with them when you return and pick up your timesheets."

He closed by saying, "Thank you again for hanging in there on this test. I know it was hard, but it's hard for everyone who is not a lawyer. And Ms. Ford, I need you to stay awake in my class if you are going to be my tutor!" He said that with a smile.

I smiled back, embarrassed. "Professor Washington, I'm so sorry, but this semester, I was pledging. I'm so embarrassed. I will do better. It's not you or the class. It's me. I stay up late studying, and in the afternoon, I get so sleepy sometimes."

He said, "I know. Congratulations, I'm your Alpha brother. You need to check with a doctor. Maybe you are anemic or something. I notice everything. As I said, I have been watching you girls. Go home and get some rest over the break and come back refreshed and ready to work."

Our response was, "Yes, sir."

With that, Kat and I were out of there. We high-fived one another and went straight to the cafeteria to celebrate. We were past starving by then, so we joined our crew for lunch and couldn't wait to tell them about our job offer. With our last final behind us, we went back to the dorm to pack our bags, and we both caught a ride with Paula to DC for our winter break. When we passed the Ferdie the Bull plant, we gave each other another high five.

That was what I liked about going to an HBCU like Lincoln. Everyone looked out for each other, and the professors looked out for, nurtured, and took care of their students. I felt blessed to be a Lincoln Lioness and to receive such LU love.

I went home to DC and went to work for Woodies before and after Christmas. I was asked to work in the children's department first, and then in the Christmas Shop, which was a special department set up at Christmastime to sell Christmas decorations, gifts, ornaments, cards, wrapping paper, bows, etc. It was fun watching how working professionals, middle-class housewives, and the Washington elite dressed their children and how they decorated their homes and Christmas trees.

Woodies had Christmas windows similar to those at Macy's in New York City. Woodies prided itself on always having the best Christmas windows in downtown Washington, with moving mannequins and toys, scenic Christmas themes with villages and trains, kids ice-skating and playing winter games, and of course a window of mechanical carolers. The buyer for the children's department invited me to walk down to see Hecht's (Woodies' biggest rival) Christmas window with her to make sure the Woodies' window looked better. Buyers could always make changes and adjustments to what the mannequins were wearing.

While there, we visited Hecht's children's department to compare what they were selling to Woodies. It was clear to me that the style and quality of the clothes at Woodies were superior by far, as were the Christmas windows. I also got the impression that the buyer was preparing me for a job offer as a buyer once I finished college. Most of the buyers back then had college degrees, and only a few were black. I got the feeling she was trying to recruit me for affirmative action reasons.

I was asked to work in the Christmas Shop the week of Christmas. Then came Christmas Eve. Woodies decided to stay open that night until midnight, especially the Christmas Shop. Though other departments would start to close at nine o'clock and most of the employees could close out their registers when things got slow and go home to their families, I was asked to work until midnight. Being single with no children, I had no problem staying late to make the extra money. Lacy agreed to pick me up and take me home, and Mama said she would wait up for me. I thought it would be fun.

Well, by noon, things started to get hectic. The line was usually six to ten people deep. By three in the afternoon, we could barely keep up. There were only three of us working the department. Two of us worked the cash register, and the buyer kept the department neatly stocked. Being a young mother, she went home at six in the evening, leaving us two salespeople to fend for ourselves.

My coworker left at nine o'clock. and I was left alone to close out, which was usually the case when I worked late. It seemed that after she left, all hell broke loose. People came in for last-minute items in droves. A lot of the customers were white men, of all ages, many of whom didn't have a clue as to what to buy, which meant that I had to help them decide. At times, I would look up, and the line would be out the door of the Christmas Shop and into the department adjacent to it.

One of the store managers would stop by periodically to pick up the cash and to see how I was doing, and the security guards made sure I was safe. We all had our hands full. One of the managers said, "Stay cool and calm. Don't let all of the people get to you, and you will get through this. Just close the register out when the last customer is gone and bring it to the office."

And I tried to do just that: keep my wits about me and keep the money straight. About ten o'clock, though, things went crazy. Shoppers started to panic and ransack the place, getting the cards and ornaments all out of place and dropping ornaments, cards, and other items on the floor. The Christmas Shop became a madhouse. Having a long line, I couldn't stop to straighten things up.

Lacy came in to check on me around eleven thirty and to let me know he was waiting outside in the GOAT. He took one look and said, "What the hell? This place looks like a war zone!"

All I could do was look at him and shrug my shoulders. I said, "I know, and I'm not cleaning up this mess. That's housekeeping's job!"

At 11:45, Woodies started to announce that it would close in fifteen minutes and to please bring final purchases to the register. My line was at the door and about twenty people deep, but no one left. I announced that I would take all of them and, as with each purchase that day, I said, "Have a Merry Christmas!"

When the bell rang at midnight, I had about ten customers left, and my cash drawer was so full of cash I couldn't close it. I left it open for the last few transactions, in sight of security. When the last person came through at about 12:15 a.m., I wiped my brow and went to work counting the money in the drawer and reconciling my receipts and cash, with a security guard standing watch.

I stuffed the cash (several thousand dollars) in the required cash bag and could barely zip it closed. I closed the cash drawer and took off to the office to turn in the money, stepping over the cards, wrapping paper, broken ornaments, and trash that customers had dropped on the floor.

I said "Merry Christmas" to everyone in the office, turned in the cash bag, and got the hell out of there.

I jumped into Lacy's burgundy chariot, and we headed to my mom's. That night, I vowed to Lacy that I would never work on Christmas Eve for anybody ever again, except in my own house, getting my kids' and my family's Christmas tree and gifts together.

That was the first time I had ever talked about having kids and a family with Lacy, and we spent the ride home talking about that, laughing all the way, while listening to Christmas music on the radio. We talked about wanting a family, at least the ideal: a boy for him and a girl for me, and perhaps as many as five kids—"a full basketball team," he said. We laughed and joked about that, but we agreed that we both wanted children, and not just one. Being an only child, Lacy said, "Definitely not just one. Absolutely not. That's no fun!"

We also vowed that if we did marry one another, with both of us being from broken homes, we would never get a divorce. I got home a little after 1 a.m. in the morning, which was my normal unofficial curfew for getting home after a date, but that was far from a date; that was from work. Dog-tired, I went right to bed.

Mrs. Lacy had the Ford women over for one of her fabulous Christmas dinners the next day. She prepared turkey and all the trimmings, with her signature sweet potato/marshmallow casserole and her famous homemade icebox rolls, topped off with her pineapple coconut cake and Mamie Eisenhower fudge for dessert. Boy, could that woman cook.

Mrs. Lacy was one of eleven children. Her dad had worked as the head cook at Howard University, and that's where some of her cooking skills came from. That and having ten siblings was also the reason she cooked large amounts of food, as though, as she would describe it, she was "cooking for an army." She usually had two shifts of guests. Me and my family and some of her immediate family (some of her brothers) and Corinth (they called Lacy by his middle name) were usually the first shift. Then her nieces and nephews and their families and friends would come as the second shift. Her house was always full when she had one of her family dinners, for everyone knew it would be a treat.

We called Mrs. Lacy the "Brown Mrs. Claus" because she loved the Christmas holidays and gave out not just the gift of food and baked goods, but Christmas gifts as well. After all those years of cooking, she had a nice round physique and a beautiful round face; therefore, she could definitely be a Brown Mrs. Claus.

She really seemed to have taken a liking to me, finally, and we were becoming good friends. She knew and understood that I was part of a "package deal," with Mama and Vee being the rest of my package. Having had so many siblings, I think she understood that better than her son did.

I spent the rest of winter break working end-of-the-year inventory at Woodies. Accounting being my area of concentration, I also volunteered at H and R Block and wrote a paper about balancing your books at the end of the year for tax purposes as my January project. I spent my spare time hanging out and partying with Lacy and making a spring wardrobe of pink and green and crimson and cream for upcoming AKA and Kappa events in their colors, respectively. Sewing was how I relaxed and expressed myself creatively; at the same time, it allowed me to keep up with the latest fashion trends.

When my grades arrived, I was shocked. I got a 3.78 that semester, my best semester grade-wise up to that point. Oddly enough, though, one of the lowest grades I got that semester was in the class I loved most. With an A– on that final he told me about, I still wound up with a B+ in accounting, the lowest grade I would ever get in that subject. Yet Professor Washington, who was a tough grader, wanted me to be a tutor? That made me wonder what kind of grades the other students had gotten. I also got a B+ in physical education, which was usually an A, but I was so tired from pledging that semester, I missed a couple of classes.

All in all, given the semester I'd had personally, coming off of pledging and all, I was blown away by my grades. I got As in everything else and an A+ in sociology. I guess all of that self-teaching and studying and those many hours spent in the library must have really paid off. It was the best semester GPA I would get during my matriculation at Lincoln. How proud was I - a 3.78 GPA, high honors, and dean's list, all while pledging AKA! Wow! It took *perseverance, hope, and determination*, (PHD).

SPRING OF 1971 WAS "WHAT'S GOING ON?"

After our January break, it was back to campus, back to the routine of campus life, and back to my strategy to graduate in three years. I signed up for another twenty-one-credit-hour semester, which meant a lot of hard work. Kat and I, being in the same major, signed up for the same classes—except she took eighteen hours that semester, which was still considered an overload. She decided to aim to graduate a semester early. In some classes, we were the only girls.

Kat and I started our new job of being accounting tutors at the beginning of that spring semester. For the first half of the semester, we continued to work at the library as we began to log in hours of tutoring, mostly guys, in accounting. Before spring break, however, we were called in by the financial aid office and told that we had too many work-study hours and would have to give up one of our jobs.

Of course, the job we quit was the one at the library. We said goodbye to the dark stacks and the smelly books and spent the rest of our work-study allotment tutoring "the pickle heads," as we called the fellas we tutored. Although we called them "pickle heads," as I have said, everyone at Lincoln was smart and capable. It's just that some students would get distracted, couldn't concentrate or weren't able to grasp the material.

And it wasn't just the pickle heads behind us who came by for tutoring. It was also some of the pickle heads in classes *with* us. They would get their homework checked by us and we would compare notes to make sure they were on the same page as we were as far as understanding the material. They would have Kat and I check to make sure their balance sheets were right, and we didn't mind working with them as well. Soon, even the girls in our classes began to join us. Some nights, our room would be packed with students, with standing room only, and some students even sat on the floor, especially at exam time.

The most popular song at that time was "What's Going On" the block buster anti-war and anti-violence hit by Marvin Gaye. I brought the album of the same name back to campus with me after spring break and would play it first thing in the morning and the last thing at night, day and night, to stay motivated and faithful to complete the tasks at hand. Tonya, Nona and Muff would often knock on my wall to tell me to cut it down or turn it off. Many of the guys who would come in for tutoring would ask, "What's going on?" to inquire about what was going on in class and what material we needed to tackle that day. Kat and I would ask, "What's going on?" to inquire about what the students needed to work on and what their level of understanding was. Kat and I asked everyone who came to us for tutoring to be serious about their studies so that we were all be on the same page as to, "What was going on!" Often, our study sessions would get intense, and we would make so much noise; sometimes, some of the girls would peek out of their rooms to see what all the commotion was about.

All Kat and I would ask in return for our services was for one or more of the fellas to make a late-night food run to *Sissy's*, the infamous local diner/grill across the road from the Lincoln Memorial Arch, to fetch some of her legendary cold-cut hoagie sandwiches (Kat's favorite) and Philly cheesesteak sandwiches (my favorite) to eat and share with one another as we often burned the midnight oil.

Sissy's was the nickname that the Lincoln University community lovingly gave to the "Ye Ole Lion's Inn," to pay homage to its owner, Luvinia "Sissy" Burress. Sissy financed her restaurant in 1961 for $2000 as a place where Lincoln Lions, neighbors, travelers and others could eat, dwell, rest, read, write, sing, study and, of course, *rabble*. Open for breakfast, lunch and dinner, the diner was open long past 12 midnight most nights to feed many hungry students, faculty members, and others, until the last customer left. Sissy, who only had one female child, playfully adopted many Lincoln students, mostly men, cheerfully serving them as a mother away from home, and serving up nourishment when students needed something to eat, sometimes on credit when they had no money, and giving them motherly advice whether they felt they needed or not. Her Italian sausage, hamburger, and Western Omelette hoagie sandwiches were Lincoln Lion favorites and would hit the spot as replacements for some of the nasty cafeteria food that students would pass on or when they were too hungry to study. Sissy was a permanent sweetheart of the Epsilon Chapter of Kappa Alpha Psi Fraternity and was considered the mother of their chapter (they loved her that much).

A *Sissy's Roadhouse* run was par for the course when Kat and I had study sessions, and she always sent her best wishes and an extra hoagie or two to nourish our minds and bodies. Attached, would be a note that would read, "Get on your material!" which was a popular phrase everyone used at Lincoln, that meant *study hard*.

Before Kat and I knew it, all of the accounting students were doing well, including all of us who were in more advanced accounting classes together. There was something to be said for and something right about studying together with peers.

My extracurricular spare time that semester was devoted to George Corinth Lacy, my AKA sorority, and serving on the Kappa Court, in that order. The highlight of that semester for me was being selected as Queen of the Kappa Court of 1971 due to my support and dedication to the brothers of Epsilon Chapter (Lincoln University). I think I was selected not only because I attended all of their campus-wide activities, but also because I tutored a lot of the Kappas in accounting and played den mother to a lot of the Scrollers who were initiated that year and the year before.

My room was often a safe haven for not only my little sisters, the Ivy pledgees of Alpha Kappa Alpha Sorority, Inc., but also for the Scrollers of Kappa Alpha Psi, who called me "Most Gracious Lady, Gwynette." The Scrollers even made me a paddle with my title on it. Both groups could come to my room to take a break and "just chill." Rather than harass them, I allowed them to relax, tell me about themselves and why they were pledging, tell me what their personal and career goals were and what their dreams and aspirations were.

I would give them advice on anything and everything they wanted to know, from how to get through pledging, courses, and school to my own personal tips about life and love. That is how pledgees spent their time when they were with me. I was not the typical big sister who scolded and harassed them. I didn't like that when I pledged, and I promised myself that I wouldn't be like that once I crossed the burning sands.

In addition, both groups could have anything I had to eat in my room, and I always had plenty of goodies from home and the cafeteria for them to snack on. The Scrollers were always hungry and knew they could come to my room for something to eat. Both the AKA and Kappa pledgees seemed to appreciate my gentle touch, even to this day. Another of my roommates, Carolyn, and I, even hid some of the Scrollers from some of their big brothers from off campus one night. In fact, I hid with them. In hindsight, I think I was practicing the type of parent I would be to my own children and the type of professor I would be to my students: very protective of them.

Anyway, I think my interaction with the Sleazy Sixteen (the Scroller line that pledged the same time I did) and the Scrollers who pledged before and after them came into play in the voting for Kappa Queen that year. The coronation was on a Sunday at the end of Kappa Weekend that spring, which started with a mixer on Friday night and a "Hot Pants Party" on Saturday night. It was one of the best Greek weekends of the semester, along with my own AKA weekend, of course.

I made all of the outfits I wore on Kappa weekend in the Kappa colors of crimson (red) and cream (off-white), to the displeasure of my pink and green sorority sisters. On Saturday, I wore a pair of off-white hot pants and a crimson-and-cream sailor top that I made to match. On Sunday, for the coronation, I wore a crimson-and-cream gown that I designed and made myself. The gown was crimson with a split up the front and Kappa diamonds cut out in the bodice section. Under the gown, I wore cream-colored long pants rather than show off a lot of leg (it was still cool in Pennsylvania that spring). I felt like "Queen for a Day" that Sunday when I was crowned.

My second year at Lincoln ended on a high note. That year was also my best year at Lincoln, grade-wise. I made the dean's list again, with a 3.6 GPA for the second semester, with a 3.7 GPA overall. I returned to DC, my two jobs, and summer school at UDC, a happy camper.

MY SENIOR YEAR: THE ENGAGEMENT

The highlight and surprise of the summer of 1971 came in August, just before it was time for me to return to Lincoln for what would be my last year. By then, I had amassed enough credits that I only needed two more semesters to complete my major in economics and business and get my degree. My goal to graduate in three years was within reach.

Summer school was over, and so was my summer job at Navy. I told them that I was entering my last year of college and would be looking for a full-time, permanent job. They told me to look no further. They asked me to consider coming to work for the Department of the Navy full-time after college at an entry-level professional civilian administrative position. I told them I would definitely think about it.

Lacy and I loved going to Hains Point, a popular picnic spot located at the southern tip of East Potomac Park near the National Mall, the Washington Monument, and the Lincoln Memorial in DC. It was not unusual for him to ask me to pack a lunch for an afternoon outing. The Thursday before I left for school, he asked, and I packed a nice lunch with all of Lacy's favorites: baked BBQ chicken, potato salad, green beans, homemade lemonade, and sweet potato pie. It was a typical hot, sunny, August, DC afternoon. Lacy seemed to enjoy his lunch—small payment for all he had done for me that summer.

However, Lacy didn't seem to be himself that day. He was quieter than usual and seemed a little nervous. I couldn't figure out why. He was usually so comfortable and jovial with me. But then, at the end to our meal, he went into his pocket and pulled out a little jewelry box. We were lying on a blanket, so he got up on his knees, and I immediately sat up straight.

He opened the box, from Charles Swartz Jeweler—it had both an engagement and a wedding ring in it—and showed it to me. He took out the engagement ring and took my hand. Then he popped the question: "Will you marry me?"

I had been hoping for that moment for some time, but I must say it caught me by surprise when it happened. In shock, I said, "Yes, yes, yes." I took him by the chin with both hands and kissed him passionately, right there. He then put the engagement ring on my finger.

I told him that I was never going to take it off, and he said, "Well, you'll have to take it off on our wedding day, silly. The wedding band must go on first."

The engagement ring was a one-carat diamond set into a silver flower on top of a gold Florentine-finished band that was to overlap on top of the wedding band. It was breathtaking and must have cost a small fortune. We had casually looked at wedding rings in several jewelry stores that December, while Christmas shopping, and I had been hoping for an engagement ring by the next Christmas. I had no idea he'd put one of the sets I liked on layaway and had been paying on it for eight months. I certainly wasn't expecting to be asked in August, when I had a whole academic year left of school and was about to return. I was hoping for a Christmas engagement at best, if at all.

Since Lacy hadn't said anything in eight months, after asking me twice before, I thought he had changed his mind about me, so I had said nothing about getting married for months. Instead, I was focusing on graduating and starting to look at jobs and graduate school. So, this was all a big surprise. I was almost speechless.

I gushed over my ring all the way home and couldn't wait to tell my mother and sister. All of a sudden, my plans for my last year of college had the major addition of wedding planning. I'd always wanted a formal June wedding, and Lacy had waited for me long enough. I decided on June 1972 as my wedding month, which gave me around ten months to plan a formal church wedding. Although Lacy was Catholic and I was Baptist, we agreed to be married at my church, in that my family was very active in our church and had been members since before I was born. I said that every penny other than my school expenses would go toward our wedding.

The day after my engagement, which was a Friday, two major things happened—one pertaining to my wedding and one pertaining to my graduation. First, I called our church for a wedding date at Mama's insistence. The number three being my favorite lucky number, I asked for the third Saturday in June as a wedding date. I was told that a church friend of mine, Betty, already had that date. While it was great to hear that my friend Betty was getting married, I had missed out on getting the date I wanted.

The church clerk, who was a dear friend to my mother, told me that the fourth Saturday in June, the 24th, was the only and last date available for a wedding in June 1972, and that our pastor, Rev. Rossie Patterson, was available to officiate. I grabbed that day, reserved it, and rushed down to the church to sign the paperwork and make sure I had that day for my June wedding: June 24, 1972.

When I returned home, a bombshell was waiting for me. My mother gave me a letter that had come from Lincoln University, my school. Having no idea what it could be about, I took it to my bedroom to open it. Basically, it said that they were reducing the amount of my scholarship and that I would have to pay a portion of my tuition. Was I shocked? No, I had been warned that as the years went on, they would cut back on the tuition scholarship. That was one of the reasons I was trying to finish in three years. But it could not have come at a worse time, during my last year and was engaged to be married. As usual, my mother said she didn't have any money to give or loan to me.

I sat down on the bed and cried. When I got myself together, I called Lacy right away. He came over to get me and instead of going out on a date that night, we went to his house and worked up a budget for our wedding. He insisted on helping financially and agreed to pick up some of the bills, such as the flowers, the cake, and tuxedo rentals. I agreed to make all the dresses, including our mothers', and my own gown and veil. I had that covered. I would buy the fabric by the bolt from Woodies with my 20 percent employee discount. I told Lacy that it was usually the groom's job to pay the minister a small fee. It all seemed so simple with Lacy at my side, working on the budget. Back then, a traditional wedding didn't need to cost an arm and a leg like today. Most of these items could be handled incrementally on a payday-here-and-a-payday-there basis. I still had my tutoring job and would work at Woodies during the holidays to pay for the fabric for the girls' dresses. I decided to put myself on a tight budget. I would buy only what was absolutely needed during my last year of college.

The biggest item left was the reception. We decided to look into having it at the party room at Mulberry Plaza, where I used to live, for a small fee, instead of at a hotel. That would have to do. The number of guests and the catering menu would depend on how much money we had left. There would be no sit-down dinner. We decided on heavy finger foods, chicken, turkey sandwiches, fruits and veggies, and a lot of desserts.

We agreed to have the wedding and reception early enough in the day so people could still go out to dinner or to dinner parties afterward. Our mothers agreed to host dinner parties at their homes for their respective families and friends, and the bridesmaids could give a get-down party with food for our young friends.

Lacy said, "Order a huge cake, all they can eat." As always, he brought calm and humor to the situation. That was one of the reasons I loved him so much and was happy to become his bride.

Lacy drove me back to school that Sunday. It was a delightful ride, at least for me, on a warm late-summer day. During the two-hour drive, we made wedding plans and talked about our future. He said he would make honeymoon plans and surprise me. I said, "Are we going to have a honeymoon? Will we have any money left?"

He said, "Hell yeah! Just leave everything to me. You concentrate on having the wedding you want. I got the honeymoon. That's what overtime is for."

So, I arrived on campus as an engaged woman. I checked in, paid for my room and board, and Lacy helped me move into what would be my last dorm room. Carolyn, my friend from Cape Cod who'd agreed to be my roommate my last year, was already there and was the first one to congratulate us. Kat and Tonya, who had decided to be roommates my last year, so that they wouldn't get stuck with someone they didn't know their senior year, were not back on campus yet. After we got my luggage into the room, I took Lacy to the student union to have dinner with me. As we were going through the chow line, someone noticed my engagement ring and congratulated us.

By the time we sat down to eat, a few more people came over to congratulate us. The gossip mill was already at work. Thank goodness not a lot of students were back on campus yet. But it was OK. Lacy and I didn't mind. In fact, I wanted to shout it to the world: "I'm going to marry this man!"

It is a tradition on most college campuses that returning students make an assessment of which upperclassmen returned and who did not, who got pregnant and who did not, who had changed (gained weight or lost weight, for example), and who got engaged. During the days and weeks that followed my return, it became clear all over campus that I was engaged to be married. Everyone wanted to see my ring. Many students commented that it was the prettiest ring on campus that year, not so much for the size of the diamond, although one carat was nothing to shake a stick at, but for its unique and beautiful design.

I think the only group I would characterize as lukewarm about my engagement, although not against it, was the Kappas. Although they openly and publicly said they were happy for me, I think they were lukewarm that their campus queen was engaged to someone who was not a Lincoln Man and not a Kappa. However, that didn't change my feelings about the Kappas. I still represented the court and carried out my responsibilities as their queen by showing up and supporting all of their activities and programs.

I did the same for the AKAs when I could, although I went home a lot (just about every weekend or so) to take care of wedding plans.

During the pledge period, often, I was not there to talk to or to protect my little sisters. My room wasn't always a safe haven, as it had been the year before. The Ivies seemed to be a little disappointed about that, especially Kat, who had finally decided to pledge AKA.

The one thing I made sure of was that I stayed on top of my classwork. I was on course to graduate with high honors, magna cum laude, and I badly wanted that distinction. To graduate in three years, magna cum laude, would be quite a feat. It wasn't easy, trying to graduate and planning a wedding at the same time. Each time I went home I tried to check something off my to-do list.

The first semester of my senior year (I guess that was what one could call it) flew by. I carried twenty credit hours the first semester and was still able to remain on the dean's list with a 3.42 GPA, though I was somewhat distracted by my upcoming wedding. During the Christmas break, Lacy and I worked on our wedding plans. We gathered addresses for our guest list. Both of us being pretty popular; we had about the same number of friends we wanted to invite from high school and college. My mom's list was about fifty people from outside of the church, including family, although it was common practice to send one invitation to the entire church membership, knowing that only some close church friends, Sunday school teachers, and church officers would attend. My dad asked for an allotment of twenty invitations for his family and friends. But Mama Lacy, George's Mom, was another story.

She gave me an old-fashioned black-and-white composition notebook full of names and addresses. Some pages were filled with people with the same last name, such as the Bullocks, the Busseys, and the Kinards. When I asked her who all those people were, she said they were all family and that she wanted them all invited, from all up and down the East Coast and the Midwest. By the time we gave up counting, we needed to plan for about five hundred guests. So, I ordered three hundred invitations to cover most of the addresses on the invitation list, since many were couples and families.

I thought to myself, *Oh my goodness, how am I going to feed all those people?* One of my cousins, my mother's brother's oldest daughter, who had just recently gotten married, told me to call her caterer, Mr. Myers, who was well-known and liked throughout Washington, DC. He had done a great job with her wedding reception, which she'd had at the AKA House in DC, a popular reception venue owned by my sorority.

When I told him the large number of guests I was expecting, he asked me, "How much money you got?" I told him I could scrape up about $1,500 for the reception food, which was a lot of money to me back then. He laughed but said he would make it work and could give me a late lunch reception, with perimeter chairs. I couldn't help but think about that biblical story where the bride' family ran out of wine and Jesus turned water into wine. Mr. Myers said that when all the food was gone, our guests would have to go home or wherever, a popular DC story that we talked about. He said that was not his normal price, but he owed my uncle a big favor, so he would do his best for me. He said not to worry and to give him all I could muster up and he would make sure everyone would be fed. I was so grateful, I cried real tears of joy.

The last item I needed to take care of before returning to school after January Break was who would be in the wedding party. Lacy told me that he had eight best friends that he absolutely had to have in the wedding, including his best man. He said that they would be renting their tuxedos.

I said, "Wow, that's a lot." I was going to have to match that number with bridesmaids, but more importantly, bridesmaid dresses. I knew that my sister, Valeria, would be my maid of honor, but of course, I would ask her formally. That meant I needed seven bridesmaids, and because the maid of honor was single, tradition had it that all of the bridesmaids needed to be single. That ruled out my closest cousins, who were already married.

So, I chose five of my closest college friends: Kat, of course; Carolyn, who was my roommate at the time; Tee, from DC; Muff, Tee's childhood friend who went to Lincoln for a year; and Paula, my ride and closest confidante. That left two more girls who weren't Lincoln

Lionesses. So, I chose to ask Antonia, of course, my play-sister/cousin who introduced me to Lacy, and Carol Gillespie, a friend who still lived in Mulberry Plaza.

All of those bridesmaids, the two mothers, two junior bridesmaids, the flower girl, and the ring-bearer (Lacy's little male cousin) made for a large wedding party and a massive sewing job for me—including my own gown. I chose none other than pink and green, my sorority's colors, as my color scheme.

I worked at Woodies during my winter break for the last time. While working there, I ordered bolts of pink and green fabric. I ordered them during the store's Christmas sale of 20 percent off and got another 20 percent off as an employee discount. The fabric was of the finest quality and, at 40 percent off, quite a bargain.

I'd decided to use a soft polyester crepe in pastel pink and green. The fabric looked like sherbet, and it was so soft. I chose a Victorian pattern to match my dress.

I rushed the fabric order in so I could at least start cutting out dresses during my January break. It was my goal to have at least half of the dresses done by spring break. Since at least half of the girls were around the same size and at Lincoln with me, fittings would be relatively easy. My sister sewed, so she could make her own gown, and the flower girl's mom sewed too, so she could make her daughter's dress. My aunt was the one who taught me how to sew, so she could make her daughter's junior bridesmaid dress. I would accept help wherever I could find it.

I put several tight deadlines together, including one for my own gown, so that if I met them, I wouldn't be insanely rushed at the end. I even hoped to make a few things for my graduation from Lincoln, the pre-wedding celebrations, and some honeymoon outfits. That was going to be a lot of sewing, but I was up to the task.

MY LAST SEMESTER

My last semester at Lincoln was delightful, but busy. Upon returning to school in February, I signed up for graduation. In a review of my transcript and courses with my academic counselor, she confirmed that I only needed four classes to graduate. That was the lightest course load I would have since first semester freshmen year. My goal of graduating in three years was within reach. All I had to do was finish my last semester.

I was also told that one more class in accounting would qualify me for most entry-level accounting positions, so of course I stayed with the accounting concentration and added one more class in accounting to assure that I would be able to find a decent job. I had put in my résumé with the career placement office that fall and hoped to hear from someone during the spring semester. Now, things had changed somewhat. Instead of a national search or East Coast search for a job and/or graduate school, I was now focused on going home to DC and settling there as Mrs. Lacy.

Sure enough, job offers started to come in during the second semester. By midsemester, there were four solid offers in my job column that I was seriously considering, one in Philadelphia and three in DC. The one in Philadelphia was with one of the then–Big Eight accounting firms, Haskins and Sells. It was a very lucrative and prestigious offer for that time. Had I not been engaged to Lacy I would have jumped at it. But knowing that he would not be willing to leave DC and his familiar surroundings, and under pressure to make a decision, I declined the offer from Haskins and Sells.

That left the three job offers in DC. Two were in accounting, and one was in general administration. In accounting, I had job offers from H & R Block and the U.S. General Accounting Office (GAO). I hadn't liked interning with Block during my January break that year, so I turned down the offer. There was also the job offer from the Navy Department, my old stomping ground, which was an entry-level administrative position. However, I'd heard that the Navy Building in downtown DC was being torn down and that they were moving into new office space in Crystal City, Virginia, closer to the Pentagon. I had my heart set on living in a nice garden apartment in Maryland, so I felt going from Maryland through DC to Virginia every day on the bus would be too tough of a commute. So, with much sadness, I told my mentors at Navy that I would not be joining them when I graduated. That decision may have saved my life, for many years later, the Navy wing of the Pentagon was hit by a plane hijacked by terrorists and many civilian employees in the building that day were killed.

That left the accountant/auditor position at GAO, which was a nice solid job offer. GAO is an independent federal agency that conducts audits at the request of congressional members and committees and works outside of the OPM (Office of Personnel Management) umbrella. It therefore was given the freedom by Congress to offer competitive salaries to compete with the private sector, salary-wise, in order to get top-notch talent coming out of college.

GAO met the salary offer I'd received from Haskins and Sells in Philly. Therefore, I jumped at the offer, which allowed me to go home at the salary I wanted. I rushed to the placement office to report my acceptance, and I heard that it was the highest offer thus far for anyone in our graduating class. I was ecstatic. I would have taken a little less just to be able to go home, where I would soon become Mrs. George C. Lacy Jr.

I went home for spring break and started making the bridesmaid dresses for the girls who went to Lincoln. I also got the fabric for and started on the mothers' dresses. Mrs. Lacy selected pink satin, so I selected green crepe de chine for Mama. When I returned to campus, there were fittings and other projects to complete.

My few months left at Lincoln quickly came to an end, and none too soon. My sorority sisters gave me a wonderful bridal shower just before finals. It was a kitchen shower, so I got lots of neat kitchen gadgets and day-to-day dishes and glassware for informal entertaining. Of course, many of my gifts were in our colors of pink and green. The refreshments were great as well, including pink lemonade and green iced tea.

Final exams were a snap. I whizzed right through them. I must admit, though, it was a little hard to concentrate, with my wedding due to kick off in a little over sixty days. However, I got through them and even had time to tutor my underclassmen in accounting during their study period. Once my senior finals were over, I made time for a review session one last time for the underclassmen to make sure they could pass their final exams in accounting. I wanted them to pass, and besides, I needed the money.

Once senior finals were over and final grades were in, it was customary for each department to give a reception/graduation party for its graduating seniors. Ours was on a Thursday evening and was held in a classroom in the economics building. I took a break from packing up my things to attend. It was delightful. Although I hadn't started out with the seniors in my department when I was a freshman, I knew most of them because we were in classes together and I had tutored many of the guys. We sat around and talked about our Lincoln experience and joked and laughed about our Lincoln days together. We ate finger foods, had desserts, and drank punch provided by the food service.

Professor Washington hosted the reception. Toward the end, he stepped up to the podium to explain the graduation procedures and the procession, which was to take place in about ten days, always on the first Sunday in May at Lincoln. He stated that we were to line up in alphabetical order and not by department. He then explained how honors would be given out. He stated that there would be a valedictorian and a salutatorian named for the entire graduation class, and that neither was from our department. We all laughed, for we all knew that. Our department was one of the hardest in the university and gave out the toughest grades. I had a flashback to junior high school, however, and my valedictorian dilemma.

He went on to say, "However, a number of you will be graduating with honors." He explained the universal college honors system to us, including *summa cum laude* (with highest honor) for students with a 3.75 or higher GPA. He explained that no one in our department was graduating with that distinction either and we all laughed again.

Then he said, "We do have several of you who are graduating magna cum laude and cum laude, with high honor and with honor, respectively." *Magna cum laude* was for those graduates with a 3.50 or better GPA, and *cum laude* was for those graduates with a 3.30 GPA or better. "The rest of you will be graduating 'Thank you, Lordy,'" he said, and we all laughed again.

Professor Washington continued, "You all probably know your GPA but will know your honors status when you pick up your cap and gown, for you will get an honors cord to go around your neck over your gown. Your honors status will also appear in the graduation program and will be announced when you cross the stage."

Finally, Professor Washington said this: "I am at liberty and happy to announce today the graduate from our department with the highest GPA in our department, who is graduating magna cum laude and will be receiving the *Wall Street Journal* Award, which is given to the best student in economics and business at every university across the country by the *Wall Street Journal*. This year, Lincoln's award will go to our very own Gwynette Ford—and she did it in three years. Miss Ford, please stand. Your award will be announced and given to you at the graduation ceremony."

I was absolutely stunned. My legs felt like rubber. I could barely get my feet together to stand up. I knew what my GPA was and that I was probably going to graduate magna cum laude, but I didn't have a clue as to where I stood among the seniors in my department, and I knew nothing about the *Wall Street Journal* Award. I was floored, to say the least. I received a warm applause from my fellow graduates and returned a warm smile.

However, as in junior high, this accomplishment was again a little bittersweet. I couldn't help but think about the fact that I had done this in three years and that I was not graduating with the class I entered with.

How did the student with the next highest GPA feel about working hard for four long years and then getting beat out by someone who came along and finished in three years? I didn't ask and didn't want to know who that student was, although I suspected it was a quiet girl who lived in my dorm and had said very little to me the whole three years I was at Lincoln. I did not want to know for sure, and Professor Washington did not announce my GPA or who the runner-up was, thank goodness. I know that person, whoever it was, would feel terrible and would not be too happy with me. I felt bad about that and was very happy our GPAs were not announced.

Anyway, the rest of the reception went well. We laughed and joked and celebrated, especially the fellas. We partied to no end.

I went back to my dorm to finish packing. Lacy was picking me up the next day to take me home. I chose not to stay on campus to party during Senior Week, for there were pressing matters that needed my attention concerning our wedding. I planned to return early on graduation morning, with my family in tow, to attend the baccalaureate church service and graduation.

Before I left the campus that Friday, I stopped by the administration building to check my GPA. Sure enough, it was 3.6, and I was graduating magna cum laude. I also stopped by my department to turn in my last timesheet to Professor Washington. I thanked him for all that he had done for me. I told him how grateful I was that he'd made me a tutor and for how much I had learned from him. I also told him how surprised I was about receiving the *Wall Street Journal* Award. I shared my feelings about getting the award after finishing in three years. I even offered to share the award with a four-year graduate.

He explained to me that the award was given not just to the student with the highest GPA but to the student who had also made the greatest difference and contribution to the department and the profession of accounting. He said that was clearly *me* by not just my GPA, but by helping to recruit students to the department and by tutoring many of my fellow Lions. He said that I ranked "head over heels," in all selection categories. He also assured me that he would keep Kat on as "chief tutor" for the following year, and he added, "I wouldn't have it any other way. Both of us are really going to miss you though!"

I returned to the dorm feeling so much better about the award. Lacy arrived, and we packed up the GTO for the last time for the two-hour ride to DC. It was a very pleasant trip home on a beautiful spring day. I couldn't wait to get home to work on some of the final details of our wedding, which included working on my wedding gown.

OUR GRADUATIONS

My graduation day came in no time. I teased Lacy that although he was three years older than me, I would graduate before he would, though only one week before Howard's graduation. Of course, that was because he went to junior college first and served in the Civil Air Patrol, and I graduated in three years, and my college happened to set its graduation date before his.

I will never forget what a wonderful day my graduation was. The first Sunday in May of 1972 was a beautiful sunny spring day, yet cool, as usual, in Pennsylvania: around 65-70 degrees. Unlike many graduates who had large numbers of family members coming for graduation, my family attendance was relatively small.

My family came separately in three cars. As was the case when I first went to Lincoln, Lacy drove me and Mama. We left at six thirty in the morning and packed a light breakfast to take on the road so that we wouldn't have to stop to eat. I wanted to attend the baccalaureate church service, which was at nine o'clock in Mary Dod Brown Chapel, which was very small, so they only gave us three tickets. Therefore, it would be just the three of us attending that service. I wore a black-and-white long-sleeve mini dress that I'd made just for graduation. It was just right for wearing under the black gown we'd had to rent.

Daddy and my sister rode up to the campus together in his car. She was home in DC from Penn State, so he picked her up from Mama's, and they rode up a little later. My mother's youngest sister, Freddie, drove my grandmother and my mother's oldest sister, Bernice, up to the campus. So, over the hills and through the towns they came, for the first time. I was so happy that they were coming, especially my grandmother, to see the second of her thirteen grandchildren graduate from college.

The baccalaureate service was great. The chapel was full of graduates and their parents. There was singing and praying and more singing and praying. The dean of the chapel gave us a graduation sermon and prayed over us and sent us on our way. The service had started on time and ended just in time for me to pick up my cap and gown for the graduation ceremony, since I had not been there during graduation week to pick them up early. I rushed over to the administration building to get my stuff. Lacy and Mama went ahead over to the new gymnasium to get decent seats for the ceremony. Our graduation was the first event to be held in the new gym.

Sure enough, the black cap and gown with a blue and orange hood in the school's colors that I'd ordered had arrived. In addition, a silver, *magna cum laude* honors cord was attached. I grabbed my order and was good to go.

There was one hiccup. By the time I picked up everything, it was time to line up to march into the gym, and I had to get all the way across the campus in heels. I took my shoes off and rushed across the campus on the grass in my stocking feet.

On my way, I ran into Walter, my guardian angel, who was on his way to the gym as well, a little ahead of me. He reached back his hand and said to me, "Come on, homegirl, you don't want to be late for your own graduation, after rushing for three years to get out, do you?" Walter was graduating in four years, and I was happy to be graduating with my male guardian angel.

I said, "Oh, hell, no," and ran to catch his hand. We laughed and joked the rest of the way until we got to the line. His last name being Mason and mine being Ford meant that I would be ahead him in line and in crossing the stage. So, while I put my heels back on, he said, "OK, little sister, I see you are going to graduate ahead of me, and with honors to boot. Go ahead with your bad self. I'm graduating 'Thank you, Lordy,' but at least I did well enough to get into law school!"

So, I yelled back, "Congratulations, Walter. I'm so proud of you, my brother." I gave him the peace sign and took my place in line.

Our graduation ceremony more than met my expectations. A lot of people these days can barely remember their college graduation, who the speaker was, or what was said. However, I will never forget who our speaker was, and some of the details of the ceremony and the day. Our orator was none other than Mr. Roscoe Lee Brown, the Emmy- and Tony-award-winning African American actor and director known for his rich baritone voice and sophisticated demeanor. Mr. Brown, an alumnus of Lincoln, gave a soul-stirring speech to our 1972 graduating class in that rich voice of his. Of course, he received a standing ovation from the commencement crowd. I don't remember all that was said except the usual, "Go out and change the world—you have the tools" etc.

Then, unlike at many of the state schools and other large universities, our small graduation class of a little over two hundred got to walk across the stage, one by one, each of us receiving our degree individually and shaking the hand of the president. I will never forget when they called my name: "Gwynette Precia Ford, magna cum laude, and the recipient of the *Wall Street Journal* Award in Economics and Business."

I could hear my small family yell, *"Yay!"* I recognized Mama's and Lacy's voices above the rest of the crowd at the calling of my name. After shaking the president's hand, I moved my tassel over to the graduate position. We hooded one another, as an entire class, when we returned to our seats.

After the ceremony, my family gathered outside of the gymnasium for a few pictures. I received a few gifts from Grandma, Aunt Bernice, and Aunt Freddie and received hugs and kisses. And then, as they had come, my family was gone—gone their separate ways. After turning in my rented cap and gown, I left Lincoln's campus as an alumna for the first time. Lacy took Mama and me to Tony's in Oxford, my favorite Philly cheesesteak place, for some of their famous subs before we got on the highway for my graduation ride home.

That first Sunday in May of 1972 was one of the happiest days of my life. I was so happy. I was proud of becoming a college graduate, proud of becoming a Lincoln Woman, proud of my accomplishments, but most of all, happy and humbled by the great education, the activities, and the opportunities afforded to me by Lincoln University. I was most grateful for the academic scholarship given to me by the university that allowed me to walk across the graduation stage, debt free. I left Lincoln that day without any student loans to pay back and indebted to no one but myself to do right by Lincoln, my ancestors, my family, and my degree. That was quite a feat. So, a happy camper was I. It was now up to me as to what my destiny would be.

I had come to Lincoln as a teenager and was leaving as an educated young woman. I had grown by leaps and bounds—intellectually, socially, and spiritually—in the three years I spent there. As with most of us who have had the experience of going to an HBCU, I often say, "I'm so glad I chose an HBCU to help start my adult life, and I am so glad that I chose Lincoln University." And to be among the first wave of women to graduate from that historic place—well, that's just special, and that's how I felt: *special*.

LACY'S TURN

On the following Saturday, the day before Mothers' Day 1972, it was Lacy's turn. Unlike Lincoln's graduation, which was sort of like a high school graduation—small, quiet, and highly organized—Howard University's graduation was huge and somewhat chaotic, yet sophisticated, elegant, boisterous, and exciting all at the same time. At Lincoln, the entire graduating classes had under 200 graduates, with fewer than 150 showing up to walk in the ceremony. By contrast, Howard had about 2,000 graduates from 13 schools and colleges, coming together from all over the world to celebrate at the same time. It was not uncommon for one school or college, such as Liberal Arts or the School of Business, to have more graduates than all of Lincoln's graduating class. You could multiply Lincoln's graduates and the crowd who came to celebrate them by tenfold to get the magnitude of what Howard's graduation was like: organized chaos.

Howard's graduation was held outside in Green Stadium, where the football games were held. The graduates marched in and were seated by school name, in order of the date their school was founded, with undergraduates going first and then the graduate programs, such as medicine, law, dentistry, and divinity. The ceremonial stage—which seated the trustees, president, deans, university officers, choir, orchestra, and other VIPs—was constructed where the goalpost to the south usually stood, near Cramton Auditorium. The graduates marched in from the gymnasium past the goalpost on the north end of the stadium.

George Lacy had six tickets to his graduation. Those tickets went to his mother and me; two of his three living first cousins, the two who were like sisters to him, Peanut and Priscilla; and to Priscilla's two little children, Marlynn and Marc, who were going to be a junior bridesmaid and the ring-bearer in our wedding, respectively. They thought it would be nice if the kids could see what a college graduation was like and that it would maybe motivate them to go to college. Marlynn was ten and Marc was four. Lacy was crazy about both of them, and Marlynn is his goddaughter.

Lacy and I drove to the campus together early that morning. Priscilla and Peanut brought Mrs. Lacy in Priscilla's car. Lacy's graduation day was sunny and quite a bit warmer than mine. In fact, it was downright toasty. Folklore has it that "It never rains on Mother's Day weekend," and that is why Howard and a lot of other HBCUs in the South chose the day before Mother's Day as their graduation day. I sat with Mrs. Lacy and her crew. The stadium was packed. The sun was beating down on us, and everyone was fanning with their programs.

There was tight security at Howard for all the dignitaries, such as Andrew Young and Coretta Scott King. There were two notorious security guards there that Howardites had nicknamed Wyatt Earp and his sidekick Doc Holliday. Wyatt Earp had shot a student for unruly behavior during registration when Lacy was a sophomore.

After the giving out of honorary doctorates and brief speeches by the recipients, followed by the oratory address, degrees were conferred in order of the founding of each school. By then, it was just after high noon and hot as hell. Because there were so many graduates in each school (hundreds), all they did was stand up, yell (boisterously), and receive applause, then hood one another and sit down. Even that took some time.

We knew exactly where Lacy was sitting and could see him from the stands. They finally called the School of Business after the College of Arts and Sciences, and they did their thing: stood up, yelled, hooded one another, and sat down. Mrs. Lacy, after applauding for her only son, said, "So, that's it? I'm ready to go!"

Overheated, overwhelmed, exhausted, and emotional, Mrs. Lacy wanted to leave, as she put it, "before I have a heat stroke." So, Priscilla took her, Peanut, and the kids to her mother's house, where the graduation party was to take place. I stayed behind to wait for Lacy.

The crowd began to thin out. After the calling of each school's graduates, many graduates from that school left; it was that hot. So, I left the stands and moved to where the School of Business graduating class was sitting and sat with Lacy until he was ready to leave. After all, he was my ride, as always. After the ceremony, we went over to the School of Business, located a couple of blocks from the main campus. Back then, you had to pick up your diploma from your particular school and sign for it.

It was there that George introduced me to two females who had played a major role in his matriculation through Howard and would later become important to me as well, as dear colleagues and friends. Their last name was Green, although they were not related.

The first was Dr. Johnnie Green, the assistant dean for student affairs at the School of Business, who also taught Management and Human Resources Management in Lacy's major. I can't tell you how many times I had heard her name at Lincoln. It was *Dr. Green this* or *Dr. Green that*. I said to myself at times, *Does Lacy have some secret crush on this woman named Dr. Green? Who is this woman and what is she to him?*

So, when he took me into her office to say hello and I saw this older woman with snow-white hair, I breathed a sigh of relief. There was never a cause for concern. He thanked her for all she had done for him and gave her a big hug. She had taught him and kept him on track toward graduation for four years, even when hope was dim. Then he said to her, "OK, I'll be back soon for graduate school and will be needing some recommendations to law school."

She responded in a deep Texas accent, "Oh, go on, boy! You? Going to law school? Well, OK, I'll be right here. I'm not going anywhere no time soon, I hope?"

Then he took me to another office and introduced me to his senior advisor, a younger woman named Jacqueline Green, who was also from Texas and Texas Southern University. He teased her and thanked her for giving him good down-home stern advice that helped him graduate on time, though his grades weren't the greatest. She gave him his diploma, and he gave her a big hug. She asked me, "Is he always such a clown?"

Little did I know at the time that I would one day teach the classes that Dr. Green taught George and little did I know that Jackie would become a longtime trusted colleague and friend, and that our children would also become Howard Bison and longtime friends.

We then hopped into the GOAT, as Lacy called his car, and headed to his aunt Mabel's house, which was just a few blocks from Howard, for his graduation party. Often, Aunt Mabel would host the Stephens' family gatherings, which gave Mrs. Lacy a break, and this was certainly an occasion for Mrs. Lacy not to have to play host—on her only son's graduation from college. She was as much an honoree as he was, and boy, was she proud.

Aunt Mabel (the widow of one of Mrs. Lacy's brothers and the mother of Peanut and Priscilla) was a peach of a woman, in terms of her soft pleasant demeanor and personality but also her plump round figure and her beautiful light brown peachy complexion. One could readily see why Mrs. Lacy's brother, Leroy, was attracted to her.

Hers was the only family I knew that hailed from Damascus, Maryland. Though not from the Deep South, Mabel could cook her butt off. She and Mrs. Lacy could have a cooking contest, and there would be a tie. Behind her back, some of us called Aunt Mabel "Mabel, Black Label" because her favorite beverage was beer. Girlfriend could toss one or two back at a time, and I could relate to that, so that endeared her to me, given my love now and again for a cold one.

Lacy and I arrived to see quite a lavish Southern spread. They didn't wait for us to arrive to start eating though. They were too hungry to wait, I guess, and I'm sure the aroma of all that good food was making their stomachs growl. They had already eaten their first round, so our first round was their second round. In addition to Mabel's fine cooking, Mrs. Lacy and other members of the family had brought their favorite culinary items as well. There was down-home fried and BBQ chicken (of course), potato salad, greens and other sides, and ham and spareribs (the Stephens family loved to eat their pork). And of course, there were lots of desserts, including three of my favorite cakes: chocolate layer cake, German chocolate cake, and pineapple coconut cake. Boy, did we pig out.

It was quite a celebration. George and I took lots of pictures to memorialize the occasion. The Stephens/Lacy clan made me feel like one of them, although we weren't married yet. Peanut's first husband, Pat, gave me the nickname *Coup de Ville* because he said I was smart, refined, and fine as the finest Cadillac. I think he was also throwing a hint to Lacy that I would be high-maintenance once we got married.

On the way to taking me home that evening, Lacy said he wanted to stop by another graduation party that one of his classmates was having in Maryland, near the Southeast border of DC. Though it was a little out of the way, I said, "Sure, I'm still in a partying mood."

So, we drove through town, out Pennsylvania Avenue past the Capitol, taking in the monuments and beautiful sites of our hometown, and through the Hillcrest section of Southeast, a very nice middle-class neighborhood where my uncle, Lawrence, lived. Just over the DC line, on the Maryland side of Southern Avenue that divides DC from Maryland, was a popular and well-kept garden apartment complex, at that time, called Penn Southern. Lacy pulled into the complex and parked and asked me to wait in the car while he checked to see if the party was still in progress.

Lacy came back to fetch me and told me that the party was still going strong. So, I got out, and we walked to an apartment near the front of the complex facing Southern Avenue and the city. He led me to an apartment on the patio level of the building. I didn't hear any music or loud conversation but thought nothing of it. He took me by the hand, opened an unlocked door, and pulled me inside. There was no party; the apartment was empty. Giving me a key, he said to me, "Mrs. Lacy-to-be, welcome to your new home."

What a surprise! While we were preparing for our graduations, Lacy had found the time to find a nice apartment for us to live in after our wedding. I was overjoyed. He took me on a tour of our modern one-bedroom apartment with a patio. He knew I liked garden apartments like my mother's and had found one similar that we could afford. It was lovely and just right. I rewarded him with a passionate kiss.

SIX
A NEW BEGINNING AS HUSBAND AND WIFE

IN THE DAYS leading up to our wedding, Lacy continued to work at his job at the post office for what he called "honeymoon money," and I spent my days sewing my gown and wedding weekend attire and scouting around for furniture for our new *crib*, as we called living quarters back then. We were now two college graduates, and I wanted our apartment to reflect that. After all, it had taken much *perseverance, hope, and determination* (PHD) to get us to that point. We'd worked hard to get through college, so I wanted our *crib* to be very nice.

The first purchase Lacy made was two Bose speakers toward a stereo component set for the living room. Like most dudes, he wanted to have nice music being played at our crib. I left those purchases to him, and Lacy had to have the latest and the best (and the most expensive): the best speakers, the best turntable, and the best receiver. But I didn't complain. Lacy had worked long hard hours while in school for everything he had, and he'd saved like crazy for our wedding, so he deserved the best sound system out there.

I found a nice dinette set (on sale) at a cute little furniture store down the street from my mother's place. It was a modern glass card table with black leather director's chairs. With that purchase, we decided to go with a mostly black-and-white color scheme for the living and dining room. That color scheme was very popular in the early 1970s: ebony and ivory. I also found a black-and-white dome lamp at that store. It was very '70s.

One of the most popular furniture stores for young, hip African Americans in DC was a store in Southeast named Curtis Brothers, known for its huge, big signature chair that stood outside. We purchased a black-and-white sofa and chair from there. We also bought a black leather chair and ottoman with a chrome base that was popular for listening to music at that time. We decided to go with red accent pillows and red area rugs. The apartment complex required that 80 percent of your floor be covered with rugs to absorb sound. Although we had a patio apartment and no one living under us, we decided not to break any of the rules. So, our final living and dining area color scheme was black and white, with red accents, except for the sound system, which was mostly dark brown wood. Our coffee table was chrome and glass, and the floor lamp was chrome.

Our bedroom suite was another story, and one of great disagreement. Lacy wanted a king-size waterbed. They were very popular during the 1970s. I wanted something more traditional. I had heard horror stories about the water getting old or the beds bursting, getting water all over the place, and I wasn't crazy about the idea of being rocked to sleep by moving water. Well, I won that argument, and we settled on a traditional queen-sized bedroom set with a firm mattress—just right for making love.

Also, in the days leading up to our wedding, we both decided to enroll in graduate school. Lacy decided to stay at Howard another year to take graduate classes in public administration at the business school. He felt he could sharpen his skills and get a good GPA while applying to law schools. His two female mentors in student affairs made sure he was accepted into the public administration program at the School of Business.

I was able to get accepted to George Washington University's MBA (master's in business administration) program as a part-time student. I had taken the graduate record exam (GRE) before graduating from Lincoln, and with my high GPA and class rank, I was a shoe-in. The federal government had a special program for professional employees: GAO would pay for two job-related classes per semester, which counted as professional development. They were also very flexible as to what classes were job-related. Therefore, it was going to be very easy to get most, if not all, of my MBA paid for by federal government.

My meeting with human resources went very well. I finalized my contract with GAO, and it was agreed that I would start working the Monday after my return from my honeymoon, which was being planned by Lacy.

MORE BRIDAL SHOWERS

As our wedding day drew closer, things started to get hectic. I was filled with anticipation and excitement. Two Saturdays before the wedding, the matrons of my church had a bridal shower for me. My mother was the host. I was pleasantly surprised. It was well attended by my former Sunday school friends, my mother's church friends, and the junior and senior deaconesses of the church. It was held in the basement level of the church where they held junior church for the young people. We played games and had great food and desserts, cake, and ice cream.

We all had a good time, except for one thing. I could have sworn that my old Sunday school teacher, the one the FBI questioned for my top-secret clearance, was there to make sure I wasn't pregnant. She gave me a nightgown, and when I held it up, she made sure to rub my belly as if she was checking to make sure there was no baby in there. I'd heard that our pastor did not marry couples in the sanctuary if the bride was pregnant; he married them at his home if she was. Well, I knew I wasn't pregnant, and other than that, the shower was quite delightful.

THE BACHELOR PARTY THAT WASN'T

Then, exactly a week before the wedding, our best man threw a bachelor party for Lacy. He decided to make it a *"party party,"* as he called it, instead of a traditional bachelor party. I guess you could call it a *"wedding party party,"* because he invited everyone in the actual wedding party except the little kids, and many of our young adult friends. He wanted both guys and girls there, so he needed my help. It wasn't going to be a traditional bachelor party. No, not at all! It was a *"party party."*

You see, over the years, David, Lacy's best man and one of his best friends, had showed that he liked most of my female friends and all of the girls I chose to be in our wedding. So, I guess that's why he wanted to have a grand party. David had attended Roosevelt High School in the Northwest section of Washington, DC, where he was a big football star, and he'd attended the University of Nebraska on a football scholarship. He had visited Lincoln several times with Lacy and had met all my Lincoln female friends and was very friendly toward them. He liked them all!

David had a fabulous bachelor pad that he shared with a roommate in College Park, Maryland, where he worked for the University of Maryland as a security officer. He decided to have the party there, where there was plenty of space to eat and boogie. He gave me enough invitations to send to the girls in the wedding and my female friends, and he said he would take care of the invitations to the males. He double checked with me to make sure that everyone was coming. He also asked if I would make a large batch of my potato salad that he was so fond of, and I agreed. He said he would provide the rest of the food and drink.

It was my intention to drop off the potato salad and leave. After all, I had never heard of the bride being at the groom's bachelor party.

MADAME PH.D.

When that Saturday rolled around, the first thing I did was wash and braid my hair, put it on rollers, and tie a scarf around it, so as not to get any hair in the potato salad. That's also how we girls at Lincoln got our bushes to look so good. Then I started to make the potato salad.

African Americans are very particular about their potato salad, and everyone loves my family's recipe. Our secret is to put a little mustard and less mayo in it, which gives it a yellow color and a little kick of flavor. Our recipe also calls for some sweet relish to give it a little sweetness to balance out the pepper, green pepper, and paprika.

While making the potato salad, I got a phone call from one of my bridesmaids. It was Muff. She said, "Nettie, my mother has two lamps I want to give you right away, today. I need you to come over by one o'clock before another lady comes to look at them. I think you will really like them, and I want you to have them. Can Vee bring you over?"

I said to her, "Muff, I am making the potato salad for the bachelor party tonight. You are coming, aren't you? I don't know if I can get to your mom's by this afternoon. Besides, I don't have any lamp tables. We bought floor-to-ceiling lighting."

My sister, who was the maid of honor, was already home from Penn State for the bachelor party and wedding, overheard us talking, interrupted us, grabbed the phone, and said, "Muff, I'll drive Nettie over to look at the lamps. We'll be there by one o'clock." Then Vee hung up the phone.

After hanging up, Vee said, "Girl, we all know what good taste Muff's mother has! If you don't want them, I sure can use a couple of nice lamps in my pitiful little apartment in Happy Valley, and if neither of us likes them, we can always sell them. Don't look a gift horse in the mouth! Go on and finish that potato salad, put it in the fridge, and I'll drive you over to Muff's. I'll have you back in plenty of time to get everything ready for the party, and you can ride with me over to David's. You are going to help David set up, right? How are you getting back home? Because I'm staying for the good food and the good time!"

I responded, "Yes, I promised David I would come for a bit to help set up. I'll probably catch a cab back home. Man, I can't wait to start working so I can get my own set of wheels."

So, I finished the potato salad, put it in the fridge (it's always best chilled), and laid out some casual clothes to run over to Muff's. I took a quick shower and slipped on a pair of brown bell-bottom pants, a fitted white polo shirt, and a pair of white sandals. I didn't try to take my hair down, because I wasn't sure if it was dry. I tied another scarf over my rollers and off to Muff's we went in Vee's car.

Muff's parents were college-educated and lived in one of the best neighborhoods in Southeast—in all of DC, for that matter—in an area east of the Anacostia River named Hillcrest Heights, not far from my Uncle Lawrence's house. They both had great professional jobs by DC standards. Her dad worked for the Department of the Interior as a scientist, and her mom worked for George Washington University in financial aid. Muff was their only child. The three of them had lived on Capitol Hill prior to moving to Hillcrest Heights. That's where Muff met Tonya, and they became best friends while attending Hine Junior High School.

After the Lincoln crew met Tonya, Muff joined us at Lincoln for our sophomore year, and we all became good friends. Muff only stayed at Lincoln that one year. She loved to party and was probably the best dancer of our group, and that is saying a mouthful. After our sophomore year, her parents thought it best that she come home to DC and finish her college education at GW, where her tuition was taken care of because her mother worked there. However, we all remained the best of friends, and I was overjoyed to have her and Tonya as bridesmaids in our wedding.

Muff's parents' house was a hop, skip, and jump from our apartment in Fort Chaplin, so we were there in no time. I loved their house; it was a large, modern red-brick split-level on an elevated lot, and as we say in the hood, it was *laid out* inside, meaning it was well decorated. Muff gave some of the best basement parties in all of DC. Everyone flocked to her house when she gave a party, often during the holidays when we were home from college.

Muff answered the door and escorted Vee and me to the basement, where she said the lamps were. When I stepped into the basement, I heard the words, "Surprise!"

Oh, my goodness! There were all of my wedding attendants and friends, coming together to throw me yet another bridal shower. I was totally blown away.

I was so shocked, yet all I could think about was that my hair was in rollers and that I wasn't dressed for the occasion. I asked Vee if she knew about the shower, and she said, "Of course, I'm one of the hosts, but I couldn't blow the surprise. Don't worry about how you look. Just go to the bathroom and pick out your hair so that we can take pictures. Surprise again!"

So, I rushed to the bathroom to make myself presentable. What a fun shower that was! Unlike the one at Lincoln and the one at my church, this one was a lingerie shower and R-rated, with adult games and alcohol. My lady friends had an absolute ball teasing me about my wedding night and drinking my favorite beverage of choice: frozen strawberry daiquiris. The gifts were wonderful, from black to white nighties and every color in between to make for the perfect wedding trousseau. Most of my shower guests were also going to the bachelor party that night, so the shower ended in time for everyone to go home to get dressed in their best house party outfits.

Vee and I rushed home so she could get ready for the party that night. I put on a sundress I had made that was maxi length, with bare shoulders and splits up both sides. My plan was to get my part of the food together, ride over with Vee, and be gone before the party started. I planned on leaving by cab after setting up the food and saying hello to a few friends, so that George could enjoy his evening as the guest of honor, alone.

Our best man did not disappoint. His bachelor pad was clean and set up for the party when I arrived. I went right to work to help David set up a buffet table with plenty of food to be enjoyed by all. While I was there, some of the guests, including some of my girlfriends who had been at the bridal shower, began to arrive—and then who should arrive but the groom-to-be, himself, George Lacy!

Upon seeing me, he asked jokingly, "What are you doing here? Is it proper for me to see the bride and her girlfriends on the night of my bachelor party?"

I explained, "I'm just here to help David set things up. I brought over my famous potato salad and a few other items. I'm getting ready to leave. I'm going to call a cab to take me home."

David then chimed in, "Welcome to your bachelor party! Man, this is going to be a *party party!*" Who wants to party with a bunch of guys and a bunch of strange women, especially with girls you don't know nothing about? So, I invited the fellas and all of our female friends over to send you off to the altar in style. So, let's get this party started!"

George laughed and seemed very pleased. The DJ was jamming with all the latest hits, and folks started to arrive in droves. I finished setting up the buffet table, put the final touches on the decorations, and started packing up to leave. I asked David if I could use his house phone to call a cab.

Then Lacy said, "No, you can't leave! Who am I gonna dance with? Your girlfriends? I don't think so! We've been dancing together all this time! You might as well stay for the bachelor party, too! After all, this party is for me! I'm marrying you, and you're marrying me, right? So, you might as well stay and be my dance partner, since we are about to be dancing partners for life."

My response was, "So you want me to crash your bachelor party? Moi? I was wondering when you were going to ask. Of course, I'll stay. When have we ever followed society's rules? Whoever said that the bride can't be at the bachelor party? What kind of rule is that, anyway? Seems like that's just asking for trouble—cutting the bachelor loose with other women before the wedding?"

So, there it was. I crashed my fiancé's bachelor party. And we both said, "So what!"

The party was *jamming*, as they say. It became a combined bachelor/bachelorette party, and that was fine by us. We had a ball, celebrating our last weekend of being single, together. Everyone had a good time at the unorthodox bachelor party, including the bride and groom-to-be.

To this day, Lacy teases me, in a complaining, playful way, that he didn't have a "real" bachelor party—not a traditional one, anyway, in the true sense of the word. He often says that he is probably the only man on earth whose bride-to-be was at his bachelor party. His was not an all-male party with guys acting horny, with a naked girl jumping out of a cake or a stripper pole-dancing. No, that was not his party. It was a get-down, coed jam. It was the bachelor party that wasn't! And when he complains now, I tell him it wasn't my idea, so blame our best man, who to me was, and still is, the "best-of-the-best," best man.

THE WEDDING

Our wedding took place exactly one week later, and what a week it was. Last-minute details and bad weather consumed my time and thoughts that week. However, the weather turned out to be our biggest problem. Hurricane Agnes decided to form in the Atlantic Ocean and threatened to ruin our wedding.

Agnes wove her way through the Caribbean Sea and made landfall as a category 1 hurricane in Panama City, Florida, on June 19, causing a lot of damage. By the time she made it to DC, she was a tropical storm that dumped a lot of rain on us that week, yet she moved out to sea just before the wedding. However, Agnes was strengthening and threatening to hit Pennsylvania and New York and points north the weekend of the wedding, with predictions for DC showers.

The rehearsal and rehearsal dinner, which were held on that Friday, went very well. I had attended many weddings at Mount Carmel, so I knew how the ceremony would flow, down to the very words that

Reverend Patterson would use, such as "love and cherish" instead of "obey." Even the reverend didn't go for that *obey* stuff, and I definitely wasn't having it. We both believed that obedience should only be promised to God. I had always thought of his ring ceremony as being one of the most beautiful I had ever heard and witnessed.

The rehearsal dinner was hosted by Lacy's godmother, Vivian, at her home, after the rehearsal. It was the usual Southern summer fare of fried chicken, potato salad, and green beans, and other sides, with a lot of baked goodies for dessert. With the large wedding party that we had, there were about fifty people there. We sat around inside and outside eating, reminiscing, laughing, "joning," (joking), and having a jolly good time. I thought to myself, *What a great life you are going to have. These people will be your family and your friends for life.*

Our wedding day, June 24, 1972, came at the end of that rainy week. If I were to pick a name for it like *My Big Fat Greek Wedding*, I would call it *My Big Fat DC Wedding on a Shoestring Budget*, for that is truly what it was. I couldn't have planned a better wedding myself. Funny, I did plan my wedding, all by myself. It was like a dream come true—what every little girl dreams about.

I woke up to the first sunny day of that hurricane week, though it was cooler than usual for the end of June due to the bad weather that preceded it, and rain showers were predicted for that afternoon from the remnants of Agnes. Boy, was I happy to see the sun that morning, and I prayed that the rain would hold off at least until after all the outside pictures were taken. And to my delight, God heard my prayers.

I had planned to take it slow and easy that morning—no running any last-minute errands, etc. I felt that everything was done, and all that was needed was to execute the plan, as we say in business. All of the dresses were ready, and last-minute details and errands had been taken care of. I stayed up late the night before the wedding putting final touches on my gown and veil and finishing a long sundress to wear to the after-parties after the reception.

I told Mama and Vee to take things slow as well—to just be ready to leave for the wedding on time. I wanted no frazzled nerves on this day, one of the most, if not *the* most important day of my life.

My two dearest sorority line sisters, Dorcas and Sharon, the two who I got in trouble with a lot while we were pledging, arrived midday. I had insisted that they stay in the bedroom to which I would never return that night. That meant there were five females in our apartment on my wedding day, giggling and laughing like schoolgirls do. All four of them left together at 1:30 p.m., after a light lunch, leaving me alone with my thoughts to get dressed and get to the church before three.

After taking a bubble bath, I calmly put on my undergarments, which included white pantyhose; climbed into my wedding dress, feet first; and zipped it up the back. It was a white cotton contemporary lace baby-doll dress with Victorian long sleeves. Because I didn't line the sleeves, my arms were quite cool, and hopefully that would continue to hold up during the wedding and the reception.

I decided not to put on the veil but carry it to the church, where Tonya's sister, NeNe, was to do my makeup. I then slipped into a pair of one-inch low-heeled white leather ballerina pumps that I hoped would not hurt my feet too much by the end of the evening.

Joe, my aunt's friend, arrived at Mama's apartment at two o' clock, as requested, in his navy blue Cadillac to drive me to the church, a quick twenty-minute ride. We had no money for a limousine, so Joe gave me a ride in his car as a wedding present. We talked, laughed, and reminisced the entire familiar ride to the church, which went by quickly. I felt like a Disney princess on my way to marry my prince. I knew that what I did on that day would change my life forever. Yet I wasn't nervous at all—not yet, anyway.

We arrived at the church before 3:00 p.m., as planned. I asked Joe to pull up to the side of the church on Third Street, Northwest, going north, so that I could slip into one of the side doors and go to a chosen choir room to meet my female wedding party and get makeup applied. As he passed the front of the church, I saw a few people starting to arrive.

But lo and behold, when Joe pulled up to park, across the street heading south, there was Lacy's burgundy GOAT. I spotted Lacy getting out of his car, looking handsome in his black tuxedo. I didn't panic too much but ducked sideways so he wouldn't see me. After all, I believed those rumors that seeing the bride before the wedding would bring bad luck. I peeked over my seat just enough to see him turn the corner to go into the front door of the church. Then I thanked Joe and hopped out to go in the side door.

Once inside the church, I rushed to the choir room where the bridesmaids and I were to finish getting dressed, have a little makeup session, and get ready for the ceremony. Before I knew it, it was time to go to the sanctuary for the big event. The wedding committee chair for the church came to the choir room and announced, "Ladies, it's time to go."

We followed her to the stairwell leading to the sanctuary. Of course, I was last this time around. When I got to the top of the stairs, I peeked outside. I could see friends and family members making their way into the sanctuary to get a seat before the wedding march. I could see the back of the church too. The church was full of people.

Then I heard the wedding committee chair say, "Let's get this show on the road." She signaled to the musicians to start the first song, "The Lord's Prayer," to begin the ceremony. I'd selected the best male voice in the choir at the time, Charles, to sing at my wedding, and he agreed—for a small fee, of course. And he didn't disappoint. He could and would sing the Lord's Prayer like you've never heard it sung, and as he closed it out, I could feel my heart beating faster and faster.

Next, it was time for the wedding party to march down the two side aisles to meet up with the groom and best man down front. In the late 1960s and early '70s, Christian churches, including the Baptist Church, found it acceptable to allow brides to use popular music in their wedding ceremonies as long as the music was tasteful and not vulgar. As a modern bride, I decided to choose popular music as well. Due to my secret love of pop music and musicals, I chose "Close to You" by the

Carpenters for my wedding party march and "Climb Every Mountain" from *The Sound of Music* and my Eliot days as the second solo to be sung. Both turned out to be great choices. "Close to You" had a perfect beat to match the steps of the bridal party as both the bridesmaids and groomsmen made their way down the aisles to the altar. The junior bridesmaids went down the aisle first, one in pink and one in green, followed by seven bridesmaids and groomsmen. The alternate pink and green dresses looked beautiful. Vee, who served as my maid of honor, followed them in her pink dress with a pink and green sash that separated and distinguished her from the rest of the bridesmaids.

Then it was time for the ring-bearer and the flower girl. Little Marc, Lacy's cousin, wore an all-white ring-bearer tux with short pants, white long socks, and white shoes. Little Leslie, my flower girl, looked cute in a replica of the bridesmaid dress made of pink and green flowered, lined organza, with a matching bow in her hair. However, she cried all the way down the aisle as she dropped real pink rose petals.

Finally, it was my turn. Daddy met me at the foyer of the church to walk me down the aisle. This had been a touchy subject throughout the wedding planning process. My mother didn't want Daddy to walk me down the aisle because she was still bitter about their divorce. But I won that battle. Since I was paying for the wedding, and since Daddy never missed a child support payment during all those years, including my years at Lincoln, he deserved to walk me down the aisle, proudly.

So off we went, to the traditional wedding march song, "Here Comes the Bride." We both smiled, all the way down the aisle. I was amazed at the number of people who showed up. There were so many guests; they had to seat some of them in the choir stands. When we got to the end of the aisle, there was Lacy, my husband-to-be, with an adoring smile. Our eyes met, and we smiled at each other as if to say, *This is it!*

Daddy held on to me until the question "Who gives this bride to be married to this man?" With an "I do," he took his seat.

From then on, it was a traditional service. Reverend Patterson did his thing. I must admit, I got very nervous when he got to the part, "If anyone objects, speak now or forever hold your peace." My bouquet started to shake a little. I closed my eyes for just a second and prayed, "Lord, please don't let some crazy person from our respective pasts stand up and say something stupid!"

Then, Rev. Patterson asked, "George Corinth Lacy Jr., do you take Gwynette Precia Ford to be your lawfully wedded wife?" Lacy said, "I sure do!" real loud. Everyone laughed, and that broke the ice. I became less nervous from then on.

Well, nothing crazy happened, and the rest of the ceremony went beautifully, especially the exchange of vows and the exchange of rings. I was so proud that the minister who baptized me when I was a little girl also married me when I became a young woman. In keeping with the times, the Baptist Church had no problem with persons of different Christian faiths marrying one another. We had our pre-marriage counseling with Reverend Patterson, and he had no problem marrying George, a cradle-to-grave Catholic, to me, a lifelong Baptist. It was the Catholic Church that had a problem. According to Catholic doctrine, I was expected to convert to Catholicism, but I wasn't about to change my religion. George and his mother, a devout Catholic, understood that. So, a Baptist wedding it was.

Charles sang the hell out of "Climb Every Mountain." I hoped that the audience would understand why I chose that song, because I viewed the marriage that a person wants as an individual "dream," with many "mountains" or obstacles to "climb" to make your dream come true. It would take *perseverance, hope, and determination* (PHD).

Finally, the vows were done, and it was time to kiss the bride. That was one kiss I will never forget—one so tender and sweet it could last a lifetime. And that was that. We almost ran out of the church, hand in hand, to get the pictures over with, especially those on the steps outside the church while the sun was still shining. After all the professional pictures were taken, we jumped into the GOAT and headed to the reception, followed by wedding party members and wedding guests in their cars, honking our horns all the way to Southeast to let all of DC know that we were now husband and wife.

THE RECEPTION

Mr. Meyers, the caterer, did a bang-up job on the decorations and food for the reception with my little budget. Although it wasn't a sit-down dinner, which was becoming popular at the time, the chicken wings; the sandwiches, mostly chicken and turkey; and the assortment of fruits, melons, and veggies were beautifully displayed and filling, and everyone seemed to enjoy the food. I also made sure that petit fours from Woodies were served. No one complained about the food, at least not to me.

The punch fountain was working, the champagne was flowing, and the DJ was pumping. We had our champagne toast using champagne glasses from Mrs. Lacy's collection of beautiful crystal, at her insistence. What more could a bride ask for, especially one who planned a wedding and reception on a shoestring budget? It was a great event by Washington, DC, standards in the 1970s, where it was common to have receptions in church basements (with no alcohol), people's houses, backyards, and anywhere that your budget would allow.

Then there was the cake. That was the one thing I didn't skimp on. We ordered our wedding cake from Clement's Bakery, probably *the* most famous bakery in Washington, DC, at the time. Its storefront was then located on G Street, NW, between 13th and 14th Streets, not far from Woodward and Lothrop Department Store, where I had worked, and the White House. Clement's, which opened in Washington in 1928 and was owned and operated by the Italian family of its founder, Clement Maggia, quickly became Washington's premiere bakery during and after WWII by providing baked goods for presidents such as Roosevelt, Truman, Eisenhower, and Kennedy; ambassadors; dignitaries; and Hollywood celebrities. Clement's was known for their extraordinary cake designs, such as replicas of famous DC monuments, buildings, and landmarks, including the White House.

To feed our many guests, I chose a design of a huge rectangular five-tier layered cake, replicating the stairs outside the church, with alternating African American girl dolls in pink or green gowns and boy dolls in black tuxedos standing on the stairs. At the top, under a gazebo, were brown boy and girl dolls representing the bride and the groom. Since Clement's was known best for its lemon- and rum-flavored cakes, I got them to alternate the layers with lemon and rum flavors, with the top layer being rum-flavored, my favorite. I would take the top tier to our apartment and freeze it, to be eaten on our first anniversary.

Mrs. Lacy was delighted with my choice of bakery and the design, given her culinary expertise, and Clement's did not disappoint. The cake was breathtakingly beautiful and a conversation piece at the reception.

We also had a groom's cake. It was a huge carrot sheet cake that George and I ordered from a DC Muslim Bakery. If nothing else, our guests were able to fill up on cake, for we surely said, "Let there be cake!" A lot of pictures were taken of the two cakes and of us feeding each other cake, as American custom would have it.

Finally, of course, there was dancing. After all, so much of our courtship involved us dancing together. After our first dance as husband and wife, the wedding party and our guests joined in. The wedding reception turned into a dance party.

By the end of the reception, the girls in the wedding party had kicked off their shoes and were dancing in their stocking feet. I tossed my bouquet, which Kat caught as a keepsake of our extraordinary friendship, and Lacy tossed my garter, which no one caught. So, he fetched it, and I kept it as a keepsake, and that was that. The reception, which was a big success, was over.

Evening was approaching as the reception ended, but the partying was just getting started. Different people who were connected to us as a couple had decided to have their own after-parties, as was suggested by me while planning the wedding. So being in Southeast for the reception, Lacy and I slipped away to our new place, just over the DC line, to freshen up and change into more casual attire to make our rounds to three parties that were a "must go-to" for us. I slipped out of my wedding gown and into a maxi dress that I'd made from a Diane von Fürstenberg designer pattern, specifically for the after-parties. As we walked to the car hand in hand, Lacy pulled me close and said, "I can't wait to get you back here tonight." I blushed and played coy.

First, we stopped by my mother's place, which was closest to our apartment. She had invited a few attendees to an after-wedding get-together for food and drinks at her apartment. There, I thanked her with a big hug for her help and assistance in making my wedding day a success. She cooperated and behaved herself. I told her that I would call her after the honeymoon. Everyone laughed, and we were off to the next stop. As we left, it hit me: My mom's place would never be "my place" again.

Our second stop was to Lacy's mother's house in Brookland where she was having a dinner party for family and friends. Her place was full of people, inside and out, eating, drinking, and making merry. Lacy had lent her our new speakers and component set to provide music for them. We floated through the house and the backyard to speak to just about everyone. Her family of well-wishers had come from all over: New York, Philadelphia, Pittsburgh, and Chicago in particular.

It took us a while to speak to everyone. By the time we left, it was a dark summer's night. Mrs. Lacy walked us to the door and began to cry tears of joy. Emotions leading up to and of this important milestone in her son's life came pouring out. It was a tough, emotional moment for both of them. It was hard on him to leave her, but he hugged her tight and we were on our way.

Our last pit stop was Antonia's crib. She was nice enough to throw an after-party for the wedding party and our high school and college friends. She wanted to celebrate the couple she had introduced to one another. She said that was the least she could do, and I was so happy she did. She had a cute little bachelorette apartment not far from Mrs.

Lacy's house. It, too, was packed with people. Everyone was in a great mood, partying and winding down from our busy day. Most of our best friends were there, with best wishes all around.

While we were there, the clock struck twelve midnight. Someone announced, "Your wedding day is over, y'all."

That was our cue to leave. It was time to leave our family and friends and start our new life together as a married couple. So, home we went. Our wedding night was magical, everything I had hoped and prayed it would be- absolutely wonderful, like fireworks on the Fourth of July.

THE HONEYMOON

While I did most of the wedding planning, I left it all to Lacy to plan the honeymoon. Since I don't particularly like surprises and needed to know what to pack, I got him to tell me where we were going and by what mode of transportation. I had only traveled up and down the East Coast and to Montreal, Canada, and that was by bus on my senior-class trip in high school. So, when he told me, "We are going to the US Virgin Islands by plane for seven days," I was surprised and excited—and a little nervous about flying for the first time. Lacy assured me that everything would be just fine and to leave it all up to him, and I did.

We weren't able to sleep in on the first Sunday morning of our new life together because we had to get up and finish packing for our honeymoon. We were to fly out of National Airport just before noon. Earlier in the week, I had started to move my summer clothes and lingerie over to our apartment and had brought my luggage over to start packing a trousseau for the honeymoon. I only had to finish packing a few more items and toiletries.

Lacy, on the other hand, had not packed and said he was only taking one small bag of casual clothes. That was my cue to take mostly casual clothes and nothing too formal. I knew that as honeymoons are supposed to go, we would be spending a lot of time in our room, so I packed a lot of the sexy lingerie I got at my lingerie bridal shower. Lacy did say to plan to go out to dinner, so I packed several sundresses I'd made for those nights. And of course, I packed several bathing suits for the beach and the pool. When it was all said and done, I had packed one large suitcase and a carry-on bag, which was par for the course, even back in 1972.

For breakfast, we snacked on leftover sandwiches and wedding cake I had been able to bring home after the reception. We then put our luggage in the GOAT. Lacy decided to stop by his mother's house to pick up a few more items for the trip, check up on her and her guests, and leave the GOAT at her house, rather than leave his fancy car sitting in the parking lot at our new place all week, where no one knew us quite yet. We would call a cab to take us to the airport from Mama Lacy's house. That sounded like a good plan to me, so off we went.

While riding, I was excited and nervous at the same time, for this new bride had never flown on an airplane before, had never been to the Caribbean, and was not a very good swimmer. I wondered what our honeymoon would be like. Lacy had been a pilot with the Civil Air Patrol after his deferment from the army and was also an excellent swimmer, so I decided to trust in the Lord and my new husband to make it everything a honeymoon was supposed to be.

When we got to Mrs. Lacy's, Corinth, as his family called him, used his key to get into the house. Everyone was still asleep. He went upstairs to the bedrooms to grab a few items for our trip and to check on the guests who had spent the night. Meanwhile, I sat in the dining room and called for a Yellow Cab to fetch us and take us to National Airport.

I heard Mrs. Lacy's voice, so I assumed Corinth had awakened her. He came downstairs, put the items in his bag, grabbed a piece of fruit from the fridge, and went downstairs to the basement to check on things. That's when I heard yelling and cursing from the basement.

"Got damnit! I'll be damn! The back door is wide open! Where in the hell are my speakers? And the component set too? Somebody done stole my shit!"

Mrs. Lacy came rushing downstairs at the same time that Corinth came storming upstairs from the basement to the dining room. Corinth was steaming hot, beet red, and mad as hell. "You can't have shit! Somebody done stole our shit?" he said. "The back door is wide open. Call the cops."

I sat there in shock. Evidently, someone had stolen our new sound system overnight and taken it out the back door. Meanwhile, the cab driver had arrived, put my bags in his trunk, and was sitting outside, waiting to take us to the airport. By that time, Mrs. Lacy's houseguests had awakened and come downstairs. What were we going to do? We needed to get to the airport or miss our flight. Everyone was cursing and fussing, yelling and screaming. Tears started to roll down my cheeks.

Lacy calmed down and got everyone else to calm down. He said, "Look, I don't have time to deal with this shit, today of all days. Mama, call the police and have them come out to get a report. There was no forced entry, so don't worry; the back door is not broken. Have them dust for fingerprints. All of you, check to see if anything else was stolen. It looks like someone left the back door unlocked and thieves came in and stole our shit while y'all were asleep. So just make a police report, and I will deal with this shit when I return. Right now, I'm taking my bride outta here, and we're going on our honeymoon."

He grabbed me by the hand, grabbed his bag, and we left. Everyone came outside to the porch, with apologies and farewells. "So sorry this happened! What a bummer! This is a damn shame, but it'll be all right. You kids just go on and try to have a good time," were some of the comments. With that, we were off to the airport, leaving me to wonder again, *What kind of honeymoon is this going be?*

Things were pretty quiet on the taxi ride to National. I think we were both in shock. Lacy had worked so hard to save the money for that component set, especially those Bose speakers, his prized possession to start off our new life in our new crib. He had worked crazy hours, a lot of overtime, and even neglected some of his studies to skimp and save for that fabulous system. I think we both were wondering, *What happened? How did it happen? Who did it? Or is this just a bad dream?*

As we neared the airport, however, he pulled me close and said, "Look, I am not going to let what happened spoil our honeymoon. I will replace the sound system when we get back, and as soon as I get back to work for the money, with the same items we had. I am *determined* that we are not going to be defeated by the thieves who stole from us. I promise you that. So, let's not talk about it for the next few days. I will call Mom in a few days to see what's going on with the investigation. But other than that, let's just go down here and have a good time." And that was that.

We checked our bags at the ticket counter, boarded our flight, and got ready to take off. We flew to the US Virgin Islands in coach. However, Lacy volunteered to sit on the exit aisle so he could stretch out his legs and no one was assigned to the middle seat. As a member of the Civil Air Patrol, he knew what to do in case of an emergency exit. That made me a little less nervous, for I knew he would get me out of the plane if there was a problem.

As the plane taxied down the runway, I got nervous and closed my eyes. Lacy grabbed my hand and said, "Don't worry; it'll be just fine. It's easier than being on a roller coaster, you'll see. Don't be a punk! You're a Lacy now. Lacys don't fold."

Sure enough, the plane took off with ease, and we were up, up, and away. I said, "Is that it? Wow, that was harmless."

The rest of the flight was smooth. It was a bright sunny day, with white fluffy clouds in the sky. I peeked over and looked out the window a couple of times. It was amazing to me how such a heavy object could fly so high in the sky and not fall. Lacy tried to explain the mechanics to me, but it went right over my head. I was not a very good physics student.

I spent a good while on our flight reading about the US Virgin Islands: its geography, its history, its landmarks, and things to do while there. Lacy spent most of the flight reading and napping. I was still too nervous to sleep.

Landing was just as exciting and nerve-racking as taking off. I grabbed Lacy by the arm as the plane descended. The pilot cruised in for a soft landing. Lacy whispered to me that the pilot had probably served in the air force rather than the navy. He said that he could tell the difference by how the pilot landed the plane. Air force pilots have more space to land the plane softly on the ground. Navy pilots are trained to drop the plane onto a naval ship, so they plop the plane to the ground. So, I was glad that our pilot was probably an air force veteran.

So that was that. My first plane ride was uneventful. I couldn't help but think that if the way Lacy took care of me and my concerns my first time up in the air was any indication of how things would be on land in the future, there was hope for our marriage.

Once we landed, we were greeted at the airport with a steel band, as was the custom for many incoming flights. The airport was lively with Caribbean music and girls dancing in delightful carnival costumes. While we waited for our bags, we were served rum punch in small cups. What a great start to our adventure!

Before leaving the airport, we rented a compact car to get around in. Saint Thomas was much larger than I had imagined. We also got strict instructions about driving on the left side of the road, as they do in Great Britain.

Lacy kept his promise. Our honeymoon was everything a bride could ask for—everything a girl dreams of. We stayed at the world-famous Mafolie Hotel in the capital city of Charlotte Amalie. It is a quaint, very popular little twenty-two-room boutique hotel nestled on a hillside overlooking the harbor near the airport. The view was breathtaking. Our room was very cozy and added to our honeymoon romancing.

Other than sleeping and making love, we spent very little time at the hotel. Most of our days were spent sightseeing and beach-hopping. On Saint Thomas, we took in most of the tourist attractions, such as Blackbeard's Castle, which was built by the Danes in the 1600's at the highest point on Government Hill as a vantage point for spotting enemy ships. We took pictures of one another sitting on Drake's Seat, where Sir Francis Drake himself sat to watch over his fleet, and we visited the Cathedral Church of All Saints.[9]

What I liked most about the Virgin Islands were their Caribbean beaches. I had never seen water so turquoise blue and clear that you could look down and see your feet and baby fish swimming around you. It was like being in a big blue bathtub, with real, friendly fish swimming all around you.

We hopped from beach to beach by car, being careful to stay on the left side of the road. We even went over to the island of Saint John by boat to check out the beaches there, which were breathtaking as well. On weekdays, very few people were on the beaches, so it was like having them all to ourselves, and just right for making out on the beach. I found a beautiful conch shell on the beach, intact, and as beautiful as the ones that people buy from the store. So, I kept it as a souvenir.

The beach at Saint Thomas's Magens Bay—touted by many as one of the most beautiful beaches in the world—was the one I liked best, where we took long walks in the sand. I couldn't swim well, so Lacy, who did, gave me private lessons on the beach. The salt water took my big butt right to the top, and by the end the week, I was floating very well, especially on my back.

Then there was the local food and drink of the Caribbean that was out of this world—like nothing I had eaten or drank before. We were adventurous and tried many new and tasty, yet mostly healthy and affordable, dishes. Fish is a mainstay of the Caribbean (of course, with all that water). So, we ate a lot a fish, especially conch, an edible mollusk known for its elaborate and colorful shell. They are plentiful in the waters of the Virgin Islands and a local favorite seafood.

For lunch, we had conch fritters, conch soup, or conch chowder with

---

[9] Zimmerman, "Lonely Planet-US and British Virgin Islands," p.5.

johnnycake, a deep-fried bread. Other lunchtime favorites were beef/vegetables *pates* (patties) and chicken *rotis*, which are pastries stuffed with meat and vegetables, yet distinctly different in terms of origin, seasoning, and the texture and color of the dough. Those pastries were very filling and would last us through an afternoon of sightseeing and swimming before a late dinner.

We went out to dinner just about every night. We tried the local favorites of grouper fish and curried or jerk chicken as main courses. Personally, I wasn't bold enough to try curried goat or oxtail. That was a little too extreme for me, as were the really spicy jerk meats. I fell in love with the rice and peas (beans) as well as the yam and fried plantain side dishes, though. I also liked Caribbean Callaloo, which was a stew made from dasheen, taro, or spinach leaves, and flavored with salted meat, fish, onions, and spices. It was sort of like Louisiana gumbo, Caribbean-style.

As for the major drink of the Virgin Islands, there was rum, rum, and more rum. Throughout the Caribbean, every major island has its own variety of rum. Caribbean rum was originally manufactured from the sugar and molasses from their sugar plantations. The US Virgin Islands are well known for Cruzan Rum, which is manufactured on Saint Croix. It is a brown rum with a sweet taste and favored by the natives.

As a college student and a casual, light cocktail drinker, my drink of choice was rum. Many college students drank rum and Coke, but I preferred the lighter and sweeter mixed frozen rum drinks, like daiquiris and piña coladas. So, I was in seventh heaven in the Virgin Islands.

They served every kind of rum drink you could think of, including some that I had never heard of before. However, I stayed mostly with my favorites and the most familiar: rum punch, strawberry or banana daiquiris, and piña coladas. Lacy calls them "girly drinks." And not to be a lush on my honeymoon, I stuck to one, or no more than two, alcohol drinks per day. Caribbean natives tend to go heavy on the alcohol, and

I had to tell the bartenders to go light a couple times, based on what other patrons were saying.

There were also a number of popular health and fruit drinks common to the Virgin Islands that we tried out. Seamoss and mauby drinks, made by boiling the main ingredient and adding spices, including cinnamon, were local favorites. Other favorites included passion fruit juice, coconut water, bush tea, and lemon tea. We tried these as healthy substitutes for sodas during our visit.

Finally, there was shopping to be done and souvenirs to get for family and friends. I was surprised that Lacy was willing to hang in there and go shopping with me, that he wanted to be part of the entire island and honeymoon experience, and the Virgin Islands did not disappoint. The shopping experience was unique and different, and we got everything duty-free.

Most of our shopping was done while walking. The downtown area of Saint Thomas reminded me a little of our Georgetown in DC, with a lot of boutiques, jewelry stores, and liquor stores. You could buy two to four bottles of liquor at a time, and they would box them up for you. The airlines would allow each passenger to carry a case of four bottles onto the plane without charging you or counting it as a carry-on. So, we bought and boxed eight bottles of rum to give to family and friends. What we didn't give away, we would keep for ourselves, especially to make my now-famous daiquiris.

There were also open markets with native vendors that I really liked. You could barter with the natives for a good price on T-shirts, casual wear, and homemade native jewelry. And then there were strip malls scattered along the roads around town that you could stop by going to and from the hotels. We bought T-shirts, jewelry, wooden statues, and other souvenirs.

Our best purchase was a huge, black wooden fork and spoon set, with African-like heads carved on top of each, that we found in one of the open markets at a great price. They were ideal for our dining area and a perfect match for our dinette set. We had no idea how we would get them home at just over three feet each, but we bought them anyway and said we would figure that out and ship them if we had to. I just had to have them. We have them proudly displayed in the family room of our home to this day.

Whether shopping or dining in the Virgin Islands, we found the natives to be very friendly and accommodating. Everyone smiled and said hello and asked whether we were enjoying the islands. The natives spoke with a British accent that I just loved.

One day while walking down Main Street in downtown Saint Thomas, someone yelled my name from a moving car. I was shocked. It was Pooggie, one of my classmates from Lincoln. He pulled over and jumped out of a sporty BMW, welcomed us to the island of Saint Thomas, and insisted that we get together one night during our stay. He said he wanted to show us the "real" Saint Thomas and a little nightlife. We explained that we were on our honeymoon, and Lacy was hesitant, but I knew Pooggie pretty well at Lincoln (we were in the same department), so I told Lacy it would be OK to go out with the natives for one night.

Pooggie came to fetch us from our hotel that Thursday night. However, we insisted on driving our rented car, so we followed him. He took us to his parents' house for dinner. I could tell that Pooggie's family was well off by island standards by their beautiful home and pool and the way they lived and dined—but I already knew that from Lincoln, by the way he carried himself there. After dinner, he took us to several clubs and nightspots where the middle-class natives hung out. We danced to Caribbean and American music until dawn and had a lot of fun. It was quite a native experience, one we would not have had if it weren't for running into my fellow Lincoln Lion, Pooggie.

Friday was our last full day and night on the island, and we made it count. We packed everything nice and neat and got most of our souvenirs into our suitcases. We took one last romantic stroll on the beach and had a fantastic romantic dinner and evening together. Saturday morning, we got up to breakfast with a great view of the island from our hotel, said our goodbyes, packed up the rental car, and made our way to the airport.

I became sad and melancholy that our fabulous honeymoon had to come to an end. But Lacy made me another promise: that we would have many more honeymoons and would go away on a honeymoon at least once every three to five years. I told him that I would hold him to that, and I have. Besides, we had fond memories of a fantastic first honeymoon—memories that would last us a lifetime. We also had that wooden fork and spoon set that the airline allowed us to carry on the plane and hold between our legs, as if they were tall, standing children.

We returned to DC tanned and happy, having had a taste of paradise. When God decided to give Earth a glimpse of paradise, he made the Virgin Islands. I couldn't have asked for a better honeymoon.

SEVEN
NEWLY WED AND WORKING

WE RETURNED TO DC from our honeymoon on a Saturday, late afternoon, July 1, 1972. We were so tired we forced ourselves to unpack, hit the shower, and hit the sack. That, in essence, was our first night back as a married couple. We only had one day, Sunday, to rest up from the honeymoon, get settled, and get ready for the rest of our lives together because we both had to go to work on Monday.

GAO

I reported to my orientation class at the General Accounting Office (GAO) as a professional auditor on Monday, July 3, 1972, with my fellow new employees. We were told that our class would be condensed into four days due to the July 4th holiday the next day. The first order of business involved collecting from us official IDs to verify who we were, for security purposes. It became apparent that some of us, if not all of us, would eventually need secret or top-secret clearances to carry out our audits. Secondly, they asked for our actual diplomas, which they had told us to bring on the first day.

Thank God I had a valid driver's license, although I hadn't driven a car since high school. I wasn't crazy about giving up my diploma for verification. I knew it was legitimate. I also reported that I had a top-secret clearance from the Department of the Navy, which they probably already knew from doing a background check on me. They checked our IDs during the day and gave them back to us before we left to go home, but they kept our diplomas and said we would get them back on the last day of orientation.

Lacy and I spent our first holiday as husband and wife together a day after we went to work after our honeymoon. We were happy to have another day off and spent it sleeping in late and lounging around, in addition to continuing to put finishing touches on our apartment. We proudly hung our painting of a Spanish dancer in the living room and the fork and spoon we bought in the Virgin Islands in the dining area. Our place was shaping up very nicely. That evening we went down to the National Mall to watch the fireworks, which were spectacular as always and something we hadn't done in a long time.

I returned to the training class that Wednesday a little melancholy. What a way to start married life! But we both needed to work to get where we wanted to go in life. We knew it would take *perseverance, hope, and determination* (PHD) to get the advanced degrees we wanted and to eventually buy a house and have the family that we wanted. I envisioned that happening four or five years down the road. We promised each other that we would put off having "B and Bs" for a while: "no bills and no babies." Yes, we agreed there would be no bills piling up and no babies while we were in graduate school. We would put all of that off until we finished our advanced education.

The rest of the week of orientation class was spent learning more about GAO's mission, how to document the data that would be needed to conduct our audits, and GAO's divisions and organizational structure. GAO is an independent, nonpartisan federal government agency that works exclusively for Congress, not the Office of Personnel Management (OPM) or the executive branch (the president).

Often referred to as the "congressional watchdog," though most federal agencies have an internal audit function in an inspector general's office, GAO is the "supreme audit institution" of the federal government, providing auditing, evaluative, and investigative services to Congress for the entire government, to help provide accountability to the American people. Any congressional committee, subcommittee, or congressman can ask for an audit as to how taxpayer dollars are being spent, and upon approval, have that audit carried out by GAO, both financial audits and managerial audits. GAO audits and reports are presented directly to Congress.

Our trainers also discussed how audits are assigned, which is by subject matter. For example, an audit on federal money being spent on interstate highway repairs would be assigned to the transportation division, and audits involving spending overseas would be assigned to the international division. We also learned about the rotation process they used to move auditors around from audit team to audit team. On the last day, we were each given our first audit team assignment and given our diplomas back before we left. Of course, there were no questions concerning my degree from Lincoln.

I was assigned to the defense audit division, perhaps because of my experience working for the Navy Department. I wasn't too happy about that, but I didn't question or complain about the assignment. Still, I said to myself, *Dag, if I wanted to stay in defense, I would have taken that permanent job with the Navy Department.*

The one thing I liked about GAO, though, was the fact that after each audit, or on a time-certain basis, one would be able to change divisions. I looked forward to moving around to new and more interesting assignments. I would not get stuck in the defense area for long and would be able to move on to a new division after my first audit.

So, after orientation, I reported to the defense division of GAO. I was assigned to the weapons systems audit team. Being a girly girl, I knew very little about US defense weapons systems, but I would soon learn all about them. The Vietnam War was raging and very controversial, so Congress was keeping a close eye on how much the Department of

Defense was spending on it. My job required doing a lot of research on defense spending, going back as far as WWI; interviewing military officers on what they were spending; and collecting data on weapon-systems costs during the Vietnam War. I didn't complain or question the assignment, for I knew I would rotate out eventually, and as they say, "God doesn't give you anything he thinks you can't handle."

During my first audit, which was being conducted out of the main GAO office at 441 G Street, NW, I immediately noticed a lack of minorities working in the building, especially African Americans in positions like mine, and particularly black females. One day, I got up the nerve to ask my manager, who was a very cool young white guy, if there were any other black female auditors in the building. He told me yes, that he had noticed another black female auditor in the building, but he didn't know her name.

It took me weeks to find out who she was. I met her while we were both doing job-related research in GAO's library. Her name was Helen, and eventually we became good friends. You could count the number of black female auditors at GAO on one hand during the early 1970s. I had hoped that with the 1964 Civil Rights Act and affirmative action initiatives, that that would have changed by the early 1970s. I certainly was willing to do what I could to bring about change in the government's affirmative action numbers. So, I joined a federal sector organization called Blacks in Government whose mission was to do just that.

To that end, one day I got a call from human resources to report to training on a Monday morning. I wondered what the training was for. It could have been any of a number of classes on my career-development list for upward mobility, including supervisory training, technical writing, or public speaking.

There were about twenty of us who arrived for the training that Monday: ten guys and ten girls. When we introduced ourselves, I noticed how diverse we were—black, white, Hispanic, and Asian. We were all from different universities and all under thirty years old.

We were immediately told that the class was designed to teach us how to become college recruiters. They taught us the ins and outs of college recruitment: how to set up a recruitment visit, the legalities, how to conduct recruitment interviews, and how to work with human resources to get the people we recruited on board at GAO. We were told that we were the best of the best, based on our performance in the orientation class, and that they expected us to be the best recruiters out there. In my mind, there was no question that would be my goal.

At the end of the three-day class, we received certificates in recruitment. Each of us was told what our recruitment budget would be and given a recruitment assignment, which would be an add-on to our auditing duties but would count toward our promotability. In other words, by getting out there and recruiting other outstanding auditors, my career progression would get a boost. To that proposition and possibility, I said, "Hell, yeah!"

I was given a $50,000 recruitment budget, excluding per diem (travel and hotel). My recruitment territory would be HBCUs (historically black colleges and universities), mostly on the East Coast, and I could pick which schools I recruited from. GAO would pick up my expenses, and our budget would pay for booth fees and other expenses charged by the universities and for flyers, refreshments for the students, and giveaways. Each recruiter was given the same budget and asked to deliver ten new employees to the orientation class by July of 1973. Each of us had a different territory that included our own alma mater.

I was thrilled and excited about the possibility of being able to give an opportunity of employment to other minorities like me. I knew that I was being used as an affirmative action recruiter, but that was fine with me if it would bring an opportunity to others. I immediately put Lincoln, Morgan, Howard, Virginia State, Norfolk State, North Carolina A&T, Spelman, Morehouse, Dillard, Clarke-Atlanta, Bethune-Cookman, and other possible HBCUs on my list of schools that I would recruit from and that my budget would allow. My plan was to set up recruitment visits on career days and special events like homecoming and spring fling.

My stated goal would be to get at least one commitment from each school listed above. That would yield the minimum of ten employees requested, but my real goal was to exceed that number and to deliver as many qualified employees from those schools as wanted the opportunity and were willing to come to Washington to work. And why not have a little fun while recruiting by going to social events, as long as I acted professionally and responsibly? I was certainly going to give it the good old college try. My strategy worked. For example, I recruited five candidates from my alma mater, Lincoln, from the department that I served as an accounting tutor for. Out of the five, three of my fellow Lincoln Lions accepted our job offer, including Kat, my sorority sister and best friend. I met the goal of getting at least one acceptance from each school I recruited from.

HOME LIFE

Until I started graduate school, most nights I rushed home from work on the bus to start dinner for the two of us—with the exception of riding over to my mother's place to visit and to pick up our wedding gifts, little by little. My sister was already in graduate school at Penn State at the time, so I would stop by to check on Mama.

At our place, I enjoyed cooking, sewing, and watching the news until my hubby got home. I was a working professional female by day and a housewife by night. As the saying goes, "I could bring home the bacon and fry it up in the pan." The only thing was, we had given up eating pork long before we got married, so there was no bacon.

Public pressure was building to end the Vietnam War, and the Watergate scandal broke wide open in the summer of 1972, during our newlywed year, following a break-in by five men connected to the Nixon administration at the Democratic National Committee headquarters at the Watergate office complex in DC. The five burglars were caught, and Nixon and his administration attempted to cover up their involvement.

Tricky Dick, as Nixon was nicknamed, and members of his administration engaged in a number of clandestine and often illegal activities that were dubbed *dirty tricks*, such as bugging the offices of political opponents and people Nixon and his officials were suspicious of. It was also discovered that Nixon and his close aides ordered investigations of activist groups and political figures, using the Federal Bureau of Investigation, the Central Intelligence Agency, and the Internal Revenue Service as political tools. [10]

During our newlywed summer, Congress, investigative reporters, election-finance officials, and watchdog organizations, including GAO, were investigating the Watergate incident. Richard Nixon and his cronies resisted these probes, which became a constitutional crisis and led to obstruction of justice and other abuse-of-power charges, and eventually to the impeachment process being initiated against President Nixon.

I was not part of any of the GAO investigations of Watergate. Although several of them were going on, other employees were not allowed to know the details. So, I would rush home after work on many an evening to watch the drama unfold on our local and national news programs. In DC, national news is often local news, so there was full coverage of every move and every step taken in the investigations daily. DC often got more details than the rest of the nation did. I would be watching the TV set while cooking dinner. This is when I became a news junkie.

I particularly liked the local news coverage, anchored by DC's first black news reporters, Max Robinson (a male) and JC Hayward (a female named Jacqueline), both of whom were anchors for the local Eyewitness News team on Channel 9 (WTOP-TV at the time). I was so proud of both of them for their Emmy-winning broadcasts, and they did a

---

[10] Fields, "High Crimes and Misdemeanors," 1978.

heck of a job reporting on the Watergate investigations. They set a professional standard of journalism for all to follow.

By the end of August, however, my evenings at home were over, for I enrolled in the School of Business at George Washington University and started working toward a master's in business administration degree. GW appeared to be the school of choice around GAO, as there were many of us at GAO in the master's program there. For one, the B-School was located in downtown DC, not far from GAO. Secondly, in order to move up at GAO and in accounting and auditing anywhere (government or private sector), everyone knew that you either had to sit for the CPA exam or get an MBA degree.

GAO encouraged its auditors to continue their education and even paid for courses after one year of employment. But you know me—I decided not to wait and to seek an MBA degree full-speed. So, I paid cash for the first year. After all, I had seen one section of the CPA exam at Lincoln—the business law section—and I wasn't quite ready to tackle the CPA exam just yet, if at all.

I worked all day and went to graduate school in the evening, as was the case with a lot of us at GAO. What was nice about it was that several of my colleagues who were ahead of me in GW's program had had the courses I was taking and were very helpful, offering advice about classes and even books and notes if I needed them. I signed up for nine credit hours, which is considered a full-time load in graduate school. Little did I know what was in store! It certainly wasn't going to be like undergraduate school, I soon found out, especially with working full time.

On the flip side, Lacy went to graduate school at Howard during the day and continued working full time in the evening. He decided to go for a master's in public administration (MPA) degree, since there were so many government jobs in DC. However, Lacy's dream was to get good grades and go on to law school to become an attorney. He applied to over twenty law schools all across the country in addition to all of the ones in DC. His plan was to go with the best offer, as I had done for undergraduate school. At the time, we wanted to stay in DC, close to friends and family, though that would soon change.

We both got home at around eight o'clock at night several nights per week, sometimes later. I got home earlier when I didn't have class and was able to prepare nice dinners for us. We had no classes on Fridays or weekends, which we spent doing what most newlyweds do: sleeping late, chilling, and hanging out at parties, concerts, and sporting events. I enjoyed having small dinner parties at our crib, especially with my Lincoln friends.

In other words, we worked hard and partied hard too, which made for two tired newlyweds. That began to take its toll, at least on me. For one thing, I had to get up early and catch the seven thirty bus into DC to get to my audit site at GAO, which was a really long bus ride—even longer than my bus ride to McKinley Tech when I was in high school. I would often get bus-sick (nauseated). On the nights when I had a class that didn't let out until nine o'clock, Lacy would pick me up. Those were pretty long days. Once we got into our schedules, our routine became hectic.

MY FIRST CAR—AND OUR FIRST DISAGREEMENT

So, I decided to buy a car. I felt I deserved it: after all, I was a college graduate with a good-paying job. I was sick and tired of riding the bus and not having a car of my own, especially on weekends to run errands and whatnot. Driving to work would lessen my commuting time by almost an hour and would allow me to sleep a little longer in the morning. GAO had underground parking at its main building downtown for employees only, since we often stayed late into the night working on audits.

I also missed my friends who were still at Lincoln, and I wanted to go see them on my own, when I wanted to. I had saved up a decent down payment by early October. So, I went to Mr. Gaither's Pontiac dealership one day after work and put my hard-earned money down on a brand-new green Firebird with white leather interior. A popular model at the time, it was a beauty. It looked feminine yet powerful, like me.

I drove my new car home, slowly and carefully, and parked it in our assigned parking space so it would get Lacy's attention when he came home. I looked at it adoringly and then went inside to prepare a nice dinner, one of Lacy's favorites: chicken, rice, and vegetables.

I thought I would surprise Lacy when he got home from work that night with my new acquisition. I was on top of the world with joy. I decided to be playful with my reveal. Lacy came in while I was looking at the evening news and getting the latest on the Vietnam War and Watergate. He seemed excited when he said, "Boy, do I have good news for you!"

I answered, "I have some great news for you, too."

I greeted him with a kiss and then he said, "Well, ladies first!"

While waiting for me to get the keys, he wasn't too happy when he said, "Somebody parked in our parking spot. That spot is supposed to be reserved for this apartment, right? Whose car is that? Do you know?"

I responded with enthusiasm, "Yes, it's mine! How do you like it? Mr. Gaither hooked me up, didn't he? Let's take it for a spin after dinner. Come, let's celebrate over dinner!"

Over dinner, my new car was all I talked about. I talked about how helpful Mr. Gaither was and what a great deal he gave me. I talked about how grateful I was to have been introduced to the Gaithers by Lacy and his mom. I gave him an update on the Gaithers' son, whom Mrs. Lacy had nursed, etc. etc.

Lacy was very quiet during dinner. So, I asked him what was wrong.

He said, "Well, you broke the rules. Remember, you promised no B and Bs—no bills and no babies! My good news is that I got my first acceptance letter to law school, to Syracuse in New York. So how are we going to move if you have a good job and a new car and a car note? You can stay in DC and I will go off to law school alone, if you want!

It's your choice, but I will be selling the GOAT and going off to law school come fall!"

With that, he got up from the table, went into the bedroom, and shut the door. I was taken aback and had to gather myself for a while. What had I done wrong? I thought everything through. Yes, I had agreed to no B and Bs, but I didn't think that applied to transportation, which every working professional needs. I thought that was a given and would make our lives easier. Since I often needed to make several stops after work and to run errands on weekends, many times when Lacy was at work, I felt I needed reliable transportation.

And yes, I wanted something cute and fun to drive. And yes, I did not like getting around on the bus. I hated the bus. So, I bought that car as a treat to myself, as a reward for all of my hard work over the years, for all of those days and nights studying, and for all of those good grades. So what?

But I also understood where Lacy was coming from. It was now his turn to follow his dreams, to get that degree he so badly wanted, and to go away to school if he wanted to. So, I went into the bedroom and apologized for not discussing the purchase of my new car with him first. We divided up the bills. Each of us would pay for half the rent and one utility—the cheaper ones being my bill to pay.

We agreed to no credit cards and no more major purchases without discussing them with the other partner. We agreed to separate bank accounts and that each of us would have our own money and our own car, but we would buy a house together down the road. That was not an issue. But until we both finished graduate school, we agreed to hold our purchases to a tight budget and that each of us would save as much money as possible.

And that was it. That was our first major disagreement. Looking back, I think that every couple should have a financial discussion early in the marriage, even earlier than we did. It lays the groundwork for how you will manage your affairs and helps to avoid misunderstandings and disagreements down the road.

So, we got through our first major disagreement without killing each other, as the saying goes, and made an unwritten agreement as to how we would manage our finances. We made up, kissed, and made love.

We both got finished with our first semester of graduate school by mid-December 1972. Both of us got 3.5 GPAs. It was Lacy's first 3.5, and he was so happy. This would surely help him in his quest for admission to law school.

I found my 3.5 hard to come by, which was rare for me. First, I had taken on three classes (nine credit hours), which is considered full time in graduate school. Nine credit hours and a full-time professional job for the first time in my life proved to be overwhelming. One course in particular, a quantitative business analysis class, really kicked my ass. I spent hours at home and on my lunch hours at work studying, even getting help from my GAO coworkers who'd had the courses I was taking at GW.

Of course, this wore my body down, and by the time final exams came around, with all that stress, I got sick, with flulike symptoms. So, I called into GAO and took the minimum three days off, without a doctor's note, to study for my finals, missing all of my first office and departmental Christmas parties.

My dad, who lived close by at the time, used to stop by our apartment on his way home from work from time to time. He'd had a minor heart attack that fall and would check in with me from time to time to let me know he was OK. One evening while I was home, I heard a bang on our door. It was my dad, concerned because I wasn't answering the phone, asking why I hadn't returned any of his calls.

I explained what was going on, that I was home sick and studying, and told him not to worry. I felt terrible! Given his heart condition. there he was, concerned about me! Being the loving dad that he was, he said he understood and went on home, relieved that I was OK.

I got through with my finals and returned to work, with my coworkers telling me that to miss the GAO Christmas parties (and organizational picnics and baseball games, which I had also missed) was a no-no for networking reasons, especially since I was a black female. They said that it appeared as though I was being standoffish and not a team player, which could be detrimental to my career. I had also learned that in my organizational behavior course that semester.

However, I had made the decision that succeeding in graduate school was more important to me at the time than picnicking, Christmas partying, and networking for my job. That was a serious decision, career-wise, but was not a priority for me at that time. I chose to take that hit to my career in the short run, hoping I could make up for it by doing my job, performing well, and being friendly to everyone in my day-to-day interactions with my coworkers and managers. So, I shrugged my shoulders and said to myself, *Oh well, we shall see how this all turns out.*

THE HOSTESS WITH THE MOSTEST

The rest of our first year as husband and wife was filled with fun and excitement, and other major decisions. Remembering my promise to Lacy, our first Christmas together as husband and wife was wonderful, but on a small budget. We bought and decorated our first Christmas tree together, and I cooked our first Christmas dinner, with a turkey and all the trimmings. Although it was an intimate day for just the two of us, followed by visits to and from the family, it was the beginning of many Christmases to come: great Christmases on a small budget.

We had great fun on our first New Year's Eve as husband and wife, painting the town green with envy with our love, bringing in 1973. We spent our first New Year's Day at our annual cousins' day with my grandma, which was always a lot of fun.

Lacy and I hosted several dinner parties at our little apartment in 1973. That January, the Redskins won the National Football Conference championship with an 11–3 regular-season record and by winning playoff games against the Green Bay Packers and their archrival, the

Dallas Cowboys, to make their first Super Bowl appearance against the Miami Dolphins. Despite being undefeated (14–0) the entire season and beating the Cleveland Browns and the Pittsburg Steelers in the playoffs to win the American Football Conference championship, Coach Don Shula's Dolphins were actually three-point underdogs to the Redskins going into Super Bowl VII due to the weakness of their regular-season schedule and the fact that they had lost Super Bowl VI by 24–3 to the Dallas Cowboys.

Lacy and I decided to host a Super Bowl VII party for family and close friends, knowing in our hearts that our beloved Redskins would win. No Redskins haters were allowed: only die-hard Redskins fans who couldn't make it to the Memorial Coliseum in Los Angeles to see the game in person. We loaded up on food (mostly soul food) and drinks and got ready for the big game. On January 14, 1973, at game time, our little place had floor-sitting-room-only space left.

However, our decision to have that Super Bowl party turned out to be a big mistake as far as entertaining goes. The Dolphins dominated the first half of the game. Under Coach George Allen, the Redskins were led by quarterback Billy Kilmer, while Shula gave the starting nod to quarterback Bob Griese over thirty-eight-year-old Earl Morrall, who had led the Dolphins to nine consecutive wins after Griese broke his ankle in the fifth game of the season. On their third possession, Miami scored the first touchdown of the game. By halftime, Miami led 14–0 after Kilmer threw an interception to set up the Dolphins' second touchdown. Our guests were pretty sad-faced by halftime, and all the food and drinks in the world didn't seem to help the mood of our party.

Some of our guests even ate and left after halftime. The only drama and glimmer of hope for the Redskins came late in fourth quarter of the game, in what was later called Garo's Gaffe.[11] Miami attempted to cap off their 17–0 perfect season with a 17–0 perfect-score shut-out of the Redskins with a 42-yard-field goal by Garo Yepremian to win the

---

[11] .Soloman, "Dolphins Finish Super Season," 1973.

game. Instead, the game and their perfect season was jeopardized when his kick was blocked by the Redskins. Instead of falling on the loose ball, Yepremian picked it up and attempted a forward pass, which was batted in the air.

Redskins' cornerback Mike Bass, who had been Garo's former teammate with the Detroit Lions years earlier, caught the ball and returned it 49 yards for a Redskins touchdown, which was followed by an extra kick, making the score 14-7 with 2:07 remaining in the game. That was the longest time in Super Bowl history that a team was held scoreless, and it had put quite a damper on our Super Bowl party. It would be a statistic that the Redskins would have to live with.

That Redskins' touchdown brought some life to our party and some hope to our remaining guests. The game had become close. We sat with our fingers crossed and hearts pumping as the Redskins got the ball back with one minute and fourteen seconds remaining. However, the Dolphins were able to stop Washington's final drive for a tying touchdown as time expired.

Super Bowl VII, and the Redskins' first, was the warmest weather-wise (84 degrees) and the lowest-scoring Super Bowl at that time, which made for a boring Super Bowl party at our place, with Washington's dreadful showing and loss. I vowed that day never to have another Super Bowl party if the Redskins were playing in it. It was much too painful to entertain and watch them loose.

Another dinner party we hosted was after a Howard–Lincoln basketball game that was held at Howard's Burr Gymnasium. Lincoln hadn't played Howard in basketball for a long time, and not ever while I was at Lincoln, so a lot of Lincoln alums (such as Paula and Walter), and a lot of my friends still attending Lincoln, including Kat and Carolyn, my old roommates, came to the game. Lacy and I made plans to bring our good friends from both schools over after the game. I bought and cooked up a lot of food, and Lacy made sure there was plenty to drink.

Our apartment filled up with people after the game—which, by the way, Lincoln won. I made sure there were plenty of strawberry daiquiris to go around, made with rum we had bought in the Virgin Islands. My Lincoln friends were in a great, winning mood, and everyone in attendance from both Lincoln and Howard—including several members of our wedding party—had a blast eating, drinking, dancing, and reminiscing about our undergraduate years together.

After those dinner parties, I became known as *the strawberry daiquiri queen*. As newlyweds, we spent the rest of the winter devoted to our jobs and to our graduate studies. We relaxed and partied on Friday and Saturday nights but spent most of our daytime hours on Saturdays and Sundays studying when we didn't have work or church.

THE KENTUCKY DERBY, 1973

The first weekend in May 1973, we took a mini spring break and went on a day trip to the Kentucky Derby with my mother-in-law and Lacy's Aunt Ruth (she was really Mrs. Lacy's cousin and best buddy), who organized the trip. We drove to Pittsburg in the GTO that Friday night after work in order to join Aunt Ruth for her bus trip to Churchill Downs in Louisville, Kentucky, the next morning. I had never been to a horse race before, so I was excited and curious. I made a pretty hot pink dress and jacket and bought a hot pink hat to wear for the occasion. Of course, I wanted to be seen.

I didn't know a lot about horse racing, so I read articles about the horses running and listened to the seasoned gamblers while on the bus. A horse named Secretariat had been favored to win the Derby for many weeks leading up to the race. Nicknamed Big Red for his reddish-brown chestnut color, Secretariat had come into the 1973 year as the most famous three-year-old thoroughbred in a generation, having finished in the money in all but one of twenty-one races leading up to the Derby. With that record, he had been named the 1972 American Horse of the Year for a two-year-old campaign that garnered seven wins in nine tries. In addition, as a two-year-old, Secretariat grew to over sixteen hands high. At two years old, he was the size of a three-year-old.

One article said that Secretariat began his three-year-old campaign toward the Kentucky Derby and the Triple Crown in grand style, with easy victories in his first two starts in 1973. With two stylish scores, he won the Gotham and the Bay Shore Stakes, respectively. However, two weeks before the Kentucky Derby, doubts arose about Secretariat following a third-place finish at the Wood Memorial Stakes, a mile-and-an-eighth race held at Aqueduct Racetrack in New York, the last prep race for three-year-olds before the Derby. A horse named Angle Light won that race a length ahead of Sham, while Secretariat finished third, four lengths behind. Therefore, leading up to the Derby, many thought that Angle Light and Sham would be the horses Secretariat would have to beat. Secretariat's third-place finish at the Wood Memorial led many spectators and sportswriters to question his ability and health. It was later found that his performance in the Wood may have been affected by a mouth abscess that was discovered just prior to the race. There was also just a tiny nagging doubt in the minds of some of his most ardent fans that the grueling distance of the Derby (one and a quarter miles) would be Secretariat's undoing.[12]

Secretariat was, nonetheless, the morning line favorite of the Derby entrants. As the race is restricted to only three-year-olds, a colt has only one shot at immortality when it comes to the Derby. This was Secretariat's chance. For some reason, I took a great liking to him. I could relate to him. It would take *perseverance, hope, and determination (PHD)* on his part to win the Derby. He'd have to be just like me, as I knew I would have to be just like him for the rest of my life to do the things I wanted to do.

As our bus arrived at Churchill Downs the day of the race, which was the ninety-ninth running of the Derby leading up to its centennial, the horse on most everyone's mind was Secretariat. Many sportswriters believed that the thirteen horses in the field possessed great speed and that the course record would perhaps be broken. That brought people

---

[12] Nack, "Secretariat: The Making of a Champion," 1988.

who loved horse racing out of the woodwork, from all over the world, to Kentucky that day. People were everywhere as we stepped off the bus. We heard the announcer say that there was a record crowd of over 134,000 people present. Many came to see what they thought would be a showdown between Sham and Secretariat, two of the greatest horses of all time.

The serious gamblers took off in one direction to place their bets, and Mrs. Lacy and Aunt Ruth stayed behind talking to the bus driver, leaving Lacy and I to fend for ourselves. We took our time walking around and taking everything in, and then we placed two-dollar bets on one horse—Secretariat to win with 3 to 2 odds and Secretariat to place—just for the fun of it.

We also stopped at the bar to sit and have authentic mint juleps. The mint julep is a cocktail best known as the signature drink of the Kentucky Derby. Consisting primarily of quality bourbon, water, sugar, crushed or shaved ice, and fresh mint, the mint julep is associated with the American South in general and the Kentucky Derby in particular, when made with the best Kentucky bourbon and Kentucky spearmint brewed and grown in the state, respectively. The drink is best served in a frosty glass or silver or pewter cup to keep it cold during warm temperatures.

We decided to have our mint juleps in traditional Derby pewter cups so we could keep the cups as souvenirs from our trip. To us, the souvenir pewter cups with *Kentucky Derby 1973* engraved on them were worth the price of the bus trip, given what we were about to see. Those cups would serve as lifelong memories of our trip and Derby experience.

We made our way into the infield of Churchill Downs, which is where the majority of the crowd stood to view the race. It was like being in the infield of a baseball diamond inside the racetrack. The space quickly filled with people, so much so that I wasn't able to see the track well, given my short height. As the race grew near, I couldn't see a damn thing. So, I jumped up on Lacy's back and wrapped my legs around his waist, making myself about seven feet tall. That way, I could see the track. Lacy was my horse and I was his jockey that day, hat and all.

As the field of thirteen horses was led into their gates around 5:37 p.m. EDT, the doubts that might have lingered in the minds of many in Secretariat's huge following gave way to hope in their hearts. However, as the field broke from the gate, Secretariat let the speed horses go and dropped in toward the rear of the pack. At the beginning of the first turn, Secretariat was ahead of only two horses. I began to worry.

A horse named Shecky Greene took the lead first and led for the majority of the first seven furlongs. People in the crowd began to yell, "Come on, Shecky, come on!" Sham took the lead from Shecky Greene close to the three-quarter-mile mark. The crowd began to chant, "Go Sham Go!"

I then said out loud, "Where in the Sam Hill is that damn Secretariat?"

Then, flying like a bat out of hell, Secretariat made his move. He broke from near the back of the pack and began to pick off the horses ahead of him one by one, which was the strategy of his jockey, Ron Turcotte. The Derby is a long race, and many of the top horses have won by coming from well behind. Secretariat was no exception. Everyone began to yell at the top of their lungs, "Run, Red, run! Run, Red, run!"

As the horses entered the homestretch, Shecky Greene began to fade back into the pack. Secretariat then passed Sham in the final furlong and distanced himself to solidify his lead, winning by two-and-a-half horse lengths ahead of Sham in a world-record time of 1 minute, 59 and 2/5 seconds. Our Native finished in third place.

Soon it was official, in the simple words that millions of Big Red fans wanted to hear: *"It's Secretariat! And he's got his Kentucky Derby!"* said the announcer.

Secretariat's winning time, and his last quarter-mile time of 23 seconds, were both Derby records. In addition, Secretariat had run each quarter-mile faster than before, thus showcasing his stamina to the world. Sham also broke the previous Derby course record with a time of 1:59 and 4/5 seconds. Secretariat and Sham were the first two horses to run the Derby in less than two minutes, and Secretariat's record still stands to this day. Shecky Greene, who had led for most of the race, finished in sixth place.[13]

My new hubby and I had just witnessed one of the greatest horse races of all time, and everyone learned the age-old life lesson that day: it is sometimes not where and/or how you start but how you finish the race that counts. My Derby experience solidified that lifelong lesson, and I hold it close and carry it with me to this day. It's not where you start in life, it's where you end up that counts.

We watched the rose ceremony and caught up with Mama Lacy and Aunt Ruth, who had charmed their way into the bleachers as senior citizens rather than stand the whole time in the infield. Our bets were so small and the lines of winners so long that we didn't bother to gather our winnings. We squeezed through the crowd to make our way back to the bus.

The entire bus ride back to Pittsburg and car ride back to DC was happy and jovial. Everyone had a great time, win or lose. Little did we know how much history we had seen that day, given what would happen to Secretariat in the days to come. He would go on the win the Triple Crown that year.

What was even more impressive and more of a lesson to me was Secretariat's response to the pressure of his fans and the media to be the first Triple Crown winner in twenty-five years. We followed Secretariat's career for the rest of the year in his quest for the Triple Crown. Could Big Red go on to become the first horse in twenty-five years prior to his Derby win to wear the Triple Crown?

Two weeks after the Derby, at the Pimlico Race Track in Baltimore, Maryland, Secretariat won the second event of the Triple Crown: the

---

[13] .Op. cit.

Preakness Stakes. The official clock malfunctioned, but hand-recorded timers had him running the mile and one-sixth race in record time.[14]

Some sportswriters felt that Secretariat gave the best performance of his career in the last leg of the Triple Crown, at the Belmont Stakes in New York, on June 9, 1973. He finished the 1.5-mile race first in a record two minutes and twenty-four seconds, knocking almost three seconds off the dirt-track record set by a horse named Gailant Man in 1957. He also won by a record thirty-one horse lengths ahead of the second-place finisher. Secretariat's win was by such a large margin that not even the widest camera angle could show him in the same shot as the next nearest horse.

Jockey Ron Turcotte, who rode Secretariat in all but three of his races, stated that at the Belmont Stakes, he lost control of Secretariat, and the horse raced into history on his own accord. With that spectacular win at the Belmont Stakes, Secretariat became the first horse since Citation in 1948, the year that George Lacy Jr. was born, to win America's coveted Triple Crown of thoroughbred horse racing.

Secretariat would race six more times, winning four and finishing second twice. The "horse of the century" would then be retired and put out to stud at Claiborne Farm in Paris, Kentucky.[15]

I never knew that you could learn so much about human life and spirit from a horse: about class and style, stamina and endurance, grace and longevity, and of course, PHD. Why of course you can, when that horse is treated like a human being—with love, respect, and tenderness; when that horse is a GOAT, one of the greatest of all time; and when that horse's name is Secretariat.

---

[14] Op. cit.
[15] Op. cit.

PICTURE GALLERY

Photograph Credit: All photographs courtesy
of the Ford Lacy Family Archive

This picture gallery was created by:

Jamaal Ellsworth
JRE Kustom Printing
Washington DC

Childhood Pictures

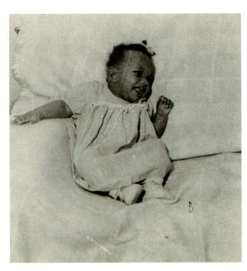

This is my baby picture, taken in 1951. I am told that I was a happy baby and a quick learner. I walked, talked, and spelled early to keep up with my big sister, Valeria.

Valeria and I were two peas in a pod. She was my first babysitter, tutor, and friend. I was her shadow and followed her everywhere.

A tomboy at heart, I enjoyed watching my daddy repair the cars of neighbors and friends as a side hustle. He was my first math teacher and taught me to count and add numbers when I was a toddler.

Our family lived in an apartment on Foote Street in the Northeast section of DC, where I enjoyed playing in the backyard until my parents separated, when I was five years old.

Childhood Continued

When my parents separated, my mother moved us into a one-bedroom apartment on 20th Street, Northeast, which was located on the fringe of Capitol Hill, in the shadow of the Washington Stadium and the DC Armory.

At Eliot Jr. High School, "I found my sea legs and my confidence." During those years, I grew by leaps and bounds intellectually and socially. A math whiz and "fly block girl" in one package, I was a co-valedictorian of my graduating class in 1966.

At Eliot Junior High School

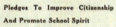

Grant Harrison Wins S C Presidency

Pledges To Improve Citizenship And Promote School Spirit

Under the able leadership of Grant Harrison, the 1964-65 student council has pledged to improve citizenship and promote school spirit at Eliot. Working with him on the newly elected slate will be Gwynette Ford, vice president, Thomas Colvin, second vice president, Mary Gordon, secretary, Jacquelyn Satterwhite, assistant secretary, Carlton West, treasurer and George Fox, sergeant-at-arms.

Newly elected Student Council Officers Carlton West, Jacqueline Satterwhite, Gwynette Ford, Grant Harrison, Mary Gordon, and George Fox review plans for the year.

At Eliot, we had teachers who really cared and provided us with wonderful experiences outside of the classroom, such as a bus trip to New York City, pictured above.

As we marched into the auditorium for our graduation ceremony, I nervously held on tight to my valedictorian speech. I was passionate about civil rights and equality for all, which was the focus of my speech.

I hand-made all of the outfits that appear in the pictures above. As a reward for my creativity, many of my classmates voted for me as the "best-dressed girl" of our class for the Who's Who List.

McKinley Tech High School Pictures

McKinley Tech High School was the best school in DC for college-bound students during the 60's. Known as "The School Up On the Hill," we had excellent teachers and we students had fun every day, "learning and playing" at anything our hearts desired.

Lacy's burgundy GTO, (The GOAT), played a major role in our relationship, from the day I met him until after we were married. When we met, it was his race car that he loved to drive fast. But it became much more. It became my "burgundy chariot" throughout our courtship that carried me to and from school and work, off to college, and back and forth to Lincoln University in Pennsylvania. Lacy's friends began to call the GOAT a "school bus" and a "taxi cab."

CHRISTMASTIME WITH THE LACYS

On our first Christmas together as a couple, my gift to Lacy was a knit and suede sweater I purchased from a popular DC men's store named "Cavalier's." Christmastime would give us a lot to celebrate from then on.

Mama Lacy was known for her fabulous Christmas dinners, so what better occasion for our mothers to meet and get better acquainted than Christmas, 1968.

Here, my sister, Valeria, and I, are enjoying Mama Lacy's infamous Christmas dinner, with turkey and all the trimmings, topped off with her famous pineapple-coconut cake and Mamie Eisenhower fudge for dessert.

McKinley Tech Senior High School

Lacy was my "hot" date to my senior prom. We also celebrated our one year anniversary as a couple that night. We were "clean as the board of health," in coordinated gold formal wear.

Gwynette P. Ford
Cheerleader—3, 4; Fr. Hon. Soc.—2, 3; V.P.—4; Hon. Soc.—4

My yearbook picture highlighted my high school activities and achievements: cheerleading, the French Honor Society, and the National Honor Society.

As a cheerleader, I was the shortest and lightest in weight on the team. I was tasked with making it up to the top of the human pyramid. I felt like I was on top of the world.

I took this picture of my girlfriends and club sisters on our Senior Class Trip to Montreal, Canada. All dressed up for a night on the town, I played "den mother" and covered for them as they broke curfew and stayed out until dawn. Left to right are Teresa, Diane, and Geraldine.

My Cheerleading Days at McKinley Tech High School

The 1968-69 cheerleaders (from left to right): Front row— Debra Iverson, Sharon Medley, Marcia Crossly, Wanda Behlin. Back row — Gwynette Ford, Denise Rutherford, Brenda Stewart, Theresa Palmer, Brenda Beckford, Diane Wilson, Francine Robinson, Linda Cacanindin.

Soulful cheerleaders lead the audience in "Sitting in the Grandstand."

These pictures appeared in the 1969 Yearbook of McKinley Tech High School.

As a Member of the French Honor Society

McKinley Honors Achievers In French Club: Communicate Truth About France

Outstanding French students found a reward for their scholastic achievements in Societe Honoraire de Francais, the National French Honor Society. Members were selected from the upper ten per cent of the student body. An A average in French and a B average in other subjects was required for each semester.

During the school year, members participated in many trips among which were visits to the National Art Gallery of Art to view French paintings and a French movie.

Affiliated with the National French Honor Society was the French Club, also sponsored by Mrs. Norton. The only restrictions for membership were an interest in France and its language.

During these meetings, students were enlightened on the many phases of life in France and were also instructed in the use of the laboratory equipment. An activity sponsored by the club was a Senior Farewell which was an after-school dance. The members also participated in the National French Contest.

Honor Society members plan for the induction of new members.

French Club members listen to a French tape to gain experience in the use of laboratory equipment.

This article appeared in the Yearbook of McKinley Tech High School, 1969.

McKinley Tech High School Picture

My Yearbook Graduation Picture
from
McKinley Tech High School, Washington, DC, 1969

Hail, Hail, Lincoln

During the summer after I graduated from high school, I made a smart decision to attend Lincoln University of Pennsylvania. Previously an all-male school, Lincoln offered me a full-tuition scholarship, as it welcomed female students with open arms, although some of the male students did not share that sentiment. Unlike students today, I arrived on Lincoln's beautiful rural campus, sight unseen.

In the aftermath of protests and marches that resulted in me losing my job as the curfew enforcer at my dormitory, I was given a new work-study assignment at Vail Memorial Library. I spent my afternoons logging in new books and re-shelving borrowed books, and my evenings studying there until closing time.

At Lincoln University

I met Katherine my first day at Lincoln at our orientation dinner. We became roommates and best friends. People called us "Mutt and Jeff" and "Salt and Pepper." We went everywhere, did everything, and studied together, eventually serving as tutors in accounting.

Walter and I met while working at Woodward and Lothrop Department Store before I enrolled at Lincoln. He became my male guardian angel. A Kappa Man, he served as my escort at the Coronation Ceremony on Kappa Weekend, 1971.

I embraced Black Greek Life at Lincoln U. I was a member of the first AKA line to pledge on campus after our Epsilon Nu Chapter was chartered. Pictured above is my line, the Ninth Dimension. I am seated, second from the right.

I had the pleasure of serving as Queen of the Kappa Court of Lincoln University in 1971, an honor that I still cherish today that I felt I earned. I fed, tutored and covered for many Kappas and their pledgees.

STEPPING AND SINGING AS IVIES DURING GREEK HELL WEEK

Alpha Kappa Alpha Sorority, Inc.
Epsilon Nu Chapter
Lincoln University, PA

Fall 1970

9th Dimension

At Lincoln University

After pledging Alpha Kappa Alpha Sorority Inc., I hit the books hard. Somehow, I managed a get a 3.78 grade point average that semester.

With sorority sisters, Patricia (left), and Hope (middle), we ventured off campus to an AKA function, along with other sorors, captured in the background.

Lacy was a frequent visitor to Lincoln's campus. Some people thought he was a Lincoln Man instead of a Howard Man. Here we are during AKA Weekend, 1971, with me in a waist-fitting pink dress I made just for the occasion.

My Graduation from Lincoln University

We arrived early, the morning of my graduation from Lincoln, so that I could attend my baccalaureate ceremony, a religious service of songs, prayers and a send-off sermon, held at Mary Dod Brown Memorial Chapel to honor our graduating class.

I was able to pick up my cap and gown just in time to march in the graduation procession. I was so happy to be graduating magna cum laude (with great honor), in just three years.

My sister, Valeria, greeted me after the graduation ceremony, to congratulate me on getting the Wall Street Journal Award, for having the highest grade point average in the Economics and Business Department.

After rushing back and forth across Lincoln's beautiful campus, exhausted, I removed my shoes as I made my way to the administration building to pick up my diploma.

Lacy's Howard University Graduation

I tease Lacy that he graduated from college a week after I did although he was three years older than me. His "bush" was so big, he wasn't able to wear his graduation cap.

After Howard's graduation ceremony, Lacy's aunt hosted a graduation party for him at her house close to Howard's campus, with all of his favorite southern dishes, including Mama Lacy's.

Lacy shared his proud moment with his family, including his little cousins, especially his god-daughter Marlynn and her little brother, Marc. On that day, I knew he would be a great father someday.

My Bridal Showers

I was blessed with three bridal showers before my wedding. The first was a kitchen shower, given by my AKA sorority sisters on Lincoln's campus.

My third shower was a surprise, R-rated lingerie shower, hosted by my bridesmaids. Looking on are guests NeNe and Regina and hosts Muff and Tanya (seated), with Kat standing with a watchful eye.

Enjoying refreshments at the lingerie shower are (left to right) guests Teresa, Susan, NeNe and me, with bridesmaid Toni.

My Big Fat DC Wedding

We were able to pull off our wedding on a shoe-string budget. I made my gown with a fine cotton lace fabric and trimmed the twenty-foot tulle veil with a string of lace from it.

"My Big Fat DC Wedding," as I call it, was comprised of twenty wedding party members, including the flower girl and the ring bearer (out of the picture), excluding the bride and groom. All of the females' dresses were hand-made, including the mothers' of the bride and groom.

For the parents' picture, our best man, David Washington (far left) stood in for Lacy's father, who was ill, with Mama Lacy in a pink dress that I made for her. My mom (in green) and dad (far right) were on their best behavior that day.

The wedding cake was the star of the show at our wedding reception. World famous "Clement's Bakery" was able to replicate the steps of the church, placing brown dolls, dressed in our wedding colors, on the stairs.

ON TO THE UNIVERSITY OF WISCONSIN

We rented a nice little modern apartment in downtown Madison, Wisconsin while attending graduate school there. Our "crib" was a first floor patio unit, just right for BBQing and entertaining.

I took this picture of my MBA classmates after class one day during the fall of 1973. After we all graduated, they left me behind in Madison and would return with stories of the "dog eat dog" corporate world.

Here I am waiting for Lacy outside of the law school, next to snow almost waist high. It was not unusual for snow to be on the ground from October until May in Madison.

Grandma's 75th Birthday Celebration

The Wright Family celebrated my maternal grandmother's 75th birthday in August, 1975. Lacy and I flew in from Wisconsin for the occasion, which was hosted by Grandma's five living children. She is seated in the middle of her entire legacy, and I am standing behind her in a big straw hat. We used the occasion to announce that we were expecting our first child. My cousins said that they were taking bets that we would return from Wisconsin with "a bundle of joy."

Wisconsin Winters

Playing in the snow was a popular past-time for students at UW. Here I am outside of the Student Union, standing on the edge of the lake, ready for a snowball fight.

My friend, Gail, a Spelman graduate from the deep south, found UW and the snow to be challenging, but nothing that we, together, would not be able to overcome and succeed at.

After completing my Ph.D. preliminary exams, law student and DC native, Lynn Sylvester (seated in the center) and others hosted a baby shower in my honor at "The Library" restaurant in downtown Madison, WI.

LACY'S LAW SCHOOL GRADUATION AND ADMISSION TO THE BAR

Lacy graduated from Wisconsin's law school in December of 1975 and was admitted to the Wisconsin Bar soon after. Here I am, four months pregnant, celebrating with him.

Celebrating with Lacy (second from the left) are fellow December graduates, Robert Buffin (far left) and Buddy Clark (far right), with their professor and mentor, James Jones (third from the left).

The December 1975 law school graduates were admitted to the Wisconsin State Bar at a ceremony held at the Madison Court House, with all of the pomp and circumstances.

After his gaduation from law school, I hosted a party for Lacy at "The Library" restaurant in downtown Madison, along with my friend, Gail, on my right, and our best man, David, on my left, who flew up from DC, just for the occasion.

CHRISTMAS, 1975

Mama Lacy hosted a Christmas dinner party that was served in four shifts. Here she is with Lacy's cousin, Priscilla (left) and his godmother, Vivian (on the right).

Christmas, 1975, was very special. Here I am, four months pregnant with our first child and Lacy having just graduated from law school. We celebrated throughout the holidays.

Hostesses at Lacy's DC law school graduation celebration included left to right, our cousin Toni, my sister Valeria, and our cousin Saundra, Uncle Lawrence's daughter.

I hosted a party to celebrate Attorney Lacy at my Uncle Lawrence's home in Hillcrest Heights, DC, right after New Year's in 1976 for our wedding party members, family, and friends.

And Baby Makes Three

After I passed my Ph.D. preliminary exams, we moved back to the DC area in February, 1976. I decided to work on my dissertation remotely and took a job in academia. Baby Gharun was born on April 15, 1976, Tax Day, three weeks earlier than expected. Here we are coming home from the babysitter's house after a day of my classes at Howard University.

We celebrated Gharun's 1st birthday with family and friends in a big party room at my mother's apartment complex, which gave us the opportunity to catch up with everyone while enjoying being new parents.

I was determined to balance the needs of my family with the demands of being a Ph.D. candidate and my job. Here we are at the petting zoo at King's Dominion, under the watchful eye of Mama Lacy.

The Gingerbread House

We bought this cape-cod styled bungalow on Chestnut Street in the Woodridge section of Northeast in 1977. I called it "our little red-brick gingerbread house." A fixer-upper, its renovations further distracted me from completing my Ph.D.

Here we are, outside of our new home, on our way to a tap-dance performance at Gharun's nursery school. I turned to organized day care as a way to ensure that our son would get a good educational start in life.

My career in academia allowed me to strike a balance between our family life and my career. Here we are on Easter Sunday, on our way to a church program. Gharun's Easter basket was almost as big as he was.

AT GEORGETOWN

Lacy pursued an advanced law degree, the LLM in Labor Law, from Georgetown Law Center, prior to opening a private law practice with a fellow classmate on Capitol Hill. I helped the fellas decorate their law office and hosted their opening party.

Mama Lacy, Baby Gharun and I represented our family at Lacy's graduation from Georgetown. After helping Lacy open his private law practice, I decided to press on to complete my Ph.D. by eliminating all distractions and interruptions. My Ph.D. journey took a lot of perseverance and determination.

All But Dissertation (ABD)

My budding career at Howard University afforded me the opportunity to work with some of the brightest minds in higher education, including that of none other than my former high school principal, Dr. George Rhodes. A mathematical genius, who also obtained a Ph.D. and retired from the DC Public Schools and the US Department of Education, Dr. Rhodes also joined Howard to teach college-age students.

While working on my dissertation, I met up with a fellow MBA classmate, Yvonne Gray, in Minneapolis, MN, to interview her as a research subject. We showed up, similarly dressed for success.

Finally, after successfully defending my dissertation, a hospital stay, and getting my Ph.D. on December 22, 1979, we celebrated my graduation with pink champagne. Joining me, on Christmas Day, was Kat (far left), my best friend, and Mama Ford, in the middle.

Ma Famille

Eventually, there would be one more addition to our small family. We welcomed a daughter, Gayna, into our lives in December, 1981. As a preemie, she was a Christmas surprise, and quite a present for her big brother. Here we are relaxing at our home after Gayna was christened, in a gown I made for her.

Four generations of Wright women are represented here. With Gayna and me are my maternal grandmother, Bellinger Golden Wright (left), and my mother, Gloria Wright Ford (right).

Lacy and I enjoyed entertaining at our first home on Chestnut Street. Here my children and I are visited by (back row) my sister, Valeria, my dad James Ford, and his second wife, Mildred.

Home is Where the Heart is

Christmastime continues to be a special time of year for the "Four Gs," as we call ourselves, which stands for (left to right) George, Gharun, Gwynette, and Gayna. I now host our Christmas dinners and enjoy preparing the delicious dishes I was taught to make by my grandmother, Mama Lacy, and Mama Ford, who have now transitioned.

The School of Business at Howard University is like a "second home" to me and my family. Many days and countless hours have been spent there by all four of us. Our kids grew up there as well as at home, playing in the hallways and classrooms, or waiting for me in my office while I taught classes and attended meetings. As Lacy's alma mater, we enjoy attending countless alumni and homecoming events there.

IN ACADEMIA

Gwynette Lacy, Ph.D.,
Chair
Department of Management

Gwynette Lacy, Ph.D.

**Assistant Dean
Of Student Affairs**

While at Howard University, I held many titles, but the one I enjoyed most is that of Ph.D. behind my name. Wearing the doctoral robe with the three velvet Ph.D. stripes on the sleeves and the Wisconsin hood has brought me much joy. I feel like I am graduating again each time I march with the faculty at graduation time.

My Work in Academia

Working with and for extraordinary colleagues, in and outside of academia, has been rewarding. Here, I am standing with colleagues after a faculty meeting.

I have had the pleasure of being honored by outstanding students. Here, I am pictured with fellow honorees, singer and actress, Vanessa Williams (third from the right), Marion Wright Edelman (fourth from the right), and golfer Rose Elder (third from the left).

Nothing has been as rewarding as raising money to further the education of deserving students. Here, I am standing next to Dean Barron H. Harvey, Ph.D. (fourth from the right), as he receives a corporate donation for student scholarships as our colleagues and students look on.

Touching the Lives of Many

My long career in academia has allowed me to touch the lives of many. I have taught thousands of undergraduate students, such as those above, who took a break from studying to attend a holiday party.

These young African leaders from fourteen different African countries, who participated in President Obama's Young African Leaders' Initiative (YALI), sponsored by the US Department of State, became like family members to me. Here we are, standing on the steps of the U.S. Capitol, prior to a visit to talk to several members of Congress.

A Wave of Pride

My life's work and career have taken me all over the United States and to other parts of the world, including South Africa, where here, I am visited by a friendly elephant outside of my cabin.

My life as a Ph.D. has been rich and rewarding, with many proud moments, but none more rewarding than seeing my first-born child graduate from college himself, as I wave to him dressed in my doctoral attire. Our son is now a Deputy Assistant Secretary (DAS) of State, and our daughter is a DPT (Doctor of Physical Therapy).

EIGHT
ON WISCONSIN?

AFTER RETURNING FROM our Kentucky trip, we spent the rest of our newlywed spring and summer making major life-altering decisions and plans. First of all, Lacy needed to make a decision about law school. Where he would go to law school was first and foremost on our minds.

For the first time in a long time, I decided not to be in any kind of rush that summer of 1973. I took the summer off to chill and relax and be a normal, everyday professional who worked during the day and came home at a decent hour in the evening to a normal life. I would make plans about my career and continuing my graduate studies once I knew what Lacy was going to do. It was now his time to make the moves that would shape and direct the rest of his life, as I had done during the summer of 1969, when I decided to attend Lincoln University. I was not going to stand in his way, nor did I want to influence or manipulate his decision. That was the least I could do, given all he did and put up with during my Lincoln years.

Lacy's mother was over the moon about his decision to go to law school. Although she had always told him not to be another lying lawyer like his dad, she really didn't mean that. She was really overjoyed that he wanted to go on to professional school and had chosen a profession that was respectable and could bring in a decent living for his family. *Like father, like son* was OK with her as well, although she never let Lacy know that.

Acceptance letters began to come in. Lacy was right on the money with his prediction, as they say in horse racing. He applied to twenty-four law schools. He predicted that he would be accepted to 20 percent, or five of them, and so it was. He was accepted to five law schools, each in a different location. They were Syracuse in Syracuse, New York; Akron in Akron, Ohio; Golden State in San Francisco, California; the University of Wisconsin in Madison, Wisconsin; and of course, his beloved Howard University in Washington, DC.

Lacy's decision would be a difficult one for many reasons. The quality, reputation, and legal curriculum of the school were first and foremost. Then there was location and cost of living; and of course, last but not least, there was my opinion and feelings about the choice. He told me that my opinion would be taken into account.

First of all, he decided to go away—to get out of DC and all of its trappings and the distractions of family, friends, and parties, as well as the temptation and desire to keep up with friends and family financially and materially. It was Lacy's time to go away. Second, he decided against Golden State Law School in San Francisco because it was so far away from home and the cost of living in Frisco was way too high.

With Howard and Golden State eliminated, we decided to visit the three remaining on the list: Syracuse, Akron, and Wisconsin. We drove up to Syracuse in New York one weekend and then to Akron in Ohio the next weekend, in that order. Both were acceptable as choices, and both were affordable. Both were in cold climates, with Syracuse being a little colder, but with Akron getting a little more snow annually. I personally liked Akron better than Syracuse. It had more of a city feel to it than a college town, with more job opportunities for me, since I planned to work.

That left one more school to visit: the University of Wisconsin in Madison, at the state's capital city and a three-hour plane ride away.

We flew up to Madison for an overnight visit and packed as much into those two days as possible. We had a thorough visit of the law school and spoke with as many people as possible, including the professors, students, and others. I toured the School of Business and collected information about transferring my MBA credits there, for I planned to finish my MBA wherever Lacy decided to go.

UW-Madison, or just plain Madison as many called it, is considered one of America's *public Ivy* universities, which refers to the top public universities in the United States, capable of providing a collegiate experience comparable to the private Ivy League schools. To me, it certainly looked and felt that way, at least at first glance. At the time, Wisconsin's B-School was ranked number ten in the country for business schools at public universities.

The campus was large, yet beautiful, and surrounded by lakes. The law school and the B-School were both located in the center of campus, almost right next to one another, on top of a steep hill named Bascom Hill. I said to myself, *Boy, we would really stay in shape, humping up and down that hill to get to class.*

Downtown Madison started at the bottom of the hill and continued up and down State Street to the foot of the state capitol, about a mile and a half away. Lacy and I had lunch downtown at one of the many eateries on State Street at the end of our campus visit our second day there.

Over lunch, Lacy said to me, "I've made a decision. This is it!"

My response was, "What?"

George C. Lacy Jr. had decided on the University of Wisconsin's law school for several reasons. First, they offered him a full-tuition scholarship as part of their LEO Program for minority students, an affirmative action program. Second, they gave him a living stipend that he felt the two of us could live on. Third, Wisconsin's law school had something called "the diploma privilege" for the state of Wisconsin, which meant if you graduated, you would automatically be admitted to the state bar without taking the state bar exam, thus assuring that you could get a job, at least in the state of Wisconsin.

The downside to going to Wisconsin was that it was a good distance from DC, some 850 miles away from our family and friends. That was about a sixteen-hour drive and a little over two hours by plane. It was also the coldest climate of all the schools we were considering.

Most important was the cultural difference. In a city where only 3 percent of the population of the university and the city was black, we would be severely in the minority. We talked things over while enjoying a deep-dish pizza, which was a signature dish in Madison. Lacy concluded that the pros far outweighed the cons, so Madison it would be. We knew that we wouldn't be able to go home a lot, but maybe that was a good thing. There would be no excuse not to study, especially during Madison's cold winters.

Lacy was sensitive to my issues. I would have to quit my job and leave George Washington midway through my MBA studies. So, he told me that he would not insist that I come to Madison with him. He said he would understand if I wanted to stay in Washington. If I didn't want to come, he said he would go to Madison alone and come home as often as he could. My initial excitement and reaction was that I would come too, but I told him I would think things through and let him know of my decision.

We left the restaurant and proceeded to quickly look for an apartment downtown, within walking distance of the school. Lacy decided on a relatively new apartment at 424 W. Dayton Street, right off of State Street. It was a large apartment building and not a garden apartment like I preferred. They had one patio apartment available on the ground floor that was affordable and somewhat secluded; it reminded me of the patio apartment we had in Maryland, yet smaller. It had yellow shag carpet, which was in style back then, so all I would have to do is change out my red accessories and pillows for yellow ones. We would be able to barbecue on the patio, like back at home, which was ideal.

So, we signed a contract and paid the required deposit. Wow, that sealed the deal. Madison, Wisconsin, it would be. With that, we rushed back to the hotel, which was also downtown; packed our things; and made it to the airport in time to catch our plane.

On a relatively quiet plane ride home from Wisconsin, I think we both were thinking the same thing: *How are we going to tell our respective families and friends that we were moving to Madison, Wisconsin?*

Although we privately told our parents and close friends by meeting or talking by phone with them one-on-one, we decided to take the occasion of our first wedding anniversary to make a formal and official announcement. Each announcement drew a different and interesting response. Some were even hilarious.

Of course, George told his mom as soon as we got back to DC. She was ecstatic and over the moon with joy, for after all, Wisconsin was her suggestion at the recommendation of George Meany, the famous labor boss and president of the AFL-CIO at the time, who was one her patients. She said she couldn't wait tell "old George Meany."

I think deep down inside, though, she was already starting to miss her only son. I could see it in her face: a subtle sadness. Women know these things. But she didn't let on. She went on to talk about us sending and bringing her cheese at her request and the fabulous dishes she would make with the different kinds. The kicker was when I asked if she was going to miss her son. She said, "Hell, if I miss y'all too much, I'll just pick up and move up there."

We quickly dispelled that notion. Lacy told her that we would call her every week and come home as often as possible, especially on holidays, and that we would always stay with her when we did. That seemed to settle things down at the time. She then went back to talking about that Wisconsin cheese and what she would cook with it.

My daddy, as always, tried to stay positive and neutral. He was genuinely happy to hear Lacy's news and told me it was my choice, of course. He told me he knew I would make the right decision and made sure not to lean one way or the other. I couldn't tell how he was feeling. He had grown to love Lacy as the son he never had. They had gotten pretty close by then. He was so proud of both of us.

My mother's response to the announcement, on the other hand, was quick and to the point. When I told her of Lacy's decision and that he had given me the choice to move to Madison or stay in DC to finish my MBA, she said, "Girl, there is no choice. You need to pack your bags and move to Wisconsin too. That's what a good wife does. Don't let that man go to Wisconsin alone. He will never forget that, and you will live to regret it."

It didn't take me long to make up my mind. I decided to take my mother's advice: old-fashioned mother wit, as they call it. I wasn't about to let Lacy go it alone in that tough environment. Deep down, I knew he wanted me with him, by his side all the way, too. So, I notified GAO that I would be leaving that August, and I began transfer proceedings at George Washington. Both were fully cooperative and wished me the best.

We began to tell friends as we ran into them here and there and started to make plans for a great dinner party/BBQ at our crib for our first anniversary celebration to make a formal announcement and say farewell at the same time.

I will never forget running into Muff, the girl who hosted one of my bridal showers, in Georgetown while we were out shopping. She said, "You're moving where? Wisconsin? You mean that place with the cows and the cheese? Y'all are joking, right?" The three of us had the biggest laugh about that.

Other friends and associates had similar and equally hilarious reactions. Many could not believe that George Lacy Jr. was leaving his beloved DC to live somewhere else, and was going to Wisconsin, no less. But slowly and clearly, it was beginning to sink in that we were stepping way out the norm for two young black natives of Washington, DC. We were being trailblazers in more ways than one in the affirmative action era. Everyone seemed to be for us, though, and wished us nothing but the best.

Our first wedding anniversary quickly arrived. We decided to invite our wedding party members and closest friends but excluded our parents and everyone over forty. Mom, Dad, and Mrs. Lacy were OK with that and understood that it would be a party for young people who wanted to "let their hair down," so to speak. As always, though, Daddy stopped by that morning to drop off a card with money in it to wish us well.

I prepared what was becoming my signature soul-food dinner menu: barbecue chicken, baked in the oven until tender then put on the grill; homemade potato salad; tuna and macaroni salad; fresh popped green beans; and a tossed salad. Lacy grilled up hot dogs and hamburgers out on the patio. For dessert, I used Mrs. Lacy's recipe and made her pineapple coconut sheet cake that stays in the fridge until served, to go with what was becoming my DC-famous strawberry daiquiris and piña coladas.

Just about everyone who was invited showed up, so we had a full house, with sitting-on-the-floor room only while eating. We ate, drank, danced, and got quite merry. And, of course, as was tradition, we unfroze the top layer of our wedding cake, cut it into small pieces, and served it on a silver platter. Because it was rum-flavored, it didn't taste bad at all; not bad at all. We made our official announcement that we were moving to Wisconsin, which was old news by then, and had a champagne toast. "On, Wisconsin!" we all said.

The music was pumping and the drinks were flowing. I just hoped and prayed that the neighbors wouldn't call the police on us because of all the noise we were making, and they didn't. What started during the late afternoon went on until around midnight, with everyone wishing us farewell as we embarked on our journey to Wisconsin. When our last guests were gone, we flopped down on the living room couch, exhausted.

George managed to get up and go into the bedroom. He came out with a small jewelry box with my first-anniversary gift in it. It was a jewelry box from an African American jewelry store near Howard University's campus. Of course, I said, "Is that for me? Oh, you shouldn't have."

Inside the box was an 18-carat, soft yellow-gold bracelet shaped into an ankh, the African symbol that stands for fertility. It was absolutely beautiful and matched my gold rings. I still have it, and I wear it just about every day, rarely ever taking it off, as with my wedding rings. That symbolic gift let me know that Lacy wanted to have children with me at some point in our future—as the song goes, "A girl for you, a boy for me!" I thought to myself, *What a wonderful gesture as to what was to come!*.

We spent the rest of the summer getting ready for our big move to Wisconsin. First on Lacy's agenda was selling his beloved GTO. He said that his racing days were over and that he wouldn't need that type of muscle car in Wisconsin. So, he traded it in for a little yellow Volkswagen Beatle. You would have thought that a member of our family had died, we mourned that GTO so. But *c'est la vie*, that's life. It was a choice and a sacrifice that Lacy felt he had to make.

As for me, I wasn't quite ready to let my beloved Firebird go just yet. I decided to take it with me to Wisconsin. I didn't know where I would be working, and I knew I would need transportation, so I decided to hold on to my Green Hornet.

Second, we arranged for a long-haul trucking company to pick up our furniture for the long trip to Wisconsin. We went with a well-known company, American Van Lines, to carry all of our possessions that we had worked so hard for during our first year of marriage, including our living room, bedroom, and kitchen items. There was one exception: our replaced stereo component set that Lacy bought after the first one was stolen. Lacy decided to take that prized possession by car. He wasn't taking any more chances. He didn't want to trust anyone with his source of music, no one but himself.

We arranged for the truck to pick everything else up before we were due to drive to Wisconsin. The van was to pick up our things on the last Thursday of July, and we would drive up on the last Friday. That way, by Monday or Tuesday, we would get our furniture.

THE ROAD TRIP

We decided to ask someone to drive with each of us for the sixteen-hour road trip so that we could get both of our cars to Madison. George asked another one of his best friends named David, David Bennett, who loved to drive, to help us make the trip. I asked my sister, Vee, and she said yes. She was used to driving a long distance from DC to Penn State and saw the trip to Wisconsin as a break she could use to clear her head prior to her return to Happy Valley and her doctoral studies.

When it was time to leave, we packed up both cars with mostly clothes, plus, of course, the stereo and Lacy's album collection. Surprisingly, he was able to get all of his stuff into his new Yellow Bug and we covered everything with sleeping bags. I was able to fit some clothes and shoes I was taking into my Firebird. Of course, we both had to make room for our second drivers and their overnight bags. When we were done, we made sure the apartment was clean and empty. We turned in our keys, took one last walk to our cars, and turned to say goodbye to our honeymoon love nest one last time: a fond farewell to a challenging, enlightening, and wonderful year. "Goodbye, Penn Southern," we said as we got into our respective cars and fled that scene.

We stayed with Lacy's mother overnight to get some sleep so we could be fresh and wide awake for the long drive to Wisconsin. We woke up about four in the morning, said our goodbyes, picked up our second drivers, and got on the road to Wisconsin around six o'clock. Lacy had mapped out our trip, and if all went well, with just one rest stop in each state, we figured that the four of us would arrive in Madison in about sixteen hours.

Up Route 70 North we went, on that old familiar road we often drove through Maryland. By daybreak, we had made it to our first stop, Breezewood, Pennsylvania—a popular pit stop when we drove to Pittsburgh to see Lacy's Aunt Ruth. We got a wake-up drink (the others got coffee, but I didn't drink coffee at that time) and a breakfast snack at a familiar restaurant. However, instead of heading to Pittsburgh, this time we were heading to Ohio.

After our first stop, we were in unfamiliar territory. It was *follow our noses* and our maps northwest through all of the interstates until we got to Wisconsin. After Pennsylvania, we hit the Ohio Interstate, where there was very little to see but farmland and rows and rows of cornfields. The same was pretty much true of Indiana until we got to see the golden dome of Notre Dame University. It was breathtaking and a landmark that would be an indicator for the next few years that we were a little more than halfway to Madison. We stopped to rest and eat.

In Illinois, there was a little more to see. Vee was driving at the time, and as we got closer to Chicago, there were factories and other industrial landmarks. As we drove around it, we could see the Chicago skyline. It was awesome. I had never been to Chicago before, so I looked forward to visits we would take there when we needed a break from Madison. We couldn't wait to get into some Chicago nightlife.

The Chicago skyline would become our landmark that we were a little over three hours away from Wisconsin and Madison. We stopped for the last time outside of Chicago to get a bite of Illinois-inspired fare. Of course, that would be the deep-dish pizza that Chi Town was known for, and Wisconsin also—the Cheese State.

We arrived in Madison around ten o'clock that night. I was so glad to see the Madison capitol dome and State Street, which would take us to our new crib. We were so tired, we barely had the energy to unpack our two cars, but we managed.

We immediately noticed how cool Madison's August summer nights were: about 65 degrees, a big and refreshing change from the hot, sticky late summer nights in DC. Vee and David loved our new crib. They kept commenting on how super-modern it was with all the latest designs in apartment living, and in the heart of downtown Madison.

Since our furniture hadn't arrived yet, Lacy and I had bought and brought four sleeping bags by car for the four of us to sleep in. Exhausted, we rolled them out on top of our shag carpet, one in each corner of the room. We had the last of the food and drinks that were left over from our trip, took turns using our ultra-modern bathroom to get into our PJs, and settled into our respective sleeping bags for a night's sleep in Madison. It felt like an adventure, as if the four of us were on a camping trip.

I don't remember anything else. We fell fast asleep. Lacy and I had finally made it to our new location and our new life together. The rest of our days and nights in Madison would prove to be interesting, enlightening, and life-changing.

NINE
TWO AFFIRMATIVE ACTION BADGERS

WE SPENT OUR first day as Madison residents unpacking the household items and clothes that we had brought with us by car and showing our fellow drivers, Vee and David, around Madison. At the end of the day, Lacy and I treated them to dinner and a movie. We had Chicago-style pizza at a pizzeria and walked to the closest theatre near our apartment. We got out of the movie around eight o'clock, just before dark.

Shocking to the four of us, it was about 45 degrees—in August. That crazy George Lacy had worn Bermuda shorts all day. He was so cold when we left the movie theatre, he left us in the dust and ran all the way home. He said, "See y'all back at the crib" and took off running. We laughed at him all the way home, and I thought to myself, *I will tell this funny story to our grandkids someday.* Back at our new crib, we spent the rest of the evening putting the stereo component set together, relaxing, listening to 1970s music, and enjoying a bottle of wine.

On our first Sunday in Madison, we helped our fellow drivers pack the one suitcase they each had brought with them for their plane ride back to DC. We drove them to the airport in my Firebird for the flight back to Washington. It was Vee's first time flying, so she was really nervous. I assured her everything would be just fine as she and David boarded their flight. Off they flew, leaving the two of us behind to fend for ourselves.

As their plane took off, I realized that it was just the two us, Lacy and me, to take on Madison, Wisconsin, together. That was it, *"Just the two of us,"* as Bill Withers would sing about. Madison would make or break us. We were determined that it would be the former.

I spent my first week in Madison looking for a job. I was confident I would land something. I was qualified, had a little experience, and was a black female who could help an organization kill two birds in the minority category with one stone. One African American and one female in one package: that was me. I had no problem with that.

By the end of that first week in Madison, I had two job offers. One was with the State of Wisconsin (the largest employer in Madison beside the university), as a management analyst, and the other was as an operations manager with Oscar Meyer, the largest wiener company in the United States and the third largest employer in Madison. Although the Oscar Meyer job seemed interesting, paid more money, and would be something different in the private sector to put on my résumé, for several reasons, I chose to play it safe and easy and go with the white-collar desk job with the State of Wisconsin.

The job I accepted was in the Office of Energy Conservation, which was a big thing in America and the State of Wisconsin in the early 1970s. My assigned immediate supervisor was a young white guy from Wisconsin who was married with a young son. He was a graduate of UW and passionate about saving the environment. Surprisingly, we had a lot in common and hit it off quite well.

My job was within walking distance from our apartment and close to the university. After all, I did plan to continue with my MBA and take one or two classes during Lacy's first semester at UW. So, I spent my second week in Madison enrolling in the MBA program at the business school at the university, which was conveniently right next door to the law school.

By the end of August 1973, Lacy and I were settling into our new life in Wisconsin. I must admit, though, I had a harder time adjusting to the culture shock than he did. I was more homesick and missed my life in DC more than he did. George, who had never lived outside of DC and had not gone away to undergraduate school, viewed Wisconsin as one great adventure, as did many of his law school classmates. There were forty incoming minority students in the LEO law school program (the largest incoming minority group in the law school's history) as part of their affirmative action plan, and they hit it off pretty well. Although the students came from all over the US and the Caribbean, they bonded together quickly. They had no choice, I guess, if they were going to make it in UW's law school.

Lacy quickly brought me into his fold and introduced me to most of his new law school buddies. There were only a handful of girls, and he made sure I met them so I would have some females to talk to. Two of his classmates were from DC and my age—one male and one female. Both were single and we hit it off right away. To this day, I remain friends with both of them. I also became friends with some of the wives of Lacy's classmates.

The LEO students quickly established small study groups based on subject matter, and our small apartment was often where those small groups met, given our close proximity to the campus. And of course, I made sure there was always food and drinks for those meetings, so 424 W. Dayton Street became one place they could come to study and get a good home-cooked meal at the same time.

As for me, I went to work at the state capitol during the day and took MBA classes in the evening that first semester. That kept me quite busy, with little time for a campus life of my own. I didn't have much time to meet or make friends with any of my MBA classmates at that time. An occasional hello or greeting before and/or after class was all I could muster. During the week, for me, it was work, study, go to class, and study some more, only to repeat the same routine the next day.

I looked forward to the weekends, when I enjoyed taking little breaks from studying to cook a nice meal for us, especially Sunday dinner. On occasion, Lacy and I would both take a break from intense studying, which could be as much as twelve hours or more on both Saturday and Sunday, to take in a movie or explore a restaurant or another attraction around downtown Madison. Those early days in Madison seemed to bring us closer together as a couple: the two of us against the world.

As a couple, we tried to stay physically fit. We walked everywhere, especially to and from the main campus, since there was very little parking on the side of the campus where we lived. The parking lots that were available were on the other side of the campus, much farther away from the law school and business school than our apartment was. It was much quicker and easier to walk everywhere: to and from school, out to eat, to the movies, and to almost all of our extracurricular activities on and off campus. Lacy worked out at the gym on campus on his short breaks to keep his mind sharp and his body strong. Immediately, he began to lose weight, and I noticed his body becoming more muscular and refined.

We also decided as a couple that we would try new things in Madison while we were there, things that we had never tried before, such as hatha yoga and transcendental meditation. I decided that I would sign up for ballet and other dance classes, such as belly dancing, while we were there. After all, it was the early 1970s, and we were living in Madison, a hippy center of the Midwest. Why not try some new things that we would never think about trying in DC? We called it broadening our horizons.

THE BIKE RIDE

When we weren't walking, we would take out our bikes, which we had brought with us from DC, to go riding occasionally along one of the many bike trails that wove around the lakes and the outskirts of Madison. One of our bike rides changed our outlook, and almost our fate, as new residents of Madison.

It was a sunny Saturday afternoon in the late fall of 1973, just before Thanksgiving and final exam time. We decided to take a break from studying to take a bike ride. We chose a bike trail a little inland but adjacent to one of the lakes. It was a lovely, somewhat cool Wisconsin afternoon, perfect for a bike ride. I wore my usual for that time of year: a pair of blue jeans that I rolled up so as not to catch into the bike petal, a warm sweater, a biker jacket, and a pair of tennis shoes. Lacy had on the same.

As we often did in DC in Rock Creek Park, we started out riding side by side, but as usual, being shorter and weaker, I would fall behind, only to have Lacy slow down periodically and wait for me to catch up. That happened about halfway into our ride. I fell behind, and Lacy was about a quarter of a mile ahead of me. The trail had a curve in it, so I lost sight of him, but I knew he would slow down and I would catch up to him once we caught sight of one another.

All of a sudden, four young white guys rode up from behind me. Two came up beside me, one on each side; the other two rode behind me. At first, I didn't feel threatened. They looked like young undergraduate students. But then they started to get a little too close for comfort. Before I knew it, I was surrounded.

So, I sped up, as fast as I could, standing up on my pedals. They pursued, and I was unable to get distance from them. One of them caught up to me and smacked me on my behind, saying, "I sure would like to have some of that!"

I swatted his hand away and said, "Stop it, you jerk!"

One of them said, "I know you liked that!"

I sped up some more, and they continued to harass me. Well, that did it. I yelled out to Lacy, "Help! Lacy, help!"

By then, I had cleared the curve in the road and Lacy could see me and had heard my cry for help. He had turned his bike around and was speeding toward us. I stopped and jumped off my bike. But so did those four guys.

By that time, Lacy was right there and brought his bike to a screeching halt. He jumped off his bike and asked, "What do you guys think you're doing?"

The smartass that felt my butt said, "What's it to you?"

Lacy said, "That's my wife, you jackass!"

The two of them by then were face-to-face, eyeball-to-eyeball. The other three came closer to Lacy as well. So Lacy, a black belt in karate, took a karate stance and began to make some impressive karate moves. I begged him not to fight those dudes, but Lacy went berserk and started toward them with his karate moves, confronting the guy that hit me on my butt. Before we knew it, Lacy had the guy in a chokehold. It was more like wrestling than karate.

I yelled, "Lacy, please don't hurt him! He's not worth it. Don't get put out of school for hurting or killing one these guys. They are so not worth it!"

Well, that did it. He must have frightened the hell out of those young punks. They jumped on their bikes and sped away, peddling as fast as their legs could go. Lacy and I had dodged a big bullet.

Pulling our bikes over from the middle of the trail, Lacy asked me if I was OK. I told him I was fine, just shook up a little—and not from getting smacked on the behind. I was more concerned about the consequences that could have resulted from a confrontation like that one—a black couple on a deserted bike trail, confronted by four white guys in a majority-white environment.

The gall of those young punks! They were testing out their dominance, and in the end, all of our egos got the best of us. I felt violated, those guys felt threatened, and Lacy felt he had to defend his manhood and his woman: a bad combination that could have been disastrous.

Standing on the side of the trail, Lacy and I were relieved. We started to laugh. We had dodged a bullet that could have ended the goals and dreams that we'd made for ourselves when we decided to go to Wisconsin. He could have been put out of school for fighting, and that could have ended his dream of becoming a lawyer, all because of my ass. We turned our bikes around, and Lacy said, "Let's go home."

For a moment, I yearned for DC, missing our families and friends and our real hometown, but I knew what he meant. Madison, Wisconsin, was now our home, and we were going to make the best of it.

We couldn't help but think of a phrase from one of James Brown's songs: "I might not know karate, but I know C-R-A-Z-Y." We laughed and sang that bar of the song all the way home. Lacy was my hero that day. We never rode on that bike trail again.

But guess what? That wasn't the only time my jeans, a biker jacket, and my ass got attention. On another Saturday afternoon that fall, while I was quickly walking down State Street on my way home from the library, another white guy, this one a little older, came up from behind me and said, "Excuse me, Miss! Has anyone ever told you that your jeans talk from behind when you are walking down the street? They dance, they talk, and they tell a story. I'm just observing!" With that, he smiled and walked ahead of me.

Well, that did it for me. Embarrassed, I ducked into the corner market, bought a couple of items for dinner, and quickly walked the rest of the way home. When I got there, I couldn't help but look in the mirror, trying see what that guy was talking about. The back pockets of my jeans had designs on them, and when I walked, those designs moved up and down. So, I said to myself, *I get it! My jeans are too tight and my butt is too round, so stop showing it off.*

I never told Lacy about that conversation. Instead, I stopped wearing tight jeans and biker jackets. I wore loose jeans, covered by longer jackets, shirts, or sweaters that covered up my butt. Now, it wasn't that I was overweight. I weighed all of 108 to 110 pounds. It's just that I had what I thought all along was a typical black girl's butt: round and curvy. I guess that was odd to some guys in Wisconsin. So, I decided not to take any more chances and became more self-conscious and conservative about what body parts I showed off. Anyways, by the time I changed up my wardrobe, it was starting to get cold in Madison;

time to shed the short jackets for longer, heavier coats, warm socks, and boots.

Between my butt, my curly bush hairstyle, and my brown skin, there were a lot of odd comments and questions thrown my way during our stay in Madison, such as "Does your brown skin turn the water brown when you wash?" and "How do you get your hair to stand up like that?" (referring to my Afro hairstyle). Lacy got similar questions. Little kids asked to touch his bush. Most of the comments, we laughed about. Although it bothered us a little, we took most of that nonsense in stride. We saw many of those inquiries more as curiosity and ignorance than prejudice. We took it all in for what it was, without getting too offended. Instead, we stayed focused on our reason for being in Madison. We stayed focused on our goals. We kept our eyes on the prize (our degrees) and not the people.

THE CULTURE SHOCK

That first semester in Madison was an eye-opener and quite interesting, to say the least. As a couple, Lacy and I got to know more about ourselves individually, about us as a couple, and a lot more about life, especially life outside of Washington, DC. We slowly adjusted to our new life away from our hometown and our familiar DC culture.

We studied hard, worked hard, and loved hard. We leaned on and loved on one another. As a couple, we got closer than I ever thought imaginable, knowing that we would make it because we had one another. I felt sorry for the black students who were in Madison all alone. I couldn't imagine being there and making it without my soul mate. That familiar tune comes to mind again and again, about our early days in Madison: "Just the Two of Us" by Bill Withers.

However, the transition into the Madison culture appeared to be more difficult for me than for Lacy. He made friends quickly at the law school and settled into a routine that he was happy with. He went to school, studied, worked out physically, and socialized with his new friends.

Balancing a job full time and school part time was not that difficult for me. After all, I had done it before in DC. My job at the State House in Madison was going well. My federal government experience gave me a leg up, and my knowledge of the federal laws and policies coming out of Washington when it came to energy conservation brought me professional respect and made me the go-to person on the subject. The money was good, and I put most of my salary in the bank toward that house we wanted to buy when we returned to DC. We lived very modestly in Madison and didn't need much money to live on to be happy. We had a comfortable lifestyle.

Yet at home and socially, I felt somewhat left out. You see, Madison was really a college town. If you weren't deeply connected with and into the university, like Lacy was and many of my work colleagues were, you didn't have much of a social life. Just going to school part time didn't do it for me. I didn't make a lot of friends that way, so I was not a happy camper. I became a loner, both at work and at school.

So, I decided to do something about that. I decided to quit my job at the end of the year, sell my Firebird, and return to school full time that January of 1974. I gave notice at my job and told them that I would be leaving in December. My young supervisor was disappointed, but understanding. He knew exactly where I was coming from in that he had very close ties to the university. His life revolved around the university.

I told him I would make sure my projects were off the ground and running smoothly and would be willing to train my replacement. He seemed to appreciate the advance notice and agreed to a transition period. I didn't want to leave them totally high and dry. They quickly found a new analyst with the help of the university's placement office, and by late November, I began the transfer of knowledge to my replacement, a new graduate of the university. That led to a smooth transition, at least to me.

As for my beloved Firebird, I sold my Green Hornet to one of Lacy's law school buddies who lived in our apartment building. Bob was a well-off New Yorker and a single bachelor who needed a nice ride to get around Madison. I made him a sweet deal. I would charge him the balance of the loan on the car if he was willing to pay cash for it, and he agreed. I paid off the loan on the car, and the fellas had the title transferred over to his name. The guys considered the transaction as one of their first legal agreements. I considered it a done deal, and that was that.

THANKSGIVING DAY 1973

Before we knew it, our first Thanksgiving in Madison was upon us. Lacy's mother reminded us that we had family living nearby. One of her sister-in-law's nieces, Martha, had recently graduated with a doctorate from UW and was a newlywed too, living in Milwaukee.

We had heard a lot about Martha. She had attended North Carolina A&T University and had taken Madison by storm. A former majorette at A&T and a professional model, she was drop-dead gorgeous and became the first black Miss Wisconsin on Madison's campus. We had talked on the phone several times. Anxious to meet two newlyweds like ourselves, we invited them to come to Thanksgiving dinner at our little place in Madison.

As I always did in DC, I cleaned up our place and went to the market and bought a small turkey with all the trimmings for a dinner for four. It was quite inexpensive and healthy, when you think about it. Along with items I already had at the house, I remember spending less than thirty dollars on the entire meal for four people. That beat going out to dinner any night of the week.

I made a Waldorf salad as our first course, and we had turkey, green beans, mashed potatoes, and sweet potatoes as our main course. Of course, I made a batch of strawberry daiquiris to serve along with nonalcoholic beverages, and I made a pineapple coconut cake for dessert, to be served with vanilla ice cream.

Martha and her new husband, a Jewish guy from New York City named Arnold (Arnie) Graf, arrived at our place right on time, at three o'clock. The Redskins were playing Dallas that Thanksgiving Day, so they arrived just before kickoff, as requested.

The game started off well, and the Redskins took an early lead. I served dinner right at halftime, with the Redskins carrying a comfortable lead of 16 to 3 early into the third quarter. You see, Dallas's star quarterback, Roger Staubach, was hurt, so they were missing their superstar playmaker. The four of us were having a good time, but I was still nervous, with memories of my spoiled Super Bowl party just that past February.

We talked about a lot of things: what it was like to be from the East Coast and going to graduate school in Madison, and what it was like being newlyweds in an environment like Wisconsin. Martha and Arnie were a little older than Lacy and me, and they gave us good counsel, having completed their journey in Madison just ahead of us. They both had doctorates in social work and were working in Milwaukee, but they planned to move to California the following year. Yet they had not ruled out moving back East. The four of us hit it off quite well.

Well, as fate would have it, the Redskins found a way to blow that lead. With a backup quarterback named Clint Longley who threw for two touchdowns in the third quarter, Dallas took the lead 17–16. As always, the Redskins toyed with my emotions and took the lead back in the fourth quarter with a touchdown, making the score 23–17.

But, lo and behold, the football gods showed no mercy, and with twenty-eight seconds to go, that Clint Longley threw a fifty-yard touchdown pass to Drew Pearson, and Dallas, by making the extra point after the touchdown, won the game by one point (24–23), making that Thanksgiving game one of the most memorable, and one of my most miserable Redskins/Cowboys games ever.

Again, I vowed *never* to have a dinner party (or host Thanksgiving dinner) when the Redskins were playing anybody, especially the Cowboys. However, although the Redskins lost the game and I was upset almost to the point of being sick about it, that Thanksgiving dinner of 1973 was quite memorable and was the beginning of a long tradition of shared Thanksgiving dinners between the Lacys and the Grafs for many years to come.

FINAL EXAMS AND CHRISTMAS

As soon as Thanksgiving was over, it was time to study for final exams. My last day on the job was November 30, 1973. I wanted to give myself plenty of time to study for my finals and to be there for Lacy as he prepared for the final exams of his first semester of law school.

My study period was a piece of cake compared to undergraduate school when I always had an overload of classes, trying to graduate early, and when I was at George Washington and working full time. I only had two easy classes, so I budgeted my time, and studying came easy. I got through my two finals like a charm. That left plenty of time for me to be a support blanket for Lacy, and did he need it.

I had never seen Lacy study and work at something so hard. He showed me a determination that I hadn't seen in him before. From Thanksgiving until his last final, he studied night and day. He studied at the library at the law school well into the early evening. I made sure I made him a decent dinner, yet not too heavy. After dinner, he studied some more. He sometimes took a short break or nap, only to study in his little study area at home well into the night. He was a night owl, and I left him up studying just about every night during finals time. I was the early bird and made sure he got up early enough to go over his notes and get to his final exams on time.

Before we knew it, final exams were all over. Boy, were we glad! Now it was wait and see, especially for my beloved. I got my results early: an A and a B for a solid 3.5 average. Lacy waited for his results. Unlike my grades, the law students got numerical scores. They needed a 70+ average to be considered passing. We passed the time by starting to pack our bags for our flight back to DC for the Christmas holiday.

Lacy periodically walked up to the law school to check for his grades. I would get on my sewing machine to calm my nerves. Sewing a new outfit always did the trick for me. After one of his trips to the law school and back, Lacy came storming through the door, with icicles hanging from his mustache, shouting, "Nettie, Nettie, where are you?"

I jumped away from the sewing machine and ran toward the front door. He lifted me off my feet and shouted, "I made it. I passed. I passed."

He had done it. He had passed all of his finals with over an 80 average, with a few points to spare. I was so happy for him. He twirled me around and around until I was dizzy. He acted as if he couldn't believe it. But I knew he could do it. I saw the drive and the determination. I knew deep in my soul that he had it in him and that he was well on his way to making it in law school and in his field. Deep down, he knew it too.

We couldn't wait to get back to DC with the good news. We caught the first flight we could get out of Madison. Back home, Mama Lacy had a hero's welcome waiting for us. She had one of the best Christmas dinners ever, with her usual delightful meals, served in shifts for both sides of the family. On my side of the family, no one was happier for both of us than Mom, Dad, and Vee.

There was gift-giving all around. Everyone was so proud of us. Knowing that we had passed our classes and would stay in Madison for the duration, everyone gave us warm gifts to get us through Wisconsin's brutal winters. We got sweaters and scarves, in Wisconsin's red and white colors, and "snuggy" underwear to keep our butts warm. That was hilarious.

We made our rounds and saw as many friends as we could, and even borrowed Mama Lacy's car and took a side trip to Richmond, Virginia, to see Lacy's dad. Well into his seventies, Lacy Sr. was bedridden in a nursing home and paralyzed from the neck down from his last stroke.

But he seemed to understand everything Lacy Jr. said to him, and when Lacy Jr. talked about making it through his first semester of law school and passing all of his classes, a tear trickled down the side of Lacy Sr.'s face. It seemed to be a tear of joy, one of approval.

Lacy Sr. was a legendary black military war hero, a Kappa Man, an attorney and Renaissance man. He had attended the infamous M Street High School in Washington, DC, for free up-and-coming colored youth, where he ran track and graduated in 1915. An accomplished musician, Lacy Sr. moved to New York City during the Harlem Renaissance and attended New York University while playing in a band. When WWI broke out, he joined the 15th New York National Guard Regiment, which later became the famous 369th Infantry Regiment, better known as the Harlem Hellfighters, who fought in France in French uniforms under French command. Lacy Sr. served as a first lieutenant, which was rare for a black man, to be an officer, at that time.

The Harlem Hellfighters spent 191 days in combat, longer than any other American unit, and never lost ground to the Germans. Their band is said to have introduced jazz to Europe. They received a regimental Croix de Guerre, a French military decoration for bravery, yet returned to the US to the same segregation and discrimination from the countrymen they'd defended that existed before the war. While in Europe, Lacy Sr. was made a member of Kappa Alpha Psi Fraternity, Inc. on November 5, 1918.

Returning to New York City to a hero's welcome, Lacy Sr. met and married classical singer Cleota Collins and moved to her native Ohio, where he attended and graduated from Ohio State, (also rare for a black man) while working as a bandleader. He later graduated from John Marshall Law School and was admitted to the Ohio Bar in 1928. He became an assistant prosecutor in Cleveland and later ran as a Democrat for public office.

He re-entered the army and served as an officer in WWII. After the war, he returned to DC as a divorcé, where he set up a law practice in the Shaw area near Howard University and met and married Lacy

Jr.'s mother. The couple settled in the Brookland home where, after divorcing, Mamie and Lacy Jr. remained.

We had dinner with Lacy Sr.'s fourth wife—who, by the way, was also a nurse. She had the same first name as Lacy Jr.'s mom, Mamie, but spelled hers Mamye. She discussed Lacy Sr.'s health and other family and legal matters with Junior, as they called him. She was very nice to me and apologized for not making our wedding, though they both were invited. She cited Mr. Lacy's health as the reason they didn't attend, and I certainly understood that. She was very gracious and seemed to be happy for Junior and his latest accomplishments.

We made our way back to DC from Richmond to enjoy the rest of our Christmas holiday and brought in the New Year in DC before returning to Madison on January 2nd to register the next day for the second semester. I carried out my plan and registered for a full-time load of MBA classes for the spring. Classes were to start in mid-January. I was able to get an affirmative action scholarship that covered all of my tuition and fees.

After registering, we went back to our crib to relax and kick back for the few days we had left before classes started. We had a few days to chill and even thought about driving down to Chicago for a couple of days to have a little fun in Chi Town. While we were relaxing and watching TV at home, the phone rang. It was the other Mamye, Lacy's stepmother. I heard him say, "What? Oh my God! OK. We will pack right away. We will get to Richmond as soon as possible."

After hanging up the phone, Lacy informed me that George Lacy Sr., Esq., had died and that we needed to quickly pack and rush back to DC to pick up Lacy's mom's car and get to Richmond as soon as possible for the funeral. He immediately got on the phone to make plane arrangements for us to get home. They only had two first-class seats available the next day, so we grabbed them. That was my first time flying first-class anywhere.

We made it back home to DC and to Richmond before the funeral; Lacy Sr.'s wife made sure of that. The funeral was small yet very nice and dignified. Lacy Sr. was buried in a Richmond cemetery with military honors, given his service as an officer in both WWI and WWII. At the repast, Lacy and I got to meet and greet several people from the Lacy side of the family, some whom he had met before, some he had just heard about, and some he had never heard of before. Miss Mamye also filled in some gaps about the Lacy side of the family in our conversations with her after the funeral. I learned a lot. We both did.

Still mourning George Lacy Sr., the two of us returned to Madison a couple of days after the funeral, just in time to start school for the second semester of the 1973–74 school year. It seemed to me that Lacy's father had waited and had died at peace, knowing that his son would be OK. He was proud that his son was on his way to carrying on his legal legacy.

The spring semester flew by quickly. We made it through our first winter in Madison and all the snow that came with it. We stayed bundled up and took pictures walking in the snow and standing on the frozen lake, taking it all in stride. We took breaks from studying by going to Milwaukee several times to see the Bucks basketball team play, with Lew Alcindor (who later changed his name to Kareem Abdul Jabbar) and Oscar Robinson, and to see Earth, Wind, and Fire and War, respectively, in concert, two of our favorite rock bands. We also escaped to Chicago for a romantic weekend at the famous Playboy Club during spring break.

We both had a successful winter semester grade-wise. I made new friends in the business school and felt like I was part of the university community, just what I had been craving. Several of the girls in the B-School had husbands in the law school or medical school, and we became instant friends. My social life expanded, and I continued to expand my horizons by taking ballet, yoga classes and transcendental meditation (TM). TM was a technique of relaxation and introspection that I took to like white on rice. It would come in handy as an important tool in my toolbox for success.

A highlight that semester for me was a call from my department chair that resulted in me landing my first consulting job. As I mentioned before, our country was struggling with the concept of *affirmative action*, which had been placed into the equal employment laws by an executive order under President Lyndon Johnson. All federal, state, and local governments were required to have an affirmative action plan to include more women and minorities into their ranks, and every public school system throughout the country was included in that.

The assistant superintendent for the Madison Public Schools (a young black guy) had called the business school asking for help in crafting an affirmative action plan for Madison's public schools. As a management major specializing in human resource management and a former federal government employee, I had learned a lot about the affirmative action guidelines set down by the Feds. I fit the bill of having the knowledge, with an added bonus of being a black woman—something known as a *twofer*. Me being a woman and a minority, any organization would get "two for one" and could count me in each category. After my interview, which went very well, I was offered the consulting job and gladly accepted it.

On days when I didn't have class and in my spare time, I proudly assisted the Madison school system in drafting its very first affirmative action plan to hire more women and minorities into every level of employment: teachers, staff, and administrators. Once again, I felt I was part of US history. I also liked the independence that consulting provided: the flexible hours and being paid well by the day. It was a rewarding experience, and I felt I made another contribution to the civil rights movement by providing more opportunities to women and minorities in the employment arena. I also fell in love with management consulting, which would become a major part of my future.

At the end of our first academic year in Madison, Lacy and I both decided to go to summer school. I would be able to finish my MBA that summer by taking two more classes, and Lacy could move toward graduating early from law school. We signed up for summer school in May while still wearing winter coats, because it was still that cold in Madison. I will never forget putting on layers of clothes, an orange wrap coat, a hat, gloves, and boots to climb Bascom Hill to sign up for summer school.

I said to myself, *People back home will never believe this!* So, I stopped to take a picture to show everyone what spring could be like in Wisconsin. Yes, snow was still on the ground, and the lakes were still icy. A native Madisonian told me that was not atypical for early May in Madison. I said, "You gotta be kidding. Snow on the ground in May? That is unheard of in DC."

Like most large universities, UW had two six-week sessions of summer school: one from mid-May through June 30, and one from early July through mid-August. I only needed two classes to complete my MBA, so I took them both the first session. Lacy took two classes at the law school also. So, at the end of the first summer school session, that was it for me. I was done with my master's degree. Hip, hip hooray!

I was the proud recipient of an MBA (master's in business administration) degree, a coveted prize that many business majors, sought from business schools around the world. At that time, the University of Wisconsin's business school was ranked number ten in the United States and as one of the best throughout the world. I considered myself lucky and was quite proud to possess such a prestigious degree from such an outstanding school.

Rather than stick around to attend the summer school graduation ceremony, we rushed home to DC, unable to stay away from family and friends for long. Our best man, David, threw me a surprise graduation party at Lacy's request at his bachelor pad in College Park, Maryland, where he had thrown Lacy's infamous bachelor party.

My graduation party was out of this world as well. All of the usual suspects, as we called our friends, were there: almost our entire wedding party and many of our friends from high school and undergraduate school. Food and drinks were abundant, and we partied until the break of dawn. At that time, David was still a security officer at the University of Maryland, but he was in training to become a Maryland state trooper, so everything was nice and legal, and everyone had a great time and got home safely. I couldn't dream up a better "Best Man," one that would have our backs for the rest of our lives.

TEN
A ROAD LESS TRAVELED

THE DAY AFTER celebrating the Fourth of July of 1974 in DC, Lacy and I flew back to Madison, where Lacy signed up for the second session of summer school. For the first time in my life in a while, I had a lot of free time on my hands. It was ironic that with a brand-new MBA degree, I was not in school and had no job, because I had not had any time to think about anything except finishing my MBA degree.

So now, I had time to think. What was I going to do with the rest of my life? Should I get a job and put my MBA to work? Should I go into real estate, which was red-hot back then? Should I have the baby that I so much wanted by that time? Or should I stay in school while Lacy was still in school, since there was scholarship money still available?

I thought long and hard. I talked to some of the MBAs who had graduated before me and to some of my fellow Lincoln Lions and Lionesses. Many were unhappy with their nine-to-five gigs, with the grind of their jobs, and with the US establishment. Some of my Lincoln classmates had even committed suicide under the pressure. One guy from DC jumped off a bridge, and one of my friends who served on the Kappa Court with me jumped out of a window. How sad, when life gets that bad!

I also thought back to my first consulting job I'd had that spring. I remembered how much freedom I'd had to be creative with my solutions, to come and go as I pleased, to set my own hours, and to work at my own pace. And the money was great, too. I was paid by the day and dealt with my own taxes. I knew I would have to work to help Lacy and live the way we wanted to live, but I was concerned about having children and a nine-to-five professional career. How would our children turn out? I had heard that so many of them wound up "wilding out" and resenting their professional parents. I remembered a quote by Jacqueline Kennedy in making similar decisions about her children: "You are only as successful as how your children turn out to be."

And what about the toll on me? What toll would working and having a family have on me, physically and mentally? And what about the toll on our marriage? I had heard awful things about that as well. Could a woman really have it all: a successful career, a good marriage, and good children?

THE PH.D. DECISION

After much thought, I decided to at least try to have it all, and if that didn't work, I could always say, "Oh well, at least I tried." I decided not to go the corporate route, though, with the nine-to-five and more—the long hours of leaving home in the dark and coming home in the dark, as many of my fellow MBAs had described to me. I decided that since Lacy had at most two more years of law school, I would stay in school too and seek a Ph.D., which would allow me to teach at the university level and do consulting work in order to make up some of the difference of what I could make in corporate pay. I knew that I would never be filthy rich like my Wall Street friends, but I figured I could make a decent high five or six figures.

I decided to let George Lacy be the chief breadwinner and my salary would be the backup to his. I wanted to be able to take our kids to school and pick them up. I wanted to be able to get home from work at a decent hour in order to cook a decent meal (at least sometimes) and to still have enough energy to play with the children after dinner and help them with their homework. Yes, I wanted a career and to be a great housewife, too. Many researchers said that was impossible. But you know me by now. I wasn't afraid to try the impossible: to do something that the average person wouldn't or couldn't do and do it well enough to prove the naysayers wrong.

So, after thinking long and hard, I went up to the university to research Ph.D. programs related to my degree in business, and I found one that was quite different and unique, one that would give me more freedom and flexibility in my life. UW had a research institute that offered a Ph.D. in industrial relations. It was an interdisciplinary degree that required you to take courses in business, economics, law, and the humanities to get a thorough understanding of the field. UW's program was well known, popular on campus, and ranked second in the world, only behind Cornell University, a private Ivy League school on the East Coast.

I found the industrial relations field and the degree to be just what I was looking for. Graduates of the program generally went on to work for human resources departments in private businesses, unions, and nonprofits, or for government agencies to help employers and employees come to terms of agreement on wages, hours, and working conditions. I felt that with a Ph.D. in industrial relations, wherever I worked, I would be able to help workers. Or I could teach and do research in the field at the university level and, in a way, accomplish the same goal. That was very appealing to me.

Dr. Miller, the director of the research institute, was very open and honest with me. He told me that the courses were rigorous and research-oriented. He told me that my MBA grades were good enough and that I met all the requirements to qualify for the program. As a side note, he added that the program was male-dominated. I just smiled about that, given my Lincoln U. experience. Then he reluctantly mentioned that there had only been three African American males and no African American females in the program. I asked if I would be the first black female then, and he said yes.

There was an awkward silence in the room. I said to myself, *I've been down this road before. What else you gonna throw at me? I've been in the minority all my life! Nothing new and nothing I can't handle!*

Finally, Dr. Miller talked about scholarship money. Because the program was small, he said that there was very little scholarship money available. After consulting with the financial aid office, I found out that because I had finished the MBA program so quickly, I still had a significant balance in my minority university-wide scholarship account that the university had given me, and that it could be used for the Ph.D. program of my choice. I was being given the opportunity and the means to accomplish my goal. I decided to go for a Ph.D. degree that would give me more freedom of time and flexibility in life. That's really what I wanted.

A NEW START

So, that August, I enrolled in the Industrial Relations Research Institute as the first African American female *ever* in the program at the Ph.D. level. Dr. Miller was happy to have a first in his program and for the scholarship that came with me. He could proudly boast about both and count them among his achievements as director of the institute.

Par for the course, I signed up for as many classes as possible so I could finish as quickly as possible. But as you know, sometimes the best-laid plans can be disturbed by obstacles and distractions. My first year as a Ph.D. candidate turned out to be quite a task, as I would face issues and challenges that I had neither anticipated nor planned for. Life can throw arrows at you that can jack you up, shake your confidence, and knock you off your game. For me, that's when *perseverance, hope, and determination* (PHD) came to my rescue to knock those arrows out of my way.

The industrial relations (IR) program was interdisciplinary in nature, requiring Ph.D. students to take classes in several disciplines, so I bounced between classes in the business school, arts and sciences, and the law school, where I was able to meet more graduate students and would get to see my husband during the day more often. And when we didn't see one another on campus, we would meet up at home for dinner.

As often was the case in Madison, summer quickly turned into winter. It got bitter cold quickly, with a sudden drop in temperature into the teens. One of those cold days, when I got home from campus, I found Lacy on the floor of our bedroom, sitting up against the bed, gasping for air. It was as if he was trying to get into bed but couldn't quite make it. He said he couldn't breathe, so I helped him to his feet, got him into the Yellow Bug, and rushed him to the emergency room of Madison General Hospital.

Immediately, the doctors knew what was wrong. Lacy was having an asthma attack, something that had not bothered him since his childhood. I didn't have a clue that he even *had* asthma. They had already treated several people since the weather had suddenly turned. They called it *cold-weather asthma*, something I had never heard of. They said that the sudden drop in temperature did not allow his body, especially his lungs, to adjust, and that his lungs had gone into shock while walking home that day, taking in the extremely cold, moist air coming in from the lake. They decided to keep him overnight to treat him with warm oxygen, medications, and IVs.

I went home to rest, but I couldn't sleep. I tossed and turned thinking about what had happened and what could happen to my husband and what my life would be like if something bad were to happen to him. I prayed to God and asked Him to deliver us from that incident stronger and better than before.

I picked Lacy up from the hospital that Thursday. The doctors sent him home with asthma medications and an inhaler, something he had never had to use before. He said that he would use the inhaler if it meant saving his life. To this day, he keeps one in his pocket at all times, just in case.

I had also had asthma as a child, with nosebleeds and all, so of course I worried throughout those fall and winter months whether I, too, would get cold-weather asthma. It's amazing how sometimes even small things can come along suddenly and knock you off your feet.

We both learned something that night. When life knocks you down, the strong get back up and, with the grace of God, "Keep on Truckin'," like Eddie Kendricks of the Temptations sang about. What a bummer! We chalked it up as a small setback, and after skipping class that Friday, we went back to class the next Monday with the determination to make it through the rest of the semester.

We learned that life can be hard on black males sometimes, even when they are trying to do the right things. For example, during my entire time in the IR program, I never got to meet the black males they told me were also Ph.D. candidates. I began to wonder if they had told me the truth and if they really existed. I was told that because they were ahead of me in their studies, they were off doing fieldwork and research on their dissertations. I was told that one guy was in DC doing research at the Department of Labor and another was teaching at Ohio State. Eventually, I learned that they were really off making money so they could stay in the program. I often felt like a lone wolf.

Sometimes when you feel alone, God sends angels without wings into your life. In my case, that angel was another black female who entered the IR program, one who came in at the master's level. Her name was Gail, and she was a graduate of the prestigious, well-known, all-girl HBCU named Spelman College, which was located in Atlanta, Georgia. She was all of four foot ten, with long black hair, and was quite the Southern belle. Her daddy was the president of another southern HBCU, so she had the grace and charm of not only a Spelman girl but also of the daughter of a college president.

Gail and I became instant friends, although I was married and she was single and I was a couple of years older. I was able to school her a little on surviving her first year in Madison, Wisconsin, and she schooled me on what it was like surviving in the all-girl HBCU environment that was Spelman "high-class" College. She lived in one of the few high-rise apartment buildings close to where I lived in downtown Madison, and we talked and laughed often as we walked to and from school, which made our journey less of a burden in more ways than one, especially on some of Madison's cold days and nights. We would talk about everything, from classwork to men, from britches to bitches. Nothing was off limits.

Gail became like a younger sister to me, and we would eventually become lifelong friends. Lacy, who was always quick to make a new friend, became a big brother to Gail and had to school her on his law school buddies, both single and married, who were always on the prowl for new prey. Gail was quite a cute little catch.

Although many of my classes were more advanced than hers, Gail and I took a couple of foundation classes together. She also took some master's classes in the business school that I'd had before, so I was able to help her with those. At the Ph.D. level, however, I was sometimes the only black person in the class, which was similar, yet different, to being the only female in some of my classes at Lincoln University, my undergraduate male-dominated school.

One of the classes I took without Gail that semester was Managerial Economics, a graduate class in the business school. It was known as an ass-kicker. Having studied the syllabus, though, I knew I could pass it. After all, I had been an economics major in undergraduate school and a management major in the MBA program, so it would be a shame if I couldn't pass a managerial economics class! But what would be my grade? The professor for the class was known as an asshole who would not give any As.

When the midterm rolled around, I was pretty confident going into the exam. Sure enough, I knew the material. My past studies kicked in. In addition, he asked some US economic policy questions that I knew the answers to due to my days at GAO and my stint with the State of

Wisconsin. Several of my classmates left the exam shaking their heads negatively.

The day the exam was returned, I sat near the back, as I usually did in that class, given the reputation of the professor. That was my strategy when the professor was an asshole. I would keep a low profile and not bring attention to myself. He came in and began to berate the class on how poorly we had done—with the exception of one person. I started to get a little uneasy and felt a pain in the pit of my stomach. He stated how clearly this one person understood economic theory and the material. I started to slide down in my chair, and then he said, "Who is Gwynette Lacy?"

Everyone who knew who I was turned around and looked at me, some proudly and some with a frown. I wanted to disappear. But I slowly raised my hand. As he passed out the papers, mine first, he turned red as a beet. I don't know which of us was more astonished!

After class, several of my classmates came up to me when we got outside the classroom and congratulated me. One friend said to me, "Well, I guess we know who is going to ace this class!"

I smiled and said to myself, *I'm sure I know who's not!*

I was right. The professor made the final exam even harder. I stumbled on a couple of items. I got an "AB" in that class, which is like getting an A- or B+ at other schools. Most of my classmates got Cs, which is like getting a D (barely passing) in undergraduate school. I think the professor made the final exam extra-hard on purpose, just for me, but I could have just been paranoid. I know one thing, though. He made sure I didn't ace the class. He certainly taught me a lesson, one that I probably already knew, and that is this: although times may change, sometimes people don't. Read between the lines.

I couldn't wait to get home to DC after my first semester in the Ph.D. program. I had gotten around a 3.6 grade-point average that semester and was relatively pleased with my grades, given the circumstances. We made our usual round of dinners and Christmas parties. Lacy and I were at our lowest weight since getting married. I was holding steady at 108 pounds. However, everyone in DC over forty years old felt that I was too small, so everyone wanted to feed us, especially Mama Lacy.

Daddy had me, Lacy, and Vee over to his crib for dinner the Sunday after Christmas. Mildred, his second wife, had prepared a nice healthy meal comprised of a salad, baked chicken, healthy collard greens, and corn bread. They both were eating healthier since Daddy's first heart attack the year of my wedding. Then, after dinner, he made a major announcement that would shake up our entire world.

He announced that he was going into Washington Hospital Center that Tuesday for open-heart surgery to have a double-bypass procedure. Although he'd had that minor heart attack the first year we were married and had stopped smoking, cold turkey, and drastically changed his diet, his arteries were clogged due to naturally occurring high cholesterol. Bypass surgery was new at the time, so to say the least, Vee and I went into shock. I was speechless for the rest of the dinner.

Daddy, a small man who had never been overweight, was chipper and in good spirits. He assured us things would go well. A God-fearing man, he asked for our support and prayers. He told us his cardiologist said he was a good candidate for bypass surgery. Otherwise, they would not attempt it, given his past history.

I was silent on the way back to Mama Lacy's house, still in shock. Lacy and I went straight home, and she explained the procedure to me. I couldn't sleep. I couldn't eat. All I could think about was Daddy up until the day of his surgery. Vee and I decided not to tell our mother until after the surgery.

We met Mildred at the hospital at seven o'clock the morning of the surgery. We were able to visit with him and kiss him on the forehead before they wheeled into surgery. We knew he was in good hands. At the time, Washington Hospital Center's cardiac surgery unit was the best in the city, if not the nation, and probably still is. They ushered us into a family waiting room where our waiting and praying began, and we waited, and waited, and waited.

Mildred and Vee were coffee drinkers, so they drank lots of coffee. I was not a coffee drinker at the time, so I read a textbook I had brought along and some magazines. We took turns getting a little something from the cafeteria. Finally, around two in the afternoon, the surgery was over and they wheeled Daddy into the ICU. Although we were able to see him briefly, he was pretty much out of it.

We met with the surgeons, who said the surgery was successful, so we sat around a little more and finally decided to leave, only to return the next morning to sit, visit, pray, and wait some more. They moved Daddy to a semiprivate room on the cardiac floor where we were able to stay with him. Being a nurse, Mama Lacy became concerned that I had barely slept or eaten in three days, and she sat me down when I got home, saying that the last thing we needed was for me to get sick. She had discussed my weight loss and anxiety with Lacy, and the three of us had a nice dinner together that night.

However, on Thursday morning, when we got to the hospital, Daddy had taken a turn for the worse overnight. He was back in the ICU, on oxygen, and had contracted pneumonia. Everything that could go wrong after heart surgery had gone wrong.

We went into shock again. I literally had an anxiety attack. Lacy escorted Vee and me out of the ICU and into the waiting area, where we cried, hugged, and began another long wait. Vee and I began to contact Daddy's family and friends and decided to go to the hospital chapel, where we prayed. That night, we went home to try to eat something and rest and decided to return on Friday with a change of clothes so that we could stay overnight at the hospital until whatever was to happen happened. Mama Lacy warned me again not to make myself sick.

I became increasingly concerned. Lacy and I were due to leave that Sunday, in that classes were due to start at Wisconsin that Monday. So, we talked and I told him I wouldn't be able to leave with Daddy in the state he was in. I told Lacy to prepare to go back to Madison without me, and that maybe I would drop out of school for the spring semester. I told him to cancel my plane ticket and that I was staying in DC for a while.

Daddy was touch-and-go all day that Friday. All we could do was pray. Mildred, Vee, and I stayed at the hospital overnight as planned, unable to leave his side. But you know what the Bible says: "Joy cometh in the morning!"

On Saturday morning, Daddy began to improve. There was a glimmer of hope. The doctors assured us that Daddy had turned the corner and would be all right. But I needed to hear that from the horse's mouth.

Later that afternoon, Daddy was strong enough to talk, and Lacy and I were able to have a private moment with him while Mildred and Vee stepped out to grab some lunch. Lacy told Daddy of my plans to drop out of school. Well, Daddy wasn't having it. He said that he would get better if he knew that I was in school. He said, "You go on back to school and make your Daddy proud!"

Well, I guess that settled that. Lacy said that he'd had to tattle on me, in that he didn't want to go back to school without me. He said that he never canceled my ticket, knowing that everything would be OK. He had the faith of a mustard seed. We went back to Mama Lacy's and packed our bags so that we could return to Madison the next day.

After our return to Madison, before we knew it, another academic year had passed. Lacy had completed his second year of law school with extra classes to boot, and I had completed my first year as a Ph.D. candidate. Again, eager to finish school, we decided to attend both sessions of summer school. We both were beginning to see the light at the end of the tunnel.

A TRIP TO CHI TOWN

Our second summer in Madison was a little different, however, than our first. Instead of us running straight home to DC at every break, family and friends decided they wanted to come to Madison to visit us and see what was keeping us so busy. To kill two birds with one stone, my mother-in-law and Lacy's Aunt Ruth organized a major road trip to Madison and Chicago to attend a family wedding in Chicago that June, which, lucky for us, would take place after the first session of summer school.

It turned out to be quite an adventure for them. Mama Lacy rounded up David, our best man, and Kat, my best friend and former roommate, both of whom had never been to Madison, along with the other David, our groomsman who helped drive us to Madison, for the long road trip to visit us. The two Davids were recruited as drivers. The four of them started out from Washington and picked up Aunt Ruth in Pittsburgh on the way to Madison. They planned to stay in Madison for one night, a Friday, and on Saturday, we all would take two cars to Chicago for the Saturday wedding. The bride was the daughter of one of Mama Lacy's and Aunt Ruth's cousins.

Can you imagine two single middle-aged post-Depression women, still looking to have a little fun, in the same car with three single baby boomers, telling jokes for sixteen hours? That's what they say they did the whole time: told jokes, listened to music, ate, and slept if they weren't driving. The guys drove Mrs. Lacy's big new Pontiac, a green Catalina, which had plenty of space for the five passengers and their weekend luggage. Mama Lacy packed a picnic lunch of fried chicken and all the fixings and lots of home-baked goodies. Her homemade peanut butter sugar cookies, with chocolate kisses in the middle that were "as big as your head," were the stars of the trip.

Kat sat in the big back seat with Mama Lacy and Aunt Ruth. The trip was a break from her job that I recruited her for at GAO. When they got to Madison, Kat said, "If I eat one more sugar cookie, I'm going to blow up!"

Mama Lacy and Aunt Ruth stayed at a comfortable hotel near our apartment for one night, while our other three wedding-party guests stayed with us in our one-bedroom apartment. That's what single people who were close to you did back in the day. They slept wherever they could find a spot: on the couch (that was Kat's spot) or on the floor.

Although our apartment was small, there was room for all three. They were like family to us.

Early on Saturday morning, we packed up our two cars and headed to Chicago. Lacy, Kat, and I rode in our little yellow Volkswagen, with Mama Lacy's big green Pontiac bringing up the rear. We stopped right outside of Madison for breakfast, which gave us time to catch up on the latest happenings in DC and Pittsburgh.

We arrived in Chicago before noon, which gave us time to rest up and catch up some more. I was so happy to see my bestie, Kat. We couldn't stop talking about what was going on in DC and with our friends from Lincoln University.

The wedding took place in a beautiful park in Chicago, overlooking Lake Michigan, which was a fashionable place to have a wedding during the early 1970s in lieu of a church wedding. It was the last Saturday in June but, typical of Chicago, it was quite cool and breezy, and the Chicago "hawk" was living up to its reputation. For us DC women, it felt downright cold.

But we were prepared. The four of us women who came to Chi Town together had decided in advance to wear long summer dresses with shawls, which was quite popular at the time for such an event. I had made a beautiful black-and-white maxi dress, with a matching shawl, just for the occasion. You couldn't tell the four of us ladies anything. We were dressed to kill, as they say.

The wedding, which took place in the early afternoon when the sun was still high, was absolutely beautiful. The bride was stunning, and the groom was quite handsome. It was a lovely gathering of middle-class attendees and families, and everyone was beaming with pride for the bride and groom, who had met in college, and their families, especially Mama Lacy and Aunt Ruth.

After sundown, the seven of us who had come to Chicago together decided to split up. The two Davids hung out with some of the single people who were at the wedding, who took them bar-hopping. Lacy drove his mother and Aunt Ruth to their cousin's house for an after-wedding dinner party. I drove the Yellow Bug into downtown Chicago to show Kat the sights and to have a late dinner and drinks.

We went to a fancy, quiet little restaurant where we could talk and giggle, to catch up with one another and our respective lives. As it turned out, we would both share a big secret with one another. Kat's secret was that she had finally met the man of her dreams and had fallen in love. Knowing her as I did, I knew this was serious. She had barely dated when we were in college.

She told me all about him. He was from Grambling, Louisiana, where his parents worked for Grambling State University. He had graduated from Howard University, Lacy's alma mater, a year before Lacy did, with a degree in economics and business, like we had, and was working as a manager at a bank in DC. I knew he was the one and that he would become her husband. I was so happy for her. But she promised me that they were taking it slow and that there would be no wedding until I returned to DC.

Having heard her big news, I decided to tell Kat my big summer secret, which I hadn't revealed to anyone except Lacy. I told her how much I wanted to have a baby and that I was trying to get pregnant, on purpose. She was shocked. "What about school and that Ph.D. you want?" she asked.

I explained that it was time, and that I didn't want to put off having a baby any longer. When that baby body clock starts ticking, the body and the heart want what the body and the heart want. Besides, I told her, I had the whole thing planned out: how I would have a baby and still get the Ph.D. I wanted. Kat thought I had gone crazy, but I hadn't.

You see, I had done the math. I planned to get pregnant by the end of the summer, finish my coursework and take my preliminary exams by January, and have my baby in the spring of 1976. I would then start on my dissertation while home with my small infant and get a job that fall wherever Lacy landed a job.

My plan was to get my Ph.D. while working a job and working on my dissertation at the same time. I was in no rush to get the degree.

Settling down somewhere and starting a family was more important and a top priority to me. All of this sounded doable to me at the time, and after all, I had studied and worked throughout my undergraduate years—but without a husband and a baby. I guess I was a glutton for punishment.

I saw it all as a math problem, given the math genius I was and the strategic business planner I had become. I had talked to my gynecologist, who gave me the science behind exactly how to get pregnant: what day(s) of the month, the body temperature, etc. I had also counted out all the courses I had left to complete in order to sit for my Ph.D. preliminary exam, and I was banking on Lacy graduating in December of 1975 and getting a job.

Of course, science and both of us had to do our part. First, we had to make a baby. We had exactly two months to do that, two shots at it, or our whole plan would go out the window. I explained the whole plan to Lacy, and he bought into it in a *c'est la vie* kind of way. It was summer, when bodies were hot and at their best, and after three years of marriage, we were still very much in love. We knew we could make a baby, and as they say, the fun was in trying.

Lacy had booked three rooms for the seven of us in a posh hotel in downtown Chicago for the night after the wedding. After parting from our family and friends that Sunday, we drove back to Madison to execute our baby plan. We both signed up for the second session of summer school and got about the fun business of making a baby.

The last month and probably the last day that my plan would work, or we would have to put off having a baby for another year, *bingo*, we made love and I got pregnant. I just think that it was divine intervention and that the Good Lord knew how much we wanted and how much love we would give a baby, so he saw fit to grant us our hearts' desire.

A BABY ANNOUNCEMENT

After summer school, we flew home with our good news for a special Wright Family Reunion to celebrate my maternal grandmother's seventy-fifth birthday—this time, hosted by her five living children rather than her grandchildren. It was a fabulous affair, with Mr. Myers, who catered my wedding, providing all the food, along with a grand birthday cake. The party was held at a historic venue in Prince George's County, near where my Aunt Bernice lived.

I don't know when I had seen my grandmother so happy. All of her living children, grandchildren, and great-grandchildren were in attendance. There were cousins I hadn't seen in ages and little children running around everywhere, with their favorite drink, Little Hugs. On that one day, our grandmother got to see her entire legacy.

A photographer was hired to take pictures, large and small, including individual pictures of each family represented. When it came time for my mother's family picture, I announced that I had a baby in the oven, to some surprise and applause. My sister, who had also visited us in Madison that summer, said she knew something was up. I had shown her some patterns of clothes I had planned on making, and she said she could tell by the loose fit of the patterns that I was planning on becoming pregnant.

My cousins were elated and said that they had been taking bets that I would not leave Madison, Wisconsin, empty-handed when it came to a baby or without a little one on the way, and they were right. Some felt that Lacy and I, keeping one another warm on those cold Wisconsin nights, would produce a little one; however, their time of year was wrong. The hot, humid summer months had done the trick.

So, in August of 1975, we returned to Madison with one last semester of coursework at the University of Wisconsin left for both of us. My other Lincoln roommate, Carolyn, visited us that fall but didn't bring clothes that were warm enough. We had to go out and buy her some warm clothes to wear during her visit.

The fall semester flew by. Before we knew it, Lacy and I were finished with all of our coursework for both of our degrees and were looking at final exams. But wouldn't you know, it was the snowiest and coldest December we had experienced since we had been in Madison, with daily temperatures averaging around 0 degrees. I remember both of us putting on two pairs of underwear, two pairs of socks, two pairs of pants, and layering up to go take our finals, topping things off with two hats and two pairs of gloves. Lacy came home with icicles hanging down from his mustache and needed to use his inhaler.

Gail called me in a panic one morning before one of our finals and said she thought that the baby would freeze inside my stomach if I came outside. She scared me to death, but I bundled up in a big red wool wrap coat I had bought to carry me through my pregnancy and went to our final exam anyway, and all went well.

A LEGAL GRADUATION

Between finals and Christmas that year, it was one occasion after another. First, there was Lacy's graduation from law school. Our best man, David, flew up for the celebration. It was very nice and not too crowded compared to the size of UW's May graduation classes. Only a couple of Lacy's buddies graduated early with him, so after a nice reception at the law school, we all went out to dinner together at a popular restaurant downtown called the *Library*. I was beginning to show a little bit, so the baby and I got a lot of attention. Between events, we started to pack up our worldly goods for our move to wherever we were going at the end of January.

Next on the calendar, just before we left for Christmas, was Lacy's admission to the State Bar. It was held at the state courthouse, which was within walking distance from our apartment. However, we drove the Yellow Bug due the cold weather and my pregnancy. That ceremony was also very nice. To be honest, I had never been inside a courthouse, with those polished wooden benches and judges' chambers and such. The swearing-in part of the ceremony was quite moving, with the raising of the right hands and the "so help me God." It was a proud moment for me to see my husband become a new member of the bar and an attorney able to practice law.

There was also a reception, hosted by the Wisconsin Law School, and of course, Lacy and his buddies went out for dinner and drinks afterward. Little Baby Lacy was getting good nourishment throughout all of the celebrations, but of course, without any alcohol. Although I was watching what I ate and drank (no pork or alcohol), I didn't pass up a good meal.

We took lots of pictures of both occasions to show everybody when we went home for Christmas. Lacy had pictures developed of many of our Wisconsin days, and I made photo albums to pass around when we got home.

This time, our holiday would not be all fun and games. First of all, we had to drive the Yellow Bug home, for good this time. That was a long, tough trip, given my pregnancy. When we got home, I spent my days studying for my prelim exams, which were scheduled for the end of January 1976. Lacy spent his days looking for a job. He had job offers in Madison and Milwaukee, where he was a new member of the bar, and in Chicago and New York, where he was not. He also had interviews in DC where all of them were with the federal government, where a lawyer could be hired if they were a member of the bar in any state.

All of Lacy's DC job interviews went well. After all, he was African American at the height of the affirmative action era and quite a likable fellow. He used his awesome sense of humor, his quick wit, and his DC charm to win over his interviewers. It was now decision time.

As with his law school decision, he narrowed his offers down to five. Of two offers in the state of Wisconsin, he preferred the one in Milwaukee. Although we had gone to school there, Madison was just too lily white and culturally homogeneous for us to live there permanently. I felt that our children would find no black identity there, as was often the case with black kids who grew up there and many who went to undergraduate school there. So, for us, it was bye bye to Madison! See you later! Lacy liked Milwaukee much better because the job offer was with an organization he had interned with in labor law, his major, and the weather wasn't quite as cold as Madison, which was surrounded by lakes that made for colder winters.

I was partial to a job offer Lacy got in Chicago, a big business town where I could easily find a job with my Wisconsin MBA. It had a large black community and culture, and plenty to do. Plus, I was OK with making a life away from DC and all those nosey family members and friends. But Lacy quickly ruled out Chicago as too expensive and too cold. He didn't like the super-cold weather there, with that hawk coming off the lake. That would be bad for his asthma, too.

Believe or not, he liked a job offer in New York City better. It involved immigration law. I talked him out of that one, though. I told him I wasn't about to raise a baby in New York City. New York City was too crowded, too fast, and too expensive for our country asses. And where would we live? Where were the garden apartments that I liked so much in NYC? He laughed and crossed New York off the list as well.

One job in DC, however, particularly caught his eye. It seemed to have everything we wanted and/or needed, and it was in labor law, Lacy's chosen specialty. None other than the National Labor Relations Board, with headquarters in downtown DC, was hiring newly minted labor lawyers. Lacy met all of the requirements, especially the one of being a member of any bar in any US state. Lacy jumped on that opportunity and accepted the job offer. It was a "good government job" and in DC. After signing his employment contract, he immediately told his mother and me his good news and told me to start looking for an apartment. Mama Lacy was ecstatic. Her only son was moving back home.

That Christmas, we had many reasons to celebrate, in addition to the birth of Christ. Mama Lacy, in her infinite wisdom, pulled out all the stops and went all out to celebrate her son's graduation, bar passage, and new job. While she prepared for Christmas dinner, cooking and cleaning her house, Lacy and I went apartment hunting. We were determined to find the right apartment in one day.

Knowing how much I loved garden apartments, we looked in nearby suburban Maryland, this time for one large enough to accommodate our growing family. We found the perfect place in close-by Greenbelt, Maryland. It had two bedrooms, one that we would use for a nursery for Baby Lacy; two baths; and a den where I could sew, study, and write to finish my Ph.D.

So many family members and friends were invited to Christmas dinner of 1975, Mama Lacy's infamous dinner was served in four shifts instead of her usual two. Both of our families; both sets of our friends, old and new, and Mama Lacy's neighbors and longtime friends came in droves to her house for her fabulous Christmas soul food dinner. She only wanted to use her best china, crystal, and dishes, so in-between shifts, I spent a lot of time in the kitchen with my friends and family, talking, laughing, gossiping, and washing dishes for the next shift, with people coming and going well into the night. Lacy's childhood friends was the last shift and were still up eating and celebrating when I retired for the night. The desserts were plentiful and included her pineapple coconut cake, strawberry cake, and those famous peanut butter sugar cookies.

That weekend, my Uncle Lawrence allowed me to host a graduation dinner party for Lacy at his lovely home in Hillcrest Heights, DC. It was well attended by family and friends. The food and drinks were plentiful, and the huge celebration cake read, "Congratulations Attorney Lacy." We danced and partied until well past midnight.

BACK TO MADISON, ALONE

This time, right after the Wright family's annual New Year's Day celebration, I flew back to Madison alone. My Ph.D. preliminary exam was scheduled for late January, just prior to the start of the spring semester, and I needed to study, hard. I had about three weeks to prepare for it. Not wanting me to lift anything heavy or overdo while I was pregnant, Lacy and I had packed most of our household items and clothes together prior to our Christmas trip back home. That allowed me to focus each day on studying, from morning to sundown, one subject at a time.

I set up a routine, mostly around studying each subject that would be on the test, stopping only to eat and take care of my health needs; a little exercise and meditation; and accepting collect calls from Lacy and close friends. On a typical day, I would wake up around five in the morning, weave around the boxes we had packed, and make my way to the sofa, where books were stacked in small piles by subject matter. My goal was to conquer one stack per day. I would review one book in the stack before I took a nap and got up for a shower and breakfast. I would review another book by lunchtime and two textbooks after lunch, stopping to take an afternoon nap for Baby Lacy and myself. After that, I would review another book or two before dinner and would talk to Lacy after dinner. I would finish my daily stack of books before I retired to our bedroom with a couple of books to review over again before I fell asleep for good, only to get up and follow the same routine the next day.

Midweek, Lacy called me, a little concerned. The apartment complex I had selected for us to live in needed a stable financial cosigner in our age bracket, in that Lacy was new to his job and I wasn't working. He suggested that we look elsewhere. We never liked to ask for financial favors from our friends, but I was determined to get that particular two-bedroom and den, so I called Kat. She was the only person from Lincoln who I knew and trusted with such a request, and besides, she had that good job at GAO. I humbled myself to ask for such a big favor, and she said, "Of course! Yes, I'll do it. I trust that y'all will be responsible and pay your rent on time!"

January was still quite cold in Madison, so Gail called daily to check in on me and Baby Lacy, with updates on the weather, still not wanting me to go outside. It was so cold, she occasionally stopped by with groceries or sent food deliveries to our apartment, always with healthy items for me and the baby.

At the end of the second week, Gail called to say, "That's it. I need you to take a break, so I'm taking you out to dinner. Put on a nice maternity outfit and walk to my place, and we'll head on down to your favorite restaurant, *the Library*, for dinner."

I did as she asked, and we got to the restaurant at six o'clock for dinner. The hostess walked us toward the back to a section that was usually reserved for private parties. As I turned a corner, I saw a large table full of my African American female friends from the B-School and the law school. I looked at Gail and asked, "What's going on?"

Then they all said, "Surprise!" and pulled out balloons, signs, and gifts in pink and blue. It was a baby shower. I was blown away. I said, "Who planned all of this?"

One of Lacy's law school classmates, Lynn, and her younger sister, Carol, had planned the shower and contacted Gail to go along with the plan. The sisters were from DC: two Southwest girls. Lynn and I were the same age and had friends in common in DC. We had become good friends during our years in Madison.

In all, it was about ten of us gathered around a large circular table. We varied in age from Gail and Carol being the youngest among us, to Lynn and I both being twenty-four at the time, on up to about the age of about thirty-five-plus for Lacy's older female law school classmates.

We ate, laughed, and giggled at first. Then we played baby shower games, including Name That Baby, which was funny since Lacy and I didn't know the sex of the baby yet. Each guest gave me a preferred baby name and a shower gift, and their gifts were as diverse as they were.

I got new-age gifts, such as something new back then called *onesies*, which were one-piece pajamas for the baby; practical gifts, from bottles to baby dishes; and heirloom gifts, including a silver spoon and a beautiful hand-knitted baby bunting, a blanket/sweater-like sack to slip the baby into, knitted by the oldest guest in attendance. I was truly surprised and so very grateful for the baby gifts, as I hadn't had time to shop for the baby yet. The shower would be one of my best memories of our days in Madison. I went home via Gail, called Lacy with the news, and exhausted, I slept through the night.

I woke up on Saturday morning with just five days left until my big exam. As the day of the exam approached, I became more and more anxious, so I increased my transcendental meditation sessions. I made one more sweep through the subjects that I was told would be on the test and tried to guess the type of questions that my professors would ask.

My preliminary exam was scheduled for a Wednesday afternoon. It was to be a four-hour exam, with short and long essay questions. It was scheduled to last from one to five o'clock, with a short break at the midway point. So, I made a special schedule for myself as to how I wanted my day to unfold. I told myself, *stick to the plan, which is the first function of management.* It became my mantra for the day.

I got up that morning at about seven o'clock after a somewhat restless night, trying to anticipate the questions on the test and how I would answer them. I went to the living room and sat on my study couch, closed my eyes, and did the same thing. I bathed and got dressed by midmorning and went over my notes one more time.

After a light lunch, I headed up to the campus. I got there a half an hour early, so as not to panic. I was nervous enough. I waited for the program director to arrive with the exam. While waiting, I went into a deep ten-minute transcendental meditation to calm myself, and it seemed to work.

The director told me to leave all of my belongings in his office and took me into a small empty office with just a couple of pens in my hand. Then he gave me a multipage eight-and-a-half-by-eleven exam and two blue exam notebooks, told me "Good luck," and left.

I looked over the exam, got myself and the blue books organized—another major function of good management—and went to work. I tackled the essays that I knew the most about first, although that was risky, but I kept track of my time so as not to spend too much on what I knew best. Still under the effect of my transcendental meditation, at times I would close my eyes and see the answers in the books and notes that I had studied during my time of isolation. That was so helpful. I quickly organized my thoughts and wrote out the answers I could remember.

To me, during the first half of the exam, the hardest section was an entire page of terms in my field that I had to define and describe. The introduction to that section of the test said that they were terms that every Ph.D. in my field needed to know and understand. So, I went right to work. I had heard of all of the terms. Some I knew well, and they were easy to define. Others were a little harder, and some I struggled to define. I left the hard ones (just a few) alone and said I would come back to them later.

Before I knew it, half of the exam time was over, and I was making good progress toward finishing. Dr. Miller gave me a bathroom break, during which time I washed my face in cold water. I was already exhausted. I then looked into the mirror and gave myself a pep talk. As I pondered the difficult questions I hadn't answered yet, I said to myself, "You can do this. It's not all bad. Now go in there and finish what you started!"

So that's what I did. I went back in there and tackled the difficult essays and short-answer questions that I had left to finish. To this day, there is one definition that haunts me: *construct validity*. I didn't understand it when I studied it, and there it was on the test. I freaked out and pondered over it. Finally, I just wrote what my understanding of it was. Construct validity is how you verify something, a construct, that you cannot see, touch, or feel, such as intelligence. Say you want to hire a CIA agent who is highly intelligent. How do you verify a test that you will use to measure that intelligence? That's called *construct validity*. I don't remember how I answered that question on the test, but to this day, I remember that term being on my prelim exam and I teach all my students, even undergraduates, what that term means.

Before I knew it, my four-hour ordeal was over. I wrapped things up and turned in the exam to Dr. Miller, who told me to come back that Friday to get my results. I thanked him for his time and assistance during that phase of my Ph.D. and left.

I stopped by to pick up Gail at her apartment on my way home, and we went out to have my favorite deep-dish pizza. I talked to her extensively about the exam and gave her some of my notes to help her prepare for her exam at the master's level. She had one more semester of coursework and her master's exam to go before graduating. She was grateful for my help. I gave her a big hug before we went our separate ways. I was to leave for DC in a few days and didn't know when I would see my southern belle friend again.

I then went straight home and immediately called Lacy to tell him the test was over. I told him that I was confident I had passed, and either way, I would be home in a few days.

That Friday came quickly. I took my time walking up to Dr. Miller's office. I walked up on one side of State Street and would return down the other side, stopping periodically to silently say goodbye to all the shops, restaurants, and landmarks I had come to love and adore. *Goodbye lake, goodbye football stadium, goodbye student union building. Goodbye Library, my favorite restaurant, and Good-bye Good Karma, my favorite concert venue.*

"YOU PASSED!"

Of course, Dr. Miller told me I had passed my preliminary exam. I knew that. I knew I had done well enough to pass. I could feel it in my bones. He didn't discuss what I had gotten right or wrong. I guess that's because they use the same subjects and/or the same questions for other prelims. What he said was that I had "obtained and understood the body of knowledge required of someone seeking the Ph.D. in my field, significantly." Even with that odd choice of words, I understood what the hell he meant, and I hope that you, the reader, understand it too. I passed.

He then explained to me what was to come. The next phase of my Ph.D. journey was called the dissertation stage—All but Dissertation, ABD. A dissertation is a very extensive research paper that Ph.D. candidates have to complete to prove that they can conduct original research that would make a contribution to the field. In other words, I had to do some work that would mean something, something new that would advance my field of expertise. But he didn't mean just a research paper, where you read a lot of articles and journals and write about what you read, like in high school and undergraduate school. He meant empirical research, to study something new.

What he meant was, I was to write a long thesis, make a hypothesis, get some human subjects (at least forty or fifty), and either prove or disprove that hypothesis. A dissertation is like a scientific experiment that scientists conduct on a new drug to determine whether that drug works to cure a disease or not. In my field, the subjects had to be people (humans), not rats or other animals. And the report, the dissertation, is like a book, around two hundred pages or longer, that explains what you studied, how you studied your subjects, and what you found, called your *findings*. That's why people who complete this process and pass the dissertation phase graduate as doctors: Ph.D. means a *doctor of philosophy*. That's what my aspirations and goals were all about, to become a doctor in my field of expertise: labor–management relations. It would take hard work, perseverance, and determination.

I told Dr. Miller that I understood the process very well. Most Ph.D. candidates clearly understand that phase of the Ph.D. process, because many don't make it past that stage to the end, for various reasons. It makes or breaks you. It takes at least a year or longer (they give you a maximum of three years). It's laborious, and you have to have *perseverance, hope, and determination* (PHD). It also takes sacrifice and deprivation. It's difficult on you, your family, and your pocketbook, unless you come from money. There is also a joke about Ph.D.s: "You either get sick or you go crazy." Dr. Miller and I discussed all of that.

I then felt obligated to discuss my plan for completion with Dr.

Miller, for I was visibly pregnant, although he hadn't said anything. I told him that I was pregnant and that we were moving back home to DC, where my husband had a job. I told him that while I was waiting for the baby to come and after the baby arrived, I would write my proposal, which was the first step in the dissertation process that explains what you would be studying and how, which had to be approved by an assigned dissertation committee.

I told Dr. Miller that I would be conducting my research remotely (as many candidates do) from DC, and that I would enroll and pay my tuition each semester as required. He said he understood, but explained that if I was doing my research remotely, I would have to relinquish my scholarship and expenses. I told him that I understood that and therefore would probably get a job teaching somewhere in order to pay for everything and help my husband financially.

He said OK but explained to me the risks of finishing my degree that way. Basically, he said it usually takes longer, and that many people don't finish. He told me that if I didn't finish in three years after the research stage started, I would have to petition to come back to the campus to finish. I told him that I would finish in the allotted time. I had come too far to be turned back or denied.

He then asked me how old I was. I said, "I'm twenty-four going on twenty-five years old." He pointed out that I would then be around twenty-eight years old if I finished within the allotted time. He said that he'd had no idea I was so young. He said that most Ph.D.s finish their degrees well into their thirties. I told Dr. Miller that I had finished my undergraduate degree in three years and my MBA two years later, while working professionally most of that time. Therefore, there was no doubt in my mind that I would finish my Ph.D. in the allotted time, if not before, and how determined I was to do so.

He then said, "Congratulations on passing your preliminary exam. We are proud of you, and good luck to you."

I shook his hand and left, stopping on the way home for what would be my last slice of deep-dish vegetarian pizza for quite a while—until

I came back to defend my paper. I then rushed home to call Lacy and tell him the good news. We laughed and giggled on the phone like old times. He then gave me strict instructions over the phone: "Pack one suitcase of clothes to carry to the airport. Don't lift any heavy boxes. The moving van will be coming tomorrow afternoon. Be there and stay out of the way."

I did exactly as I was told. North American Van Lines showed up on Saturday afternoon to pick up all of our furniture and worldly goods. After they left, I laid out the clothes I was going to wear to the airport, turned up the heat, and slept on the floor in my pajamas and socks, with my winter coat as a blanket and winter scarf as a pillow. I actually slept well that night.

On Sunday morning, I got up, prayed, bathed, got dressed, finished some milk and a bagel that was left in the fridge, turned in the key to our apartment, and caught a cab to the airport. After a light brunch to nourish myself and the baby, I boarded my flight. The preliminary exam part of my Ph.D. requirements was over. As the plane took off, I said goodbye to Madison, Wisconsin. I would not be returning for some time. At that time, I had no idea where life was about to take me or how long it would take for me to come back. I knew, however, that there would be at least one more trip back to Madison to complete my Ph.D. journey.

ELEVEN

HOME, SWEET HOME AND BABY MAKES THREE

LACY PICKED ME up from the airport in the Yellow Bug, and we stayed at Mama Lacy's house until the moving van arrived in Greenbelt to deliver our furniture and belongings to Seven Springs, the largest upscale garden-apartment complex, by far, that we would live in. There were hundreds of apartments and townhomes to pick from at Seven Springs. The two-bedroom and den apartment we chose was a third-floor unit, with walking trails and one of several swimming pools nearby. We chose a third floor unit for the privacy of having no one walking around over our heads while I worked on my dissertation during the day and at night while the baby would be sleeping.

The moving van arrived at Seven Springs on February 1, 1976. Lacy's childhood friend, Donny, the guy who had always called me Hots when I was in high school and helped me move out of my college dormitory when the Klan came calling, was there for us, as always, this time to move us into our new crib. After studying architecture at Howard University, Donny had landed a job as a draftsman for the DC government. He loved all the space that our new apartment had to offer. He helped us to place our furniture strategically to maximize the use of space and gave me tips on how to decorate.

Although our apartment would stretch our budget, we felt our comfort was worth the sacrifice. We were grateful to Kat for cosigning to get us into the apartment. Donny compared our floor plan to one of the finest expensive apartments one can find for thousands of dollars in New York City.

We couldn't afford a lot of new furniture, so we went back to our original black, white, and red color scheme. We reused all of the living room furniture we had before and bought a black leather loveseat for the den, where we used Lacy's law-school desk as my dissertation desk. Our lease required that three-quarters of the floors be carpeted, so we had the living room, dining room, and den covered with red/burgundy speckled carpet, which brightened up the black and white furniture and accessories.

Greenbelt, Maryland, was an ideal location for two young, college-educated, up-and-coming professionals back then. It was about twenty minutes by car to DC by way of New York Avenue, which was a major artery into DC, closest to where both my mother and Lacy's mother lived, so that either of us could get to either one of them quickly if we needed to. Seven Springs was about ten minutes by car from the University of Maryland, where I planned to go to the library to study and conduct some of my research.

Because we were down to one car between us, Lacy decided that he would leave the Yellow Bug with me during day, since I was pregnant, as a precaution, and that he would commute by bus to work and back. A bus stop for the public bus that went into downtown DC was a block away from our apartment. So yes, that guy who once owned one of the hottest cars of the decade had now reduced himself to riding the bus to and from work so his wife could have access to their compact car for herself and their baby.

IT'S A BOY

While waiting for my delivery date, I spent my days unpacking, decorating, studying, and writing my dissertation proposal, stopping to nap and make dinner. I enjoyed being in our new apartment. I also enjoyed driving into DC to see both of our mothers. One of the first things I had to do was to see Dr. Edwards, my first gynecologist, whose office was in my mother's apartment complex.

Dr. Carl Edwards was one the best-known and most accomplished OB/GYNs in DC, known for his huge practice, serving hundreds of black women. He was also known for his extravagant lifestyle. He was handsome, sophisticated, and well educated, and was known for owning several homes (one in the Caribbean), a mink coat, and a private jet. That brought him a lot of attention and scrutiny from the Feds and the DC government, because many of his patients were on Medicaid. Articles about him had even been written in the *Washington Post* and *Jet Magazine*. But after being audited, he was given a clean bill of fiscal health by the IRS and the DC and federal governments and was praised for the excellent health care he provided to his patients.

An older man, around my mother's age, Dr. Edwards was wise, patient, and attentive. He had a lot of patients, his office was always packed, and his wait time was in the hours, but when you finally got to see him, he treated you with familiarity and kindness, as if you were a family member. I had heard that he treated all of his patients that way, including my mother, who was also one of his patients and had recommended him to me before I got married.

On my first visit back to see him after the years we had been away in Madison, I was surprised that he remembered me—or at least he pretended to. He asked me, "Where have you been, young lady?"

I told Dr. Edwards that I had been away at the University of Wisconsin in Madison for almost three years and that I was ABD—All but Dissertation. We talked about that and my early pregnancy for a while, and then he examined me and checked all the vitals of Baby Lacy. He told me that I was over six months pregnant and that Baby Lacy and

I appeared to be doing well. He gave me a due date in the second week of May. He teased me and said that the baby would come probably just before Mother's Day and that I would be able to celebrate Mother's Day that year as a brand-new mom.

He then said that he normally didn't begin to treat and deliver a woman as late in her pregnancy as I was. However, he said that since he knew me and my mother, and since I appeared to be in great health and shape due to the clean living and exercise I had been getting in Madison, he would deliver my baby. I was overjoyed. I wanted a doctor that I knew to deliver our baby.

Before I got down from the examination table, he took a weird picture of my stomach, called a sonogram, which showed what looked like our baby. After explaining to me what the new sonogram device was and what it showed, he printed out the picture, gave to me, and said, "Here, take this picture home and tell your husband that the two of you are having a boy."

I was absolutely elated. I immediately went over to my mother's apartment to tell her the good news and show her the picture. Neither one of us could see how Dr. Edwards could tell that it was a boy. We also called my sister, who was still working on her Ph.D. at Penn State, to give her the good news. She told me that she would be coming home for an Easter break and couldn't wait to see me pregnant.

I then rushed home to prepare a nice dinner before Lacy got home. Over dinner, I told him all about my visit with Dr. Edwards. I then whipped out the sonogram picture and told him that Dr. Edwards said we were having a boy. Lacy jumped up and down with joy. You know, they say that one of the best things a woman can do for a man is to give that man a son. We stared at that picture until bedtime to see how Dr. Edwards knew it was a boy. I said, "He must have seen his little ding-a-ling somewhere in there!"

A RED AND WHITE NURSERY

I added one more chore to my to-do list as Easter approached: preparing Baby Lacy's nursery. I would take welcomed breaks from working on my research proposal to decorate the nursery. It was a regular-size second bedroom, so I had plenty of space to work with. Since I still couldn't tell how Dr. Edwards knew we were having a boy, I didn't want to take the risk of using a blue color scheme if our baby turned out to be a girl. So, I decided to go with a neutral color scheme. Since the rest of our apartment was back to our original black, white, and red, and in memory of my days as Kappa Queen back in college, I decided to go with Kappa colors of crimson and cream. Lacy said he was OK with that.

We bought a white baby crib that Lacy put together, which was truly a labor of love. I found some red-and-white gingham crib bumpers that had sheets and a lightweight quilt to match. I found some red gingham fabric at a fabric store and made some curtains for the nursery window. I also found a child-size white French-provincial dresser at Sears. Although it wasn't a baby dresser, it fit the color scheme perfectly. They also had a new baby furniture item that came out back then called a changing table. We bought one of those, in white, that Lacy also had to put together. We also bought a large red area rug and a large white trash can for the dirty diapers.

The nursery was big enough for a bookshelf. I found a large white one at a thrift store and filled it with children's books and toys. We also installed a record player on it and put records on the shelf that we would play to rock the baby to sleep. And to do that, we bought a white rocking chair.

With most of my decorating complete, and since I wasn't working and the two grandmothers-to-be were, as April approached, I decided to host Easter dinner for our immediate family. It would double as a housewarming dinner, since none of the ladies had seen our apartment yet. The most important females in our lives agreed to come.

I spent Holy Week preparing for my Easter dinner: cleaning,

decorating, and collecting ingredients for a few desserts that could be refrigerated, such as a cherry cheese pie and Mama Lacy's famous pineapple coconut cake. The Wednesday before Easter, I had a doctor's appointment with Dr. Edwards. He told me that things were moving along nicely toward my due date in early May, which was less than four weeks away. He gave Lacy and me an appointment to meet with him the Tuesday after Easter Monday at Women's Hospital of Washington so that he could walk us through the delivery process. He also signed us up for birthing classes, which were to start the week after Easter also.

On my way home from my prenatal appointment, I went shopping for some new bathroom rugs and other items for the guest bathroom, since we were having Easter dinner. I also stopped to get my hair cut. The guy who did my hair said, "Girl, let me hurry up and get you out of my chair. You're scaring me! Don't go into labor while you're in my chair!"

I laughed all the way home at how animated that hairdresser was. When I got home, I put the new rugs down and finished cleaning and decorating the guest bathroom. I described my lovely day to Lacy over dinner. Lacy wrote down the dates Dr. Edwards had given me in his day planner, and we worked on our taxes, which were due the next day, before retiring early. I remember saying, "If we'd had this baby last year, we would have a little tax write-off. Oh well, we will have one next year!"

IS IT TIME YET?

Around three in the morning, which was the time I usually woke up to go the bathroom during my pregnancy, I felt some warm water coming out of my crotch area that wet the sheets. I sat up in bed quickly and tried to wake Lacy up, saying, "Honey, wake up, I had an accident. Wake up, I wet the bed!" A hard sleeper, Lacy didn't wake up.

Never having been a bed wetter, I got out of bed and rushed to the bathroom. When I wiped myself, I saw a little streak of blood, but nothing alarming. So, I went back to the bedroom to wake Lacy, more forcibly this time. Pulling on the sheets, I said, "Get up, get up, I need to change the sheets!"

He jumped out of bed to help me, and I told him what had happened. He then said, "Maybe you should call Dr. Edwards."

After a little cajoling, I got Dr. Edwards' number from the nightstand and called him. I wasn't in pain, nor had I had what I thought was a contraction. But when I told Dr. Edwards about the bed wetting, he said to get dressed and go to the hospital, just as a precaution. He said it was probably a false alarm, and since the baby wasn't due for another three weeks, not to worry. Besides, first babies usually take their time coming into the world. He said he would call the hospital to let them know we were coming and would meet us there.

I was a little embarrassed calling Dr. Edwards in the middle of the night like that. What if it was a false alarm? What if that long drive to the hospital was for nothing, because everybody knows that first babies are usually late? But then, while I was packing an overnight bag, a little contraction hit. It was mild, so I thought I might be having what they call Braxton-Hicks or false labor. How embarrassing would that be, to go all the way to the hospital on a false alarm!

I finished packing anyway, and Lacy and I headed to the Yellow Bug. When we got there, I told him I would be more comfortable if I lay across the back seat. After all, it was around 3:45 a.m. in the morning, and I was still sleepy. So that's what I did.

Once we got going, I felt a sharp pain across the bottom of my belly, like a bad cramp, but one like I'd never had before. I then told Lacy, "Step on it, honey, the baby's coming!"

He took off, like he was racing in his old GOAT. We got into town in what must have been record time. When we pulled up to the emergency room door, an attendant in scrubs was waiting there with a wheelchair. Lacy jumped out of the car and helped me into the wheelchair. The attendant told him where to park the car and where to go with our insurance papers to get me admitted. By that time, I think I must have been in full labor.

They rushed me to the labor and delivery room and got me into a gown and onto a delivery bed. A resident came into the delivery room and said that he would examine me while we waited for Dr. Edwards and Lacy to come. He showed me how to put my feet into the stirrups, and after one look, I heard him say, "Oh my God, she's crowning. The baby's head is here. Where's that Dr. Edwards? She's one of his patients! He needs to get here quick!"

With no time for an epidural (numbing medication), no Dr. Edwards, and no Lacy, the resident and the nurse started telling me to push, and with two pushes, out came the baby. It was a boy, just as Dr. Edwards had said it would be. They let me hold him briefly and then took him away to clean him up. By then, Lacy had come into the room in a surgical gown and a mask, looking like a doctor, saying, "Look at me! I'm ready to help! Let's go!"

Little did he know that our baby was already born. I hated to disappoint him, but I said, "The baby is already here. It's a boy! You have yourself a son!"

I could see the shock on his face, even behind the mask he was wearing. By that time, the nurse was back with our baby boy, wrapped in an Easter bunny receiving blanket. She gave our baby to Lacy to hold.

Then Dr. Edwards came rushing in, bigger than life, saying, "What in the world happened? You must have been nesting when you came to see me yesterday! What were you trying to do, have that baby on the Baltimore–Washington Parkway?"

Shaking Lacy's hand, Dr. Edwards said, "So you must be that young attorney who had sense enough to marry Gwynette. You're the lucky man! Congratulations, you have a son!"

The three of us laughed and had a light moment. Dr. Edwards said that it must have been all that walking I did in Madison that made me strong and flexible enough to push the baby out so fast, but he wanted to watch me for a day or so in that I didn't have an epidural or anything.

He then asked if we wanted to have our son circumcised. When we said we did, he said he would come back within twenty-four hours to take care of that, and that I would be home for Easter Sunday dinner. Then he left the room.

However, when he stepped outside the door, Lacy and I overheard a conversation that he had with the resident, the young white doctor who had delivered our son. Evidently, Dr. Edwards was pissed. He said that he heard the young doctor had complained that he had to deliver "one of his patients." Dr. Edwards asked the young doctor what he meant by that. He told the young man not to assume that all of his patients were poor and on welfare, and then he added, "You'd better watch your attitude! You don't know anything about her. Do you know who she is? She's a future doctor, too, and much smarter than you'll ever be. And her husband is a lawyer, so you'd better be careful before you get sued for discrimination!"

Our son was born a little after four in the morning on Good Thursday, April 15, 1976, on Tax Day, weighing in at seven pounds and six ounces. He was feisty, wiggly, and full of energy and personality. After seeing him in action for the first time, I understood why he came into this world early. A little over an hour of hard labor, and it was all over, yet it was just the beginning of what I knew would be a joyful life for him.

We named our son Gharun Stephen Lacy. *Gharun* was a name I created because we wanted a name starting with a G, like ours. I made it up from an Arabic name, *Harun*, meaning "the exalted one." Harun was the Arabic version of the biblical name, Aaron, the brother of Moses. His middle name came from Mama Lacy's maiden name, Stephens, without the final letter *s*.

We couldn't wait to tell the family about our surprise delivery: Mama Lacy, my mom, Vee, and Daddy. Vee was coming home from Penn State on Good Friday and told me she had planned a surprise baby shower the Saturday before Easter, but the surprise was on her, because the baby had surprised all of us. So, I told her to cancel the shower and reschedule it for the next holiday she would be home for, perhaps during the Labor Day weekend. Her little nephew would be the guest of honor.

EASTER SUNDAY

We brought our little bundle of joy home on Easter Sunday morning. Since I had planned to have Easter dinner and a housewarming, Mama Lacy insisted that we go ahead and have the dinner at our new apartment. Our mothers would bring dinner, potluck, and would come to meet their first grandchild.

My dad slipped over to our crib before the females got there. He wanted to be the first to see his first grandchild, and a grandson at that. He was over the moon and back about that. He finally had a male descendant. He came with both his Polaroid and a regular camera and didn't stop taking pictures until we told him he needed to leave before the ladies came, so that they wouldn't be jealous that he had seen the baby first. We didn't want any drama on our baby's first holiday.

Since I was still tired and sore from giving birth, Lacy and Baby Gharun played hosts to the women who would play such important roles in this baby's life: his mommy, his two grandmothers, and his aunt. Our three female guests took turns holding, changing, and spoiling the baby.

Not long after dessert, I excused myself and Baby Lacy, and we retired to the nursery, where I breastfed him and got him down to sleep in a white bassinet we had bought in addition to the crib, which I had decorated in blue bedding. Lacy stepped in to check on us, and I asked him to please escort Mama and Vee to Vee's car and for him to drive his mom home. I was absolutely exhausted. They would have stayed all night if they could.

Since the baby came three-and-a-half weeks early and the shower didn't happen, I gave Lacy a list of items to pick up from the twenty-four-hour drugstore on his way back. He came home loaded down with baby pajamas, toiletries, and diapers from the drugstore. We both went to bed exhausted, only for me to have to get up for Baby Gharun's night feedings, which was a preview of what was to come.

So that was Baby Lacy's first dinner party, but there would be several more. Since I was homebound and breastfeeding, I took welcome breaks from caring for the baby and my studies to host small dinner parties for our closest friends, one or two at a time. Kat was one of the first to come over after work to see the apartment she had cosigned for and Baby Gharun. Then there was Paula, my riding buddy from our Lincoln days, and her new husband, Joe, the newly named tenor for the famous male group, the Drifters. Of course, we played lots of music and sang to Baby Gharun during their visit, with Joe singing the lead for "Under the Boardwalk" and "On Broadway."

And of course, I had several dinner parties for Lacy's crew. There was one for David Bennett, who helped drive us to Madison; one for Donny and his brother, Doug, and his young family; and one for David Washington, our best man, who we asked to stand as Baby Gharun's godfather. Tanya, my other DC dorm-mate at Lincoln, agreed to be Gharun's godmother. She was pregnant with her second son, and we agreed that they would grow up as godbrothers and playmates. We had Baby Lacy blessed at Mount Carmel Baptist Church, where we were married, at the end of the summer of 1976.

We also hosted several dinners for Lacy's law school buddies when they came to Washington to visit. I enjoyed having small, intimate dinners so as not to overwhelm the baby, the kitchen, the apartment, or me. To me, small and intimate dinner parties to say "thank you for supporting us" were better this time around rather than the big and crowded house parties, with people stepping all over each other, that had been the case at some of our dinner parties in the past. This would be our life for a while: Lacy, me, and baby makes three.

Our first trip together as a threesome was to Penn State to see Valeria receive her Ph.D. We drove all the way to Happy Valley in Pennsylvania for her graduation ceremony, with my mother riding with Baby Gharun in the back seat. What a proud moment that was for our family! My dad came separately. Boy, was he proud! My big sister was now a Ph.D., and as always, a role model for me.

BACK TO WORK

In between the dinner parties, caring for Baby Gharun, and writing my research proposal, I was also looking for a teaching job—and if you know me by now, you know that I was strategic about it. I was looking for a job with fewer direct contact hours during the day, not the normal nine to five, which can become ten-to-twelve-hour working days when you add in grooming and commuting time. I had put in a lot more education to have more time at home as a wife and mother. The trade-off would be more time working at home, preparing for classes, and grading papers and exams. After getting my proposal approved, I started my job search.

First, though, I needed to wean my baby off my breasts. He had gotten all of the great nutrients that only breast milk provided. I felt that four months was enough and that I needed to introduce him to formula. He absolutely loved the sweet taste of breast milk and knew nothing else. It was even difficult to get him to take water from a bottle, much less formula. He also didn't take to the nipples of any of the bottles I had been given as gifts. He wanted no part of any bottle.

One day, we both got so frustrated, I called Lacy at his job and asked him to stop by the drugstore and get at least three types of bottles we hadn't tried. There was a new bottle on the market that I decided to try that they said was close to the shape of the breast, called the Playtex Nurser. I didn't give Gharun the breast for the entire afternoon, regardless of how much he cried. When Lacy got home, I opened a can of Similac formula and poured it into the Playtex Nurser to try it out. And wouldn't you know it, it worked. The little fella was so hungry, he took right to the shape of the nipple of that bottle and lapped up the formula. So that was it. Cold turkey was the way to go.

My second task was to find a babysitter for my small baby. Gharun would be a little over four months old when college classes started in late August. My mother, who was still working at the Bureau of Engraving and Printing at the time, said she wouldn't be able to keep him. But her upstairs neighbors, the Kramptons, a retired older couple, were home during the day and keeping their five-year-old grandson, Jamie. So, we approached the Kramptons and asked if they would be willing to keep Baby Gharun also. We negotiated a great weekly price with them that, for the elderly couple, would help them pay their monthly bills.

Lacy and I were comfortable with the arrangement and comfortable with the Kramptons, whom we had known for years. It would be like Baby Gharun would be staying with a great-grandmother and great-grandfather, and both grandmothers agreed to be backups when the Kramptons were not available. The Kramptons agreed to keep our son during the day so that I could work.

With babysitting arrangements in place, I set my sights on five colleges. Four were inside DC, within driving distance of Fort Chaplin, where the Kramptons and my mother lived. I also applied to the University of Maryland, which was closer to our apartment. Hopefully, one or more of these schools would need a business professor to teach that fall. The other four were George Washington, Georgetown, and Howard universities, along with the University of the District of Columbia. I was able to get interviews with all five schools. I found each to be very interesting, yet different.

As August first rolled around, I had gotten job offers from the University of Maryland and two schools in DC: Georgetown and the University of the District of Columbia. I then narrowed my choices down to the two in DC, since my babysitting arrangement was in DC. The schools could not have been more different.

Georgetown was an old, majority white, Jesuit Catholic school rooted in history and tradition in the old Georgetown section of DC where rich and famous millionaires and politicians have lived, including the likes of John F. Kennedy, Elizabeth Taylor (while married to Senator

John Warner), and Julia Child. Its McDonough Business School is old and famous, and its reputation is storied. It is ranked high among the nation's best and best-known.

On the flip side, the School of Business and Public Administration at the University of the District of Columbia (UDC) was a new school within an HBCU (historically black college/university). HBCUs were just beginning to develop professional business schools, and UDC was no exception. In fact, UDC itself had grown out of several mergers of older HBCUs under DC's mayor at the time, the Honorable Marion Barry.

Although staunchly different, both schools came in with offers that were roughly the same. Professional business schools at the college level were at their peak of popularity in the 1970s, with large student bodies and growing class sizes, so all of them needed professors with the proper credentials. However, colleges and universities in DC were not known for paying their instructors that well, in that like waiters who make more money with tips, instructors could earn more money consulting in a city like Washington, DC.

I discussed the two job offers with Lacy and told him I was torn between them. My decision was going to be, in part, based on which school needed someone like me the most, with my Wisconsin credentials: the notable Georgetown, which badly needed more diversity within its faculty ranks, or UDC, with an up-and-coming business school trying to provide a mostly black student population with the best business education possible.

And yet, I had not yet heard from Howard University, Lacy's alma mater, with its storied HBCU past, but a relatively new business school. Lacy was president of the senior class of the second graduating class of Howard's new School of Business in 1972, the same year that I got my undergraduate degree from Lincoln University. The founding dean and the assistant dean had taught him accounting, and he had taken a music class with the world-famous jazz musician, Professor Donald Byrd. Lacy's classmates were none other than Donnie Hathaway (who had already recorded a record with the famous Roberta Flack), Debbie Allen, and her sister, Phylicia Ayers Allen.

At Howard, I had interviewed on campus with the chair of the Department of Management and Marketing and its faculty at Howard's newly built Blackburn Student Center in a small, private conference room. The faculty looked like something out of the United Nations, but there was not one African American. There were two women in the department: an Egyptian and a Turk.

The chair was an older man from India who seemed to be quite traditional and used to women walking three paces behind him. He didn't warm up to me, and the women asked me a lot of personal questions. I left that interview somewhat doubtful, although I knew I was qualified and would bring a lot of US experience and knowledge to the mostly African American student population that Howard served at the time. Yet I had not heard from them.

When I laid out my choices, and the fact that I had not heard from Howard, Lacy took a day off from work. We dropped Baby Gharun off at Lacy's mother's house, which was about ten minutes away from Howard's campus. He drove the Yellow Bug down to Sherman Avenue, in the then rough DC neighborhood known as Shaw. He pulled up to an old-looking worn-out converted warehouse with a sign that read "School of Business" on it. I was not impressed and not pleased that the School of Business was not located on the main campus, which was very traditional and quite beautiful, a short walk away.

Lacy pulled up to the building and said, "Get out! If you are going to be an underpaid college professor, I want it to be here, at my alma mater. Now get in there, ask for the dean, and get yourself that job! I'll be at Mom's. Call me when you're done!"

I looked at him like he was crazy and rolled my eyes at him. But without a word, I got out of the car to do what I had been asked to do. With not another word spoken between us, I knew exactly what he meant and what he wanted me to do, and dressed in a suit to impress, I went about my task. It also became crystal clear what Lacy's position and desires were about my job choice. His choice was Howard, and he wanted me to be assertive and take the bull by the horns.

From the inside, the building took on a different atmosphere and ambiance. It was well decorated and appointed and looked like a traditional school, with a nice lobby, bulletin boards, statues, artwork, and large classrooms. However, like a warehouse, it had a lot of open space, long hallways, and nooks and crannies with closed doors that had been converted into offices. Internally, the space was very quaint. I found my way to the office of the dean, which was well appointed with leather furniture and looked like an executive suite. I took a deep breath and said to myself, *Gwynette, this is it. Be Taurus the Bull! Go in there and do your thing!*

Once inside the suite, I met two very nice older African American women, one named Mrs. Ferguson, who was the receptionist, and another attractive older woman named Mrs. Ruby Washington, who looked as if she could be one of my family members. She was the dean's executive assistant. I asked to speak to the dean and, while waiting to see him, to calm my nerves, I started a pleasant conversation with those two ladies. I had been taught to always be nice to the staff.

I found out that both of them were from DC, which we had in common, and that both had attended Dunbar High School, which was not far from Howard. It was the premiere high school when they came through, although it was the school that beat up on McKinley students that infamous night when we beat them in basketball. I told them that I had attended McKinley Tech, and they seemed quite impressed. I also told them that Lacy was one of their Howard graduates. When they asked about how he was doing, I talked a little about our escapade in Wisconsin. I told them that he had just finished law school and we had recently moved back to the area. I said that I had heard from other business schools but not from Howard, and I needed to make a decision soon.

They seemed a little confused and apologized that I had not been called in for an interview with the dean, who was always the last one to meet every candidate up for a teaching position. It appeared to me as if something had fallen through the cracks. Those two ladies made me feel more comfortable and helped calm my nerves.

The dean emerged from his office, and I was introduced as one of the candidates for a teaching position in the Department of Management and Marketing. He was a short, stocky, round-bellied older man with wavy, mixed gray hair. He told me that the chair had not sent my résumé and paperwork to him for my last stop in the interview process. He called the chair to ask what had happened, and the chair said it was on his to-do list and he would send my information along. It was apparent to me by then that something had fallen through the cracks all right, and that one of the cracks was the chair. Always prepared for the unexpected, I had an extra copy of my résumé and a transcript from Wisconsin in my leather folder, which I presented to the dean to look over.

I had also done my homework on Dean Wilson. He was from Texas, an accountant (the first black CPA to practice in the state of Texas), and one of the first African American males to receive a DBA (doctor in business administration) degree from Indiana University's world-renowned Kelley School of Business. Given his stature and reputation for being tough, I must say, I was nervous and somewhat intimidated.

The dean seemed impressed with my résumé, especially my stint at the General Accounting Office. He said that in addition to management courses, he would keep me in mind to teach accounting, which was a position always in high demand that didn't carry with it the requirement of necessarily having a Ph.D. We talked for a long time—about the Midwest and my experiences at the University of Wisconsin, about his expectations for the faculty and the school, and about his plans to build a new School of Business building on the main campus.

One of his plans was to get the school accredited at the highest level possible in the nation at that time. He said that when you are an HBCU, you needed to be "better than the rest" to be on a level playing field with the white business schools. I agreed.

I was very impressed by Dean Wilson's philosophy and plans for the school, and he seemed to be impressed with my credentials and potential. He specifically asked when I planned to complete my Ph.D. I responded that I was ABD and just finishing my dissertation proposal and had gotten it approved by my dissertation committee. He impressed upon me the need to finish, and that it would be expected of me if I were to come on board. He stressed how important that was for me and my academic career, to the school in its quest to seek the highest level of accreditation, and to African Americans, not just in business but in general, as a race.

We then talked a bit about the need for African Americans in higher education and the general debate as to where they were needed the most: in majority white universities like Georgetown and George Washington, to integrate and bring diversity to their faculties, or at HBCUs in order for students of color to be taught by professors who look and live like them. I told him that where I would teach was a big decision for me on those grounds as well. He told me that, having taught in both of those types of institutions, that his experiences at HBCUs were far more rewarding.

I told him what schools I had interviewed with, that I had received job offers from two of them, and that they were waiting for a decision from me. That got his attention. Looking at me over his rimmed glasses, he said, "OK. We will get a decision to you as soon as possible."

Finally, without asking my age, he said that I could pass as one of Howard's students, and he cautioned me to be careful about that and to demand respect for my position and authority, especially from the male students. I assured him that my age would not be a problem and that I would have command of the classroom and would demand the respect that I deserved. With that, the interview was over. By the end of that visit, the powerful grizzly bear had turned into a soft, fatherly teddy bear of a man.

On the Monday afternoon after the weekend that followed that interview, if you could call it that, I received a phone call from Mrs.

Washington notifying me that a formal job offer was on its way. The offer was for $2,000 more than my smallest offer, which was from the University of the District of Columbia, leaving me to think that someone had done some homework. That salary offer was equivalent to a GS-9 in the federal government, which was what I would have been making starting out with just my MBA and little experience. That didn't make me very happy, having gone to school longer. But lifestyle-wise, I thought it would be worth the trade-off due to the more flexible hours and more time at home with my family. To me, that would make for a happier life.

The title Howard offered me was that of a full-time instructor, with the understanding that I would be promoted to assistant professor, on the tenure track, when I received my doctorate degree. In other words, as a result of my talk to the dean, he was giving me incentive and time to get my Ph.D., and I needed the time to finish. He wasn't putting me in the pressure-cooker of getting the doctorate and getting tenure at the same time, but setting the clock for getting tenure until after the doctorate.

With the exception of the low salary, it wasn't a bad deal, and it carried with it a little less pressure. Maybe I would come out with the doctorate being a little less crazy than most people. So, when I got the paperwork, I accepted the job at Howard.

Although I wasn't crazy about my salary, I was fine with mine being secondary to Lacy's. He was making a decent amount of money for a lawyer just starting out in the federal government. We split up the bills, as we had always done, with me taking the smallest of them. With that, we agreed that I would save at least one paycheck, if not more, each month. We decided to start saving for a house and a second car, which we would need eventually, and for a second baby, down the road apiece.

TWELVE

NEW BABY, NEW JOB, NEW HOUSE = CRAZY!

IN LATE AUGUST of 1976, I began a career that would become my life's work. If you had told me when I graduated from Lincoln University in 1972 that I would be teaching at the college level in 1976, I would have said you were crazy. My goal after undergraduate school was to get my MBA and make a lot of money in corporate America in some big city, like other MBAs. Where and how, I wasn't quite sure. So, teaching at the college level and making the same salary I would have been making if I had stayed in the federal government was the furthest thing from my mind. But my aspirations and material needs changed once we decided to have children.

EARLY DAYS AT THE MECCA

My first year of teaching at Howard University—the Mecca, as they call it—was a big adjustment from being a graduate student at Wisconsin, and with Baby Gharun added to the mix, life was no picnic. Although

I still got up early, my daily schedule was quite different, starting even earlier.

Actually, I usually got up at three o'clock in the morning for the last baby feeding before daybreak. Baby Gharun was not an all-night sleeper. For one, he had to wear a brace to correct the angle of his feet or he would have been significantly pigeon-toed. Although we tightly tied his feet on to the brace, he didn't like it, so he would cry and somehow wiggle his feet free. Since I had weaned him from the breast, Lacy was a big help and took the first shift to give Gharun a night bottle before going to bed at midnight or one o'clock in the morning, while I tried to get some sleep. Baby Gharun was usually up again at three o'clock, wanting another bottle and often not wanting to go right back to sleep. He must have thought it was playtime when he was with me!

I would often have a difficult time getting him back to sleep. I tried everything in the book: walking back and forth across the floor with him in a burping position, rocking him back and forth in the rocking chair, and playing with him on the floor and in his crib, to no avail. I would get so jealous when I heard other mothers talk about how their babies slept all night without waking up. They would tell me wild stories and tricks of how they made that happen, including letting the baby cry all night for a week. I thought they were lying or something.

I did try some of their tricks, like cereal before going to bed on a full stomach or withholding all naps. Letting him cry all night didn't work either. That just kept us up all night, and we would go to work the next day drowsy and frustrated. I even took him to the doctor and asked, "What's wrong with this baby? I can't get him to sleep all night!"

My OB/GYN, Dr. Edwards, referred me to Dr. Robert Crawford, who was known as the best black pediatrician in all of Washington, DC. He examined Baby Gharun and examined me and took my history: the bloody noses and asthma and all I'd had as a child. He said that in addition to his crooked feet, our baby had inherited my crooked nose structure and upper respiratory issues. Jokingly, he asked if I had I gone crazy at night yet. I wanted to say *yes*, but I didn't. In other words, he was saying to me, *Suck it up and deal with it. You are the cause of this problem. It's hereditary!*

There was nothing that Dr. Crawford could or would do. He gave me some more tips and old wives' tales and sent me on my way. I left his office almost in tears. There was no magic cure to get my baby to sleep all night, and Dr. Crawford said to definitely not to let him cry all night. That was too risky in Baby Gharun's case. In other words, he was saying, *get your lazy ass up and tend to your baby!*

So, we were left to figure things out on our own. I added a warm bath to our regimen, per Dr. Crawford's advice, and continued to put the baby to sleep on a full stomach. I cut out playing with him. The one thing he and I liked best of all was hearing soft music on the record player in his room and slow-dancing. And no, I didn't play the traditional lullabies. I played old-school *rhythm and blues* slow jams, as they are called today. His and my absolute favorite was "Betcha My Golly Wow" by the Stylistics. Maybe that's why he loves, writes, and produces a lot of rhythm and blues songs as a hobby today.

I would finally get Baby Ghurun back down to sleep around four in the morning. By then, I was often wide awake, so I would read my textbooks, plan my lectures, grade papers, or work on my dissertation until I got sleepy again, which was between five and six. Then I would go back to bed for a short nap until around seven thirty, when it was time to get Lacy off to work and get Baby Gharun and myself ready for our day.

THE COMMUTE

My first class didn't start until nine-thirty or eleven a.m. on alternate mornings, so I drove into DC via the Baltimore–Washington Parkway at the end of rush hour in order to drop Baby Gharun off at the babysitter's place in Fort Chaplin in Northeast and head on over to Northwest to Howard. It took about an hour on a good day. But if you know anything about that parkway and taking New York Avenue into DC, you know that you never know what you're gonna get. One little snafu, and you're stuck in traffic.

But I made it to class within the ten-minute grace period *always*. I *never* missed class for anything, to the chagrin of the students—except when the university called off classes for special occasions, such as convocation, to celebrate the beginning of the school year, Charter Day (Founder's Day), or snow days.

Teaching and talking to my students were an enjoyable and easy part of my day. I loved engaging with the students at Howard. They came from all over the country, the US territories, and around the world, representing some seventy countries, mostly from the black diaspora. When I started at the School of Business, the male/female ratio was about 55/45 male-dominated, although the university-wide ratio was just the opposite, 60/40 female. I quickly had to command respect from both genders, as well as from my faculty colleagues, who were overwhelmingly male.

My life experiences—being from DC, McKinley Tech, Lincoln University, GAO, and Wisconsin—made my command of respect a piece of cake and gave me confidence. When the male students tried to get a little too friendly for one reason or another, I would flash my left hand and my ring finger and say, "Check out the finger!" That's all that was needed.

This time around, unlike at Lincoln, the young ladies particularly gravitated toward me. Not only was I their professor, responsible for making sure they got the knowledge and skills they needed to be successful in their business careers, but I was also their surrogate sister, mother, and/or aunty. The same was true for many of the young men. One thing I did and still do is refer to my students as Mr. and Ms. followed by their given surname. I believe that if you give respect, you can command respect in return.

It was fun to get up each day and go to work. There was never a dull moment, and I learned something each day, mostly from my students. I had found fulfilling work that made me very happy.

Sometimes I gave the young ladies professional and career-planning advice, as well as personal and romantic advice. Several times, I had to give them advice on how to handle sexual harassment from their male professors. One egregious case led to the immediate retirement of a male professor. I was pleased with how the dean handled that case, although there were others that could or would not be handled.

Likewise, many of the young men saw me as a mother or sister figure who they could talk to about just about anything. I heard it all, including some things I didn't want to hear about. They also reported to me about "slips falling" when it came to their female classmates giving "it" up to "some" professors. And, on some very rare occasions, I was propositioned myself. I made it quite clear that there was nothing that they had financially, and especially physically, that could or would convince me to jeopardize my job, livelihood, or reputation.

I would tell both my male and female students that there are two things in life that once you lose, you can't get them back: your integrity and your reputation. Every day, I tried to have a positive impact on any and all of my students. That was also true of my colleagues.

My trip back home from Howard in the afternoon was just as dicey and usually worse than in the morning, although better than most people who came in and out of Washington by car. I finished my classes and office hours around three o'clock and would rush over to Mrs. Krampton's to pick up Baby Gharun, always trying to beat the rush hour traffic on the Baltimore–Washington Parkway. Most of the time, I didn't make it. It seemed as if just as soon as I thought I had beat the traffic, when we got to Capital Plaza, which overlooked the parkway, traffic would slow to a crawl. So, I would turn up the radio and play more rhythm and blues, loudly, to keep myself and Baby Gharun awake for the rest of the ride home.

Other than Dada and Mama, two of Baby Gharun's first words, two other of his first words were "Brick House," from the song by the Commodores. It was a popular song back then, and when it came on the radio, we would both sing it as we made our way home.

I normally got home around five in the evening, just before the top of rush hour began and just in time to cook dinner, wind down, and start my daily routine all over again. I did not envy my college friends and other women who had young children and worked nine to five. I wondered how they did it without losing their minds.

The HU School of Business had no classes on Friday, so on that day, I dropped Baby Gharun off a little later, only to come back home or go to the library to work on my dissertation. Or I would keep the baby at home with me, and I would write or grade papers when he slept. Fridays were considered my research days, but being a new mom, I often used them to take Baby Gharun for his doctors' visits and/or to run errands, too.

On weekends, with Lacy's help, I reverted back to my days at Wisconsin. Lacy would watch Baby Gharun, and I became a graduate student again. I would go to the University of Maryland's library as often as I could and stay until dinnertime, trying to get some work done on my dissertation. Slowly but surely, I was getting into the literature review and the research.

BABY'S FIRST CHRISTMAS

My first semester of teaching at Howard flew by quickly. I hustled to get my grades in on time in early December, in plenty of time to pull together Baby Gharun's first Christmas. We hadn't put a Christmas tree up since the first year of our marriage, and although we took our huge artificial Christmas tree with us to Wisconsin, we never put it up the whole time we lived in Madison because we always came home to DC. So, we dragged it out of storage and put it up with ornaments that matched our décor and added one that said, "Baby's First Christmas."

It was fun playing Mr. and Mrs. Santa for the first time as parents. Everything under the tree was for Baby Gharun: wooden toys, a xylophone to bang on, a train set, a hobbyhorse, toys to help him learn how to walk and talk, and of course, a Mr. Potato Head. As with most first-time parents, we overdid it. He wasn't one year old yet, so we knew he wouldn't remember his first Christmas. "Baby's First Christmas" is more for the parents than for the child. However, we exchanged gifts with one another and vowed to never forget one another at Christmas, no matter how many children we had. After all, it was because of the two of us that our babies would be made.

My daddy came over early Christmas morning to see his one and only grandson, who he was so proud of. You should have seen the joy on his face. After exchanging gifts with one another as usual, we went to Mama Lacy's house for her famous Christmas dinner. I spent the rest of the holiday working on my dissertation, paid my tuition for my required research class at Wisconsin, and returned for my second semester at Howard in January, back to the same routine as before.

SUBURBAN LIVING WEARS THIN

Living in the suburbs was beginning to get to us. I was getting tired of the commute by car and the traffic that tied me up most days, and Lacy didn't like the commute by bus to and from Greenbelt at all. Nor did he like living in an apartment. As an only child, Lacy had grown up in his mother's detached house in the Brookland section of Northeast Washington, with plenty of space and a big backyard to play in.

So, when February rolled around and the end of our first year's lease, Lacy decided not to renew it and instead cut a month-to-month deal. He asked me if I had been saving one of my paychecks each month, as we agreed. In fact, I had been saving money since my days at GAO and the State of Wisconsin. We had a nice little nest egg. That had been our agreement, hadn't it? So, with an affirmative answer from me, he asked if I would start looking for a house.

He said he would leave it up to me to find it—any house I wanted, as long as we could afford it. He asked for two things. One, that the house should be located in DC, inside the beltway and inside the city itself, and not in the suburbs. Secondly, he asked me to find a detached house with a decent-sized backyard, that we could afford, of course. He wanted space between neighbors and a backyard for kids to play in. That was a tall order, given the housing market in DC and our limited finances. In response to his request and those parameters, however, I agreed to start looking.

Always being able to read my husband's mind and being tuned in to his needs and desires, I knew exactly the type of house he wanted. I had sensed that he was homesick for DC and that he simply wanted the type of house he had so happily grown up in for his son. I understood that, loud and clear. But he said to me, "Just find something you like. Just make sure it is in DC and that I can afford to make the mortgage payment."

The problem for me was that I needed to be working on my dissertation rather than looking for a house. I didn't want the house hunting to cut too much into my research time. So, I began to check the *Washington Post* real estate section briefly every Sunday to get a feel for the market and I decided to go out looking, in earnest, during the week of Howard's spring break.

THE GINGERBREAD HOUSE

Most of the houses in DC were a lot more in price than those in the close-by Maryland and Virginia suburbs, but I stuck to Lacy's desire to move into the city. I decided to concentrate my limited time looking into modest homes in Northeast and Northwest, close in proximity to Howard University and not too far from, but just the right distance from Mama Lacy and Mama Ford. I knew that mother and son would like that, and because both grandmothers were our backup babysitters, I'd liked that too.

On the Sunday before spring break started, as if God was directing my eyes, I saw a house listed that was located in the Woodridge section of Northeast DC, right off of South Dakota Avenue as you come into DC off the Baltimore–Washington Parkway, the same route I took into

DC every day. Woodridge is located right near the Brookland section of Northeast, where Lacy's mother lived, but closer to the DC–Maryland dividing line. In the back of my mind, I said to myself, *how convenient! God, are you trying to tell me something?*

So, I called the number of the listing agent and asked if I could see the house that was listed. At first, I thought it was a mistake. It was an all-brick detached house, listed as having four bedrooms, a sun porch, and two baths, for $55,000. I couldn't believe my eyes! Was I dreaming, or was that a typo or something? That was dirt cheap for real estate in DC in the seventies, as the housing market was beginning to skyrocket, with prices in favor of the sellers.

Marian Jones, the listing agent, told me that no, it was not a mistake. She said that it was an estate house, meaning that the person who owned the house had died, and the family wanted or needed to sell the house as part of the owner's estate. She said that was the reason for the lower-than-market-value price, as is often the case with estate homes. She said that she and her daughter, an agent-in-training, would meet me there on Monday morning, because the house would not sit on the market for long, given the shape it was in and its market value. She also said that she was obligated to show me two other houses for sale in the same area, for comparison's sake.

So that Monday morning, I dropped Baby Gharun off to the babysitter's and off I went, like going to work, to see the three houses for sale in the Woodridge section of DC, where the houses tended to be old and sturdy, with lots of character. I was not disappointed. As soon as I crossed the line into DC, I made a right onto Vista Street as the agent had instructed. It had old and quaint country-style frame houses on both sides and lots of trees, with the branches meeting high up in the middle of the street. That street took me to a street named Chestnut Street, where I turned left to find the house for sale, the second house from the corner of Monroe Street, which takes you back into Maryland. What I liked about the houses in that neighborhood was that no two houses were the same. Each was custom-built and architecturally different.

The house for sale was the cutest little red-brick Cape Cod–style home at the bottom of a slight hill on the right, with a long driveway on the left-hand side of the property leading to a detached garage in the back. I liked that the garage was separate from the house. The house had a long, deep backyard with a red-brick patio.

Inside of what looked like a little red-brick gingerbread house was everything that was described in the *Washington Post* ad. I entered an odd-shaped wooden door that led me into the living room on the left and a separate, nice-size dining room on the right. Separating the two was a tall center-hall staircase that gave each room individual space and privacy. The living room had a beautiful wooden fireplace, and behind the dining room was an old country kitchen leading into a sunroom with jalousie windows. The fireplace, crown moldings all around the living and dining rooms, and staircase were done in fine mahogany wood with a rich shellac finish. The carpentry was professional excellence at its best.

One drawback to that lovely little house, however, was the location of the bedrooms. As with many Cape Cods, the bedrooms were not all on one floor. In this case, there were two large bedrooms and a master bathroom upstairs and two bedrooms and a bath on the first floor.

I was told that the house had been owned by an old DC public-school teacher who used the small bedroom behind the living room as a sewing room/office. The other bedroom, behind the sewing room, was a guest bedroom, which had a guest bathroom beside it, separating it from the sunroom, which led to the backyard. That schoolteacher had died of cancer, and the family was anxious to sell the house and settle her estate. They had left several items that would convey with the house, including a beautiful wooden sideboard in the dining room, an antique Singer sewing machine with a foot pedal, a wooden secretary, and several pieces of artwork in the den/sewing room, all that conveyed with the house. Some of the items left in the house were worth a lot of money.

In looking at a house for sale, you can always imagine yourself in it. I, too, would use the small bedroom on the first floor as a sewing room/office. As a college professor, I too needed a den to prepare my lectures and do my research. Also, I imagined the den as being able to second as a sewing room, although it was very small. I imagined the guest room on the first floor as a playroom for Baby Gharun and having a playroom right next door to my study/den would be ideal. That room had a small closet in it and I imagined using it to store my fabric and sewing projects.

The realtor finally showed me the basement, which was divided into two rooms: a finished recreation room with a fireplace and old-fashioned knotted-pine wood paneling and a large unfinished washroom, complete with a relatively new washer/dryer. The basement and the sunroom led to a large, deep backyard that backed up to woods that divided DC from Maryland. It was very green and very private and had a bricked-in patio in the middle of it, just right for an outdoor picnic table. Although it needed some work, at $55,000, that little Cape Cod was a bargain.

The realtor then took me a little farther into Northeast into a section of DC known as Michigan Park, which is between Woodridge and Brookland, with houses built along Michigan Avenue and all around it. If you didn't know you were in DC, you would think you were in DC's close-in suburbs, such as Hyattsville or Bladensburg, Maryland.

Michigan Park is a subdivision of Northeast known for its beautiful tree-lined streets and colonial brick houses that pretty much all look alike. All are three-bedroom, modest-sized colonials with the center-hall staircases that DC is known for. Most of the houses in Michigan Park are cookie-cutter, with just about the same floor plans.

I was shown two of them. One was located next to a popular Presbyterian Church, and the other was located a little deeper into Michigan Park. Both were all-brick with living room, dining room, kitchen, and porch on the first level. They were priced at about $75,000 each, which would stretch our budget a bit, but we would be able to bite the bullet if we really wanted to. They both were very nice and would meet our needs, but they were so "cookie-cutter." They both needed a little work (mainly new kitchens) to make them ours, but were otherwise pretty much in move-in condition. Although all three bedrooms were upstairs on the second level, and both had finished basements, nothing jumped out about either of them that said, *I am for you! Buy me!*

So that concluded my tour, and I was left to go home and think about the three houses I had been shown that day and discuss them with Lacy. I couldn't wait for him to get home that evening. Over dinner, I described each house in detail. We could afford all three, but home ownership was scary. We would have to put ourselves on a strict budget, sacrifice, and be unselfish. We would also have to spend money on each house to make the one we chose our own in terms of comfort.

I knew that one of them would work for us, and I didn't want to spend any more time looking. I needed to get back to work on my dissertation. The location was right, and the prices were right. I felt the need to get the house hunt behind us and to make a decision. We needed to get it over with and move.

The next step was to show Lacy the three houses. So, I called the realtor that night and told her we were ready to make a decision and that I wanted to show my husband the same three houses. We decided on the upcoming Saturday morning, when Lacy was off and we could bring Baby Gharun along.

So, on that Saturday morning, we gathered up Baby Gharun and off we went. Personally, I was ready to make a deal on one of those three houses. Spring break was almost over, and I didn't want to spend any more time house hunting.

For some reason, that little gingerbread house on Chestnut Street had stuck in my mind all week. It was as if it was made just for us three: the sewing room/study for me, the two bedrooms just for us three, the playroom for Baby Gharun, and the big back yard. After looking at all three houses, sure enough, Lacy was sold on the first house I had looked at as well. It was as if God directed my path that Sunday morning when it showed up in the paper and said, *this is the one I have chosen for you!*

Sure, it needed a little work, but it was so cute, so quaint, and so different. I envisioned new carpet and a new kitchen to start. That would be enough to make the house just right and comfortable for the three of us to begin with. The biggest drawback was the lack of a third bedroom upstairs if we were to add to our little family. If we really wanted to stay there long-term, however, there was enough space and enough land to add a bedroom or two to the top or the bottom level. And Gharun's bedroom would be large enough for a bunk bed if we had another boy. We certainly had enough time to think about and deal with all of these things. So, we came back to the gingerbread house and wrote out a contract for it, as it was, for $55,000 with no contingencies, and that was that.

We moved into our new address on April 1, 1977, fourteen days before Baby Gharun's first birthday. Always in support of us, Lacy's crew, some of the fellas who served as groomsmen at our wedding, were there to help us on both ends—to move out of our apartment and into our house. All I had to do was feed them brunch on the front end and dinner on the back end. We made it a celebration of sorts, and they were very happy for us—and for a new place where they could come and hang out. Personally, I was overwhelmed by the awesome responsibility of both the move and the financial obligation of home ownership, but I knew it was good for our family, good for our marriage, and good for our son.

BABY'S FIRST BIRTHDAY

After we moved, I would come home from work and be surrounded by boxes that needed unpacking. I also needed to plan a birthday party for Baby Gharun. Lacy was so sweet and patient and told me to take my time. He was so happy to finally own his own home and said I had all summer and a lifetime to make our house a home. So, I unpacked the things we needed right away and took to planning Gharun's first birthday.

Since our home wasn't ready, we rented my mother's party room over at Fort Chaplin for the party. I invited all of our family and friends, which was over fifty people: cousins (old and young), aunts, uncles, friends (old and new), college friends, high school friends, colleagues, and of course the grandparents. Since we'd just bought a home and money was short, I decided to serve my usual soul food barbecue meal to our guests and not cater the event. The menu consisted of barbecue chicken and baked beans, and I asked Mama to make her famous collard greens and potato salad. Mama Lacy chipped in a couple of items as well. We bought a huge sheet cake from the Giant in blue and white and decorated the party room in the same boyish theme.

Lacy served as our photographer and took great pictures. Everyone had a great time, especially Baby Gharun, who had just started walking and was learning to tackle the stairs in our home. He was King for a Day, although I am sure he doesn't remember a thing.

Again, as with Christmas, as first-time parents, we overdid it, but we had a ball, too. Of course, we overspent, but we got a chance to entertain and see a lot of family and friends we hadn't seen since we had moved back from Wisconsin. All three of us went home exhausted, but happy.

THIRTEEN
HELL'S KITCHEN VS. THE MECCA

THE REST OF April 1977, including my twenty-sixth birthday, flew by in a flash. Mama Lacy babysat while Lacy and I went out on a real date alone to a fancy restaurant like the good old days when we were dating. We celebrated my birthday and our new home. I thoroughly enjoyed myself and tried to forget, for one night, that I was still ABD: All but Dissertation.

However, that rarely left my mind that spring as I turned in my final grades and wrapped up the academic year. In addition to teaching one summer school class three days a week for six weeks, I spent that summer working on my dissertation and getting our house in order. I was determined to accomplish two major projects that summer: finish my literature review and get a new kitchen built in our home.

A NEW KITCHEN

My Uncle Lawrence had introduced me to an old friend of his named Kenneth Woods, who was a fantastic carpenter. He had designed and renovated a kitchen in Uncle Lawrence's house in the beautiful upscale Hillcrest Heights section of Southeast Washington. My Aunt Audrey's country-style kitchen, with modern appliances and a light-up modern ceiling, was the talk of the family. So, I hired Mr. Woods to build us the same type of kitchen in our home. That turned out to be "more than a notion," as the old folk say.

Our home was right inside the DC line in Ward 5 but still not too far from the University of Maryland. So, on most of my free mornings, I would let Mr. Woods in to work on the kitchen, drop Baby Gharun off at the babysitter's upstairs from my mother's apartment in Ward 7, and head to the library at the University of Maryland to work on my paper. What was so nice about Mr. Woods was that he would turn the gas back on and hook my stove back up before he left so that I could cook dinner when I got back home. Lacy and I would say that God broke the mold when he made Mr. Woods.

After spending my summer days and weekends at Howard's and the University of Maryland's libraries, I finished my literature review and submitted it to my research committee for approval. I then turned my attention to designing my survey to study attitudes toward women managers in government.

By the end of July, my kitchen was done, my literature review was finished, and my survey was drafted, but I was exhausted. My kitchen was quite beautiful, with everything I wanted in it—something every woman would envy. However, there were days when I was so tired I couldn't see straight and was certainly too tired to cook in it. I was so grateful to Mr. Woods, though. He had done himself proud.

To make things even better, I asked if he could also update the first-floor bathroom. He asked for another week and a couple more thousand dollars, and he also renovated the guest bathroom on the first floor. I had more than enough money left over from my summer school check, so by summer's end, I had both a new kitchen and a new bathroom. Our house was becoming a home, to say the least. I'd had enough of the renovations, though, so I called the new kitchen, "Hell's Kitchen."

As a family, we were beginning to get adjusted to our new

neighborhood, which was friendly and familiar. The neighbors opened up their arms and homes to us as a new young family in the neighborhood. There was an older couple on each side of us who proved to be excellent role models. One couple had grown children, and one had older teenagers. Both couples fell in love with and loved on Baby Gharun.

Both couples also gave us great advice on home ownership and upkeep, such as cutting the grass and caring for the beautiful shrubs around our house. We also found that old friends as far back as elementary and high school also lived in the neighborhood. Baby Gharun's godmother and my Lincoln friend, Tonya, soon moved in around the corner with her two boys, and a friend from McKinley Tech, with a young daughter, lived across the street. So Gharun soon had several new playmates.

FROM BABYSITTER TO NURSERY SCHOOL

One day, I stopped by a neighborhood store with Baby Gharun and ran into an old friend. I recounted my schedule and house projects with her and how I was ripping and running all the time. I must have looked tired and real bad to her, or she must have felt sorry for me or something. She immediately told me that she had her daughter in a fantastic nursery school near my house that took in babies and toddlers under two years old. It was a five-minute drive or a ten-minute walk from our house and would cut way down on my ripping and running. She said, "Girl, you need to put that sweet little baby in that school. You will really like it."

The next day, I looked into that nursery school. Not only did I like it; I loved it. I applied, and Gharun was accepted. So, when Howard University opened back up in August 1977, we said goodbye to the Kramptons and Fort Chaplin and hello to Second New Saint Paul Baptist Church's Child Development Center of Woodridge, DC. It was a very sad goodbye, with tears and all, but a happy hello, with smiles and joy.

I immediately fell in love with that church-related, religion-based nursery school. It reminded me of my upbringing at Mount Carmel Baptist Church in Northwest DC. They provided reading readiness and math, bible stories and holiday programs, music lessons, and extracurricular classes like tap and even karate—all of which I planned to sign Baby Gharun up for. The student/teacher ratio for his age group was 5 to 1, which was fantastic. But the best thing about it was that the nursery school was a hop, skip, and a jump from our house and to Howard University.

SECOND YEAR AT THE MECCA

My second year teaching at Howard was very similar to the first, but with the addition of new challenges and adventures. This was also true of Lacy's parallel career. I was finding my sea legs and my passion for what would become my life's work. However, working at Howard University brought with it many unexpected and unplanned issues and opportunities that often took my attention and focus away from working on my dissertation.

I often say that all you have to do is go to class and/or go sit in your office and an issue or opportunity will either knock on your door, walk into your office, or ring your phone. It could be a student, the dean's office, a colleague, a federal agency official, or the White House, even. I continued to help my students in and outside of the classroom. Many continued to seek out my advice as a confidante and friend.

For example, that year, the DJs at Howard's famous commercial radio station, WHUR-FM, went on strike, and the student interns were asked to sit in for the striking DJs. One of those interns, Mr. Melvin Lindsey, who was in my labor–management relations class, came by my office to talk about the strike for a better understanding of what was going on.

Lindsey told me how nervous he was having to DJ the seven-to-midnight time slot. He said he was so nervous that he hardly said anything and just played "soft, quiet" R&B music all night—mostly love songs, one record after another, along with the required commercials. We laughed and talked about that, and I gave him tips as to how to overcome his shyness. That format, originated by Lindsey, is now one of the most popular evening and late-night rhythm-and-blues radio formats, used throughout the United States and the world, which Lindsey named "The Quiet Storm" after the love ballad and blockbuster hit single by Motown's Smokey Robinson. My student, Melvin Lindsey, also a DC native, became one of the most famous American DJs of all time and later died at age thirty-six from complications of AIDS. Many more students like Lindsey would touch my life, as I would touch theirs.

OPPORTUNITIES COME KNOCKING

During that same year, I began to add consulting projects to my portfolio. The dean added a new associate dean to his School of Business executive team, Dr. Lawrence Johnson. An older black man, Dr. Johnson was a distinguished marketing professor and expert who had served as president of a college in Massachusetts in his own right. That year, the HU School of Business received a grant to train minority women in management, and the dean appointed Dr. Johnson as the principal investigator (PI). As the only black female faculty member in the Department of Management, I was added to the grant as a Co-PI to bring legitimacy to the topic, the project, and the program. In other words, it made sense to have a black female delivering the goods. I fit the bill.

Dr. Johnson and I traveled all over the East Coast conducting seminars and workshops to help minority (mostly black) women hone their management skills, traveling by plane as far away as Boston and Atlanta, two of Dr. Johnson's favorite cities. The plane trips didn't agree with me much, as they caused my sinuses and upper respiratory system to act up. However, on the flip side, those ailments caused me to lose a lot of weight, so I dealt with it when people asked what my weight-loss secret was. All of my "baby weight" had disappeared, plus some. I would later know the cause.

I got teased a lot by the staff and several faculty members at Howard about Dr. Johnson behind his back. They called us "the old professor and his protégée." It was true that the two of us couldn't be more different. He was much older and single (divorced), and I was just over twenty-six and married, with a young child. He was described by some as a "stiff and proper" Bostonian, and I was described by some as a "hip and southern" Washingtonian. We were two oddballs, but we got along well, especially on the road: the Bostonian and the Washingtonian.

Dr. Johnson was a genius at marketing and product delivery and I at managing and writing, which turned our grant into a tremendous success and became the blueprint for many grants to come. He was one of my first and most trusted consulting mentors, who taught me the ins and outs of private consulting. He would always tell me, "Don't let any client take advantage of your talent, and make sure you get paid well for what you do!" Johnson would become the next dean of the School of Business at Howard.

Also that summer, I got my first individual consulting job within the federal government. I got a call one day that spring from the Department of Commerce and was asked if I would come to the Maritime Division during my summer off and assist with their Employee Development Program, an office within their Human Resources Department. That was the first of many federal and local government programs like it that I would work for as a consultant throughout my career.

That same year, after leaving the National Labor-Relations Board and a short stint with the Department of Labor, Lacy decided to take the DC Bar in order to go into private practice. He had taken the Pennsylvania Bar in Philadelphia and passed it with flying colors. We had both agreed that rather than take the DC Bar, one of the hardest to pass in the country, he would wave in from Pennsylvania or Wisconsin after the required five-year waiting period. During that waiting time, he went back to law school to pursue an advanced degree in labor law and received his LLM (a master's in law) degree from the Georgetown Law Center in DC. His graduation from Georgetown was another proud moment for Mama Lacy, Baby Gharun, and me.

However, impatient to start his own practice, he decided to take the dreaded DC Bar right away rather than wait things out. And guess what? That lucky dog passed it on his first try. Boy, did we celebrate, big time.

Lacy and I would stop periodically to take a break and have a romantic weekend or short vacation—or as we called them, second-honeymoon getaways—somewhere where there was a beach. We would hop down to Virginia Beach close by or go as far as Florida or the Bahamas for a few days. So, we decided to celebrate his new degree that way.

SLOW AND STEADY WINS THE RACE

Both of our careers were taking off. It appeared to me that Lacy's was taking off a little faster than mine because I hadn't finished my doctorate yet. I was getting a little concerned, but we needed to stop every now and then to smell the coffee, as they say. So, I took my work everywhere we went and tried to get something done toward my degree.

Mama Lacy was a great babysitter. The more time she had with Baby Gharun, the better for her. She enjoyed introducing him to all of her favorite dishes. After Lacy graduated from Georgetown and passed the DC Bar, we flew off to the Bahamas for three nights and four days for one of our second honeymoons.

Immediately upon our return, Lacy began to look for office space and a partner. The partner came in the form of Charles Ailstock, a DC native I just so happened to know. Lacy had met Charles at Georgetown Law, but I knew him from my old neighborhood in Northeast DC where I grew up. He lived on 17th and D Street, NE, the same block as Darren and Candy, my two elementary school classmates who called Valeria and told her I was being bullied back in the day when I was in deep trouble. The Ailstocks were a fine family with solid values. Charlie, as he was called back then, had a younger sister that everyone called Baby Sis, who was cute as could be and very popular, especially with the boys in our neighborhood. I remember Charlie being very protective of her. When Lacy announced Charles Ailstock as his legal partner, I was totally on board with that.

So, the law firm of Lacy and Ailstock, LLC, was born that summer. In finding office space, rather than settling for something downtown in a big office building, the two friends decided to rent an office townhouse in the historic Capitol Hill section of DC because of its closeness to Capitol Hill and the courthouse. It was a cute, historic, quaint little white brick two-story house that had been converted into office space at 8th and Pennsylvania Avenue, SE, near the Capitol and Senate Office Buildings.

NEW CHALLENGES

Having little money, the guys asked me to help them decorate the space and plan the office opening party, including designing and getting out the invitations. I chose a tried-and-true brown earth-tone color scheme and took Lacy with me to pick out an oriental rug, client chairs, and tan curtains. Lacy and Charlie picked out their own mahogany desks and bookshelves. The three of us felt the resulting space and furniture was inviting and comfortable and would not feel too imposing to potential clients.

We quickly pulled together the office opening party and got the invitations out. We had the party catered and filled in the menu with our mothers' favorite homemade items, such as chicken wings, potato salad, and Mama Lacy's desserts, which were a big hit. The partners provided a well-stocked bar. It was a great party on a shoestring budget, which the Lacys were getting well known for. It was well attended by family and friends, (the usual suspects, as we call them), Lacy's and Charles's classmates and acquaintances from elementary through law school, and many of their colleagues, old and new. The party was a big hit and the talk among our circle of friends and the guys' legal community for days, which was pleasing to the new partners and to me. Lacy was happy to finally be his own boss, and I for him.

To say the least, all of these activities and projects were distractions and side trips on the road to finishing my dissertation and my Ph.D., causing what I had been warned about: procrastination and delay. The clock was ticking. Finally, I said, *enough is enough! Get this thing out of the way!*

I was determined to get done with my dissertation and my degree my third academic year at Howard (1978–79), which was also the end of the second year from when my dissertation timeline started. My contract, my job, my career, and the rest of my life the way I wanted to live it depended on it. I would carve out every free moment I had to get my research finished and write my chapters.

I sent chapter after chapter back and forth and back and forth to Madison to my committee. There was one young professor on my dissertation committee who was trying to give me a hard time, but the older professors didn't appear to care much. I even hired an editor in Bethesda, Maryland, to help me edit the paper, and the two of us went back and forth with my committee to try to get things right. I needed their approval so very much, but it was slow in coming. It reminded me of pledging my sorority, and I understood why the big sisters would give us a hard time sometimes. They were preparing us for life, when things got tough. So, I would say to myself, *This is like pledging! You can do this!*

Lacy was very supportive of me, every step of the way. There were so many times when I wanted to just throw in the towel and quit. When that happened, he was right there to pick up the towel, tell me a joke, or hold me in his arms. He would always say to me, "A Lacy never quits. Finish what you start!"

FOURTEEN
SICK OR CRAZY? MY DEFENSE

AFTER THREE LONG years of *perseverance, hope, and determination* (PHD), during the summer of 1979, I believed that I was finished with my dissertation. I had been back and forth and back and forth with my committee, spent thousands of dollars in research tuition dollars, and finally felt that I was through.

ENOUGH IS ENOUGH

I was exhausted and tired of the entire ordeal. I felt as if I had pledged another sorority all over again, or a fraternity in this case, in that my research committee was comprised of all white males: five of them. My committee chair, another Dr. Johnson, seemed tired too. An older professor at Wisconsin, he seemed to feel that I had done enough to earn my degree. It was as if we both felt that I had been hazed enough. My time was up. It was the twelfth round. We both had had enough.

After my final edit, I mailed off the final draft of my dissertation to my committee prior to returning to teach at Howard on a new two-year contract that fall. I was proud of what was considered back then to be groundbreaking research, which I had titled, "An Examination of Attitudes Toward Women Managers in Government." Being from DC, I had been used to seeing a lot of female supervisors/managers in government, at both the federal and local levels all of my working life, many of whom I knew personally, so I had plenty of subjects.

For some reason, I felt a little pushback from some of my committee members, as if they didn't want to be affiliated with the label *breakthrough research* about women managers. My research found mostly positive attitudes toward women managers in government, which I found was the case back then and has been exponentially the case ever since. Look at what women are doing today!

The fall of 1979 was an important time for the School of Business at Howard University, too. We were preparing to go up for reaffirmation of the highest level of accreditation a school of business can seek, so Dean Wilson was in beast mode in making sure that all of our ducks were in a row for what was his claim to fame: making sure that all of his business programs were accredited and remained that way.

Each fall, each faculty member was called in with his or her chair for what Dean Wilson called a management-by-objectives (MBO) session, which was one part of his performance evaluation process (PEP) that examined your teaching, research, and service productivity. I remember my PEP clearly that year. I had received the "Teacher of the Year" award the spring before for outstanding teaching, which was a piece of cake for me. Both the dean and my new chair congratulated me on that accomplishment. They also gave me kudos on my service to the school, based on the committees I served on, for my consulting to the federal and local governments and my grant work. We also talked about my specialty area of labor–management relations and plans for a grant that they wanted me to serve as the principal investigator for.

When we got to the research area, both the dean and my chair zeroed in on the progress I was making toward finishing my Ph.D. At that time, there were three of us—myself and two foreign faculty members—trying to finish our degrees out of over seventy faculty members within the School of Business. The dean was gentle, but I could tell he was concerned. I was the only person in my department without a Ph.D.

He stressed how important it was to him, to the school as it sought accreditation, and to me professionally to "get the job done." I assured the dean that I had finished the dissertation, that it was sitting on my committee chair's desk, and that I would have my Ph.D. by the end of the semester.

The dean and my chair stressed that they wanted the Department of Management and Marketing to have 100 percent of its faculty terminally qualified for our accreditation. Dean Wilson asked if there was anything I needed him to do, including time off, to help me get to the finish line, and I responded, "Nothing." I assured them both that I would make it happen.

With that promise, the dean said, "OK, we're counting on you. Don't let us down!"

I left my MBO session sweating bullets. The pressure was on. I knew what I needed to do. I immediately went to my office, which was right across the hall from the dean's office, and called my dissertation committee chair, Dr. Johnson, in Madison. I asked him to schedule a date for me to come to Wisconsin to defend my dissertation and receive my degree. I was very persistent and would not accept *no* for an answer. He said he would get back to me with a date.

A DATE WITH MY FUTURE

I went home to tell Lacy about my day and my MBO session and to strategize with my beloved and domestic partner. Lacy always gave me good advice as to how to handle my business. He told me to be persistent about getting a specific date for my defense and offered to go with me to Madison to have my back.

I told him, "No. I started this journey, and I will finish it alone. Just stay on this end and watch over our son, and I will bring home the trophy."

After a couple of weeks of going back and forth with Dr. Johnson, I finally got a date that I will never forget: Tuesday, December 11, 1979. That was the date set for my defense, which would come after giving my final exams at Howard and two weeks before Christmas.

That fall semester was a difficult one for me that year. It wasn't the teaching or the students that semester. Those were always a joy. I told my students what I was up against, and they were rooting for me. It was the stress and anxiety of getting ready for my defense. It was also about preparing myself mentally and physically for it.

I went back and forth with Dr. Johnson and Dr. Miller with minor changes on the final copy of the dissertation, which had to be approved by my department and filed with the Wisconsin Library and the Library of Congress, as all dissertations in the US are housed there. Further, the fall weather in DC that year was wet and raw, which left me with a chronic cough that wouldn't go away, and I certainly wasn't looking forward to the colder weather that I would face when I got to Madison.

As December 11th approached, I had to get everything in order for my trip to Madison. First, I had to close out the fall semester by giving my final exams. I warned my students not to miss their final, given my *no-makeup policy*. I told them that I would not be around to give any makeups before my trip. However, knowing my students and thinking ahead, I gave my finals two days early, on the Tuesday a week before my defense, because of course, as always, a few students missed the final and had doctors' excuses for a makeup, which I scheduled for that Thursday, the last day I would be able to give an exam before my trip.

So, I went back to campus early that Thursday morning to give makeup exams. I was also able to schedule an appointment to see a pulmonologist that afternoon at Howard University Hospital to get something for that nagging cough I was having. I had been referred to Dr. Earl Armstrong by an old high school friend, Carolyn Lang, who was his head nurse.

Newly named as the assistant chief of pulmonary diseases, Dr. Armstrong was trained at Johns Hopkins University and had been at

Howard for about the same length of time as I had. We hit it off well with stories about our adjustment to the Howard University culture from our respective graduate schools. We talked about my medical history, the asthma I'd had as a child, and my lifestyle as to its effect on my health. He listened to my lungs. He also asked me about allergies, my physical environment (such as the type of trees that surrounded our house), and the materials that our house was made of, such as plaster vs. drywall and whether I thought there could be mold in the house. I guessed that he was trying to figure out what I was breathing in that could be causing that chronic cough and whether I could be allergic to something.

He gave me a sample of a prescription-strength cough syrup, asked me to get a chest X-ray on my out of the hospital, scheduled a follow-up appointment for the next week, and sent me on my way. Although I needed to pick up Gharun from the day care center, I managed to get the X-ray done before they closed and made it to the day care center in time, without having to pay a late fee.

I spent all day Friday in my office at home, in isolation, grading exams, going through my dissertation, and making mental notes as to what kind of questions my committee might ask and what kind of oral answers I would give. I spent the weekend packing and hanging out with Lacy and Gharun, and preparing them for a few days without me.

BACK TO MADISON

My two fellas watched from National Airport as my flight took off to Madison that Sunday afternoon—the same flight number we used to take flying back as graduate students, a flight that had played a major role in our lives. After deplaning, I stepped out of Madison's airport to catch a cab to my hotel, which was in downtown Madison near where we used to live and walking distance to the campus. With one big gulp of that cold, moist December Madison air, I knew I was back, and I started to cough. My lungs began to burn, so I went straight to my room at the hotel to take the cough medicine I had packed in my luggage. I changed into my pajamas and climbed into bed to study a copy of my dissertation until my cough got better and I was able to fall off to sleep.

That Monday, after taking breakfast in my room, I walked up to the campus to make a round of visits before my big day, which was to come on Tuesday. My first stop was to see Dr. Miller, the director of the research institute, who shared with me all the steps and forms that I needed to complete to finalize the doctoral process. The most important step, of course, was to complete and pass my dissertation defense the next day.

All of the members of my dissertation committee would have to sign off that I passed my defense. Dr. Miller would then certify the completion of all my requirements and make sure that the registrar got all the paperwork needed to issue my degree. My last task would be to drop off two copies of my dissertation to the library to be bound. One copy would be sent to the US Library of Congress, where it would be permanently housed, and one would be housed at UW's library.

My second visit was to Dr. Johnson's office. As the chairman of my dissertation committee, he explained the defense process. He said that I would be asked to explain my research and go through each chapter of my dissertation and answer questions. Since I had been teaching for three years, I decided to treat my defense as if it were a lecture on my dissertation. I asked Dr. Johnson to let me treat it that way, to allow me to do the talking and to only step in if he felt I was having a problem with a question, for no one knew my research better than I did. I knew exactly what I needed to say and do. He agreed.

My last official stop of the day was to fill out paperwork at the registrar's office, which would certify my graduation and get my degree to me and send transcripts wherever I needed them to go. It was a cold day in Madison, so cold it made my bones ache, so I quickly grabbed a bite to eat on my way back to my hotel room, where I put on warm pajamas and curled up in bed again with my dissertation, a cup of tea, and my prescribed cough medicine. I spent most of that time studying the statistics chapter of the dissertation, which was sure to be a major and the most difficult area of questioning from my committee. I was determined not to get tripped up by the math; not the math whiz, not me!

I called home to check in with my fellas, and Lacy said that Dr. Armstrong's office had called and to give them a call when I could. However, it was late and after his office hours, so I wasn't able to make that call. I went to sleep a little nervous and not feeling that well, but confident I would make it through the next day successfully.

TWO HOURS AND DONE!

After a somewhat restless night, I got up early on Tuesday. I went over my dissertation once more and was dressed and ready to leave the hotel at nine in the morning for the fifteen-minute walk to the campus. I stopped for a croissant, juice, and cough drops and arrived at the test site, Dr. Miller's conference room, at around nine thirty, about half an hour early. The thirty-minute wait for everyone to arrive felt like a lifetime. I just wanted the whole ordeal to be over. I sucked on two cough drops while I waited.

Eventually, everyone arrived and took their place around the conference table. I took my place at the front of the table with a dry-erase board behind me if I needed it. Dr. Johnson took the first seat to my left. The defense started on time at ten o'clock sharp.

I went through the introduction, my reasons for conducting the research, and the literature review with ease. As I'd expected, my explanation of my statistical method choices and quantitative analysis was the most difficult part, but I got through it. The findings, results, and conclusions were easy. Yes, my research showed that attitudes toward women managers in government were positive back then, as they are now, and yes, that conclusion was statistically significant. There were just a few questions during my lecture.

Before I knew it, it was eleven thirty, and my lecture, as I chose to call it—my part of my defense—was over. It was now time to take questions. I took a deep breath and tried to keep from coughing. I seemed to have impressed most of the committee members with my poise and demeanor, the organization of the paper, and my presentation of the facts. After all, I had been teaching at the college level for almost three years.

But then, the youngest professor on the committee, as I knew he would, took me to task on the technical and statistical analysis of my data. He started in on me, and I got stuck on one of his questions. I then looked to Dr. Johnson, and he stepped in to rephrase the question in a way that he knew I could answer it. That was a big help, and I seemed to answer the question to the professor's satisfaction.

After the question-and-answer period, they dismissed me from the room, and I was sent to sit in the reception area, where I sucked on more cough drops. What seemed to be forever was about fifteen minutes, and then they called me back into the conference room. I was sweating bullets! When I walked in, everyone was all smiles and stood up to shake my hand individually. I had passed my defense successfully. I was done. Dr. Johnson said, "Congratulations, you passed!"

With that, it was all over: the long hours of studying and writing, the sleepless nights, the thousands of dollars spent, the days I wanted to quit, and the sacrifices. Ten years of college, and with a two-hour defense, it was all over. A Ph.D. was mine, at 28 years old.

Dr. Miller came out of his office and joined my committee in congratulating me. Dr. Johnson said that the committee or the chair usually takes the candidate out to lunch, but that his wife needed him to come home. I think that he was uncomfortable taking me, the only black female candidate he had probably sponsored, out to lunch, so that left me to celebrate all by myself. That stung, but I wasn't feeling well anyway, so I gathered my papers and headed back toward the hotel.

On the way, I stopped by the library to turn in the two copies of the dissertation that needed to be bound, and I also stopped by the registrar's office to make sure all of my fees were paid, especially my graduation fee, so I could get my diploma. They asked if I would be attending the graduation ceremony on December 22nd. I told them I would not be there because I needed to get home to my young son. So, they told me December 22, 1979, would be the graduation date that would appear on my diploma and on my transcripts and that they would mail them to me. I ordered six copies of my transcript, three to be sent directly to the dean's office at Howard and three to be sent to my house.

On what turned out to be my final walk down State Street in Madison, Wisconsin, I stopped to get my last deep-dish pizza and a bottle of Italian wine from my favorite pizzeria. I felt like I was walking my last mile after being sentenced to life somewhere and stopping for my last supper. In a way, it was—the last supper before the rest of my life.

I got back to the hotel early that afternoon, celebrated alone, and crawled into bed. I said to myself, *No celebration? No party for me and my classmates? I should be standing on top of a mountain somewhere!*

Instead, it was just, me, myself, and I. I realized how difficult being the first at anything truly is. It's hard work to get there, and then you stand alone at the top of that mountain, which can be very lonely. Exhausted, feverish, and coughing like the heavy smoker I was not, I took the cough syrup I was prescribed to knock myself out and took a long nap.

I woke up about six p.m. in the evening and made three special telephone calls (collect, of course) to the three most important people in my life—Lacy, Mama, and Vee—to tell them my good news. In fact, I joked with each of them at first and told them I didn't pass, and then told them I had made it through just before nearly giving each of them a heart attack. They were ecstatic to hear the good news. Lacy told me how much he loved me and to hurry home. Still feeling exhausted and drained, I hung up the phone, packed my bags for my flight the next morning, finished off my medication, and went back to bed, thanking God for allowing me to complete such an important phase of my life.

I was now done with my Ph.D. and ready to go on with the rest of my life. It took a lot of *perseverance, hope, and determination* (PHD), but I did it. Feeling pretty bad physically at that moment, I fell off to sleep. I couldn't wait to get back home to DC the next day. My answer to the sick or crazy question for me was I ended my Ph.D. journey *sick*, instead of crazy.

FIFTEEN
IT'S NEVER OVER, UNTIL IT'S OVER

I WOKE UP the next morning sick as a dog: feverish, achy, and coughing. I couldn't help but think about that myth that you either go crazy or get sick while working on a Ph.D. I concluded that I was one who got sick during my ordeal. I said to myself, "Oh well, I'd rather be sick than crazy."

Knowing that I was an hour earlier time-wise than they were, I called home to catch my fellas before they left for day care and work. I told Lacy I wasn't feeling well, and he told me that Dr. Armstrong's office had called the house again the day before while he was at work and left a message for me to call his office as soon as possible. I told him that I had finished my medicine and promised that I would call the doctor's office as soon as I could catch his office open.

I talked to Gharun and told him that his mommy had passed her final school test. I phrased it that way because I knew that there would be other tests in my life to come. I told him to go to nursery school and do well, that Mommy was coming home, to mind his daddy, and to be a good boy. I told them both how much I loved them and that I couldn't wait to get home to celebrate with them. Worried about how I was feeling, Lacy said he would drop Gharun off at nursery school and pick me up from the airport after checking on a few items at his office on Capitol Hill.

I struggled to get dressed, check out of the hotel, and get to the airport for my nine o'clock flight. I stopped to pick up some more cough drops and a hot cup of tea before getting on the plane. I couldn't wait for it to take off and take me home. I slept through the first leg of the flight to Chicago and arrived in Washington by midday EST. As I deplaned, there was my sweetie standing there, waiting for me with open arms.

I melted into his arms and the tears began to flow. Everything just came down on me at once. There were tears of joy that the years of hard work were finally over and that I had achieved my goal of attaining my Ph.D., but also tears of exhaustion and frustration over how I was feeling. Lacy seemed to understand that, as he always does, so he picked up my bags and helped me to the car.

He said, "You don't look so hot, so I'm gonna take you straight home so you can call your doctor, and then I'm gonna go pick up Gharun. He's been asking for you!"

HOME AGAIN!

When I got home, I went straight to the phone while Lacy went to the nursery school. I was able to reach Dr. Armstrong's office while Lacy was gone. He told me he had been trying to reach me for several days. I told him where I had been. He said he had the results of my chest X-rays and needed me to go to Howard Hospital as soon as possible, and he would meet me there. I was stunned. What could possibly be wrong? I felt bad, but I thought it was just a bad cold and emotional exhaustion from what I had just gone through.

I told him I had been coughing and felt lousy and tired the whole time I was in Madison and that I would get to the hospital as soon as I was able to see my son. He said that I had walking pneumonia and to plan on staying in the hospital a couple of days so he could run some tests. The hospital would call him as soon as I got there. With that, we hung up.

I went to take my suitcase upstairs to unpack but couldn't make it past the first couple of steps, I was so weak. So, I pulled the street clothes I wore in Madison out and left the pajamas and toiletries in the suitcase. By that time, Lacy was home with my sweet little Gharun. I greeted him with a big hug and told him all about my trip and gave him some gifts I had gotten him from the Wisconsin bookstore: a Badger T-shirt, a banner, and a toy. His little eyes lit up with joy.

I told Lacy and Gharun at the same time that Mommy needed to go away again, this time to the hospital for a couple of days; but he would be able to come to see me, and I would be home soon for that celebration party that we had planned as a family.

I asked Lacy to go upstairs to get another pair of pajamas out of our room. While he was gone, I talked to Gharun. I told him that Mommy had a bad cold and needed to get some rest in the hospital, and that I needed him be a good boy for his daddy and Nana. He said he would, and I told him I believed him. With that, we headed out to drop him off at Mama Lacy's house and me at Howard Hospital.

VIP TREATMENT

Employees of Howard University are treated like royalty at its hospital, especially its professors and administrators. In addition, I had the best employee health insurance money could buy: Blue Cross/Blue Shield, high option. So, I was placed in a private room in the VIP wing of the hospital. By the time I got settled in, Dr. Armstrong was there, Johnny-on-the-spot. All he had to do was walk over to the hospital from the doctors' offices.

Evidently, he had met and talked to Lacy before coming into my room. The first thing out his mouth was, "What were you doing walking around with walking pneumonia in Madison, Wisconsin? I've been calling your house since Monday, and no one was home. Your husband just told me you were defending your dissertation? Did you pass? I hope it was worth it!"

Dr. Armstrong told me he didn't like the looks of my X-rays or my test results, and having examined me the Thursday before I left, the way that I looked and my overall health wasn't good either. He gave me another thorough examination and listened to my lungs and that nagging cough I was having several more times. Yes, it appeared to be pneumonia all right, with some wheezing that gave him concern also.

He ordered some blood tests, an oxygen tube, and an antibiotic drip. He brought Lacy into the room and told us that I looked pretty tired, beat up, and run down, given the fact that I had been burning both ends of the candle for some time, and that I needed to stay in the hospital for a few days of R & R. He said that he was going out of town to a conference and therefore turning my care over to the chief of pulmonary, Dr. Hackney, whom I knew by his outstanding reputation. I felt I was being left in pretty good hands.

He asked who would be caring for my son and to tell him that his mommy needed some rest but would be home in a few days. He said that he would be back to see me on Monday morning to let me know if and when I could go home. With that, he left.

Lacy and I looked at each other in disbelief. I had no idea I was so bad off that I needed to be in the hospital at least until the weekend was over. I knew I was tired and run down, but that bad? That myth about Ph.D.s getting sick or going crazy came to mind again, and Lacy and I laughed about that.

So, I decided to make the best of it and get some much-needed rest. I asked Lacy to bring me some more pajamas and my final exams for grading the next day and to explain everything to Gharun and his mother. Feeling lousy and weak, I couldn't wait to get some sleep.

I had never been away from my sweet child for more than two or three days at a time. With me just getting back from Madison and then having to go right into the hospital, the poor little guy had to be wondering what was going on with his mommy.

Lacy said he would keep his schedule as close to normal as possible. He said he would pick Gharun up from Nana's, Gharun's name for his grandmother, and take him home and to nursery school each day until that Friday, and then they would do guy stuff all weekend, like going to the movies and to a ball game. The VIP wing of the hospital allowed twenty-four-hour visitation from family members, including small children, so Lacy said he would play that by ear. With that, he gave me a big hug and was gone, and I was left all alone to get some much-needed rest.

While Dr. Armstrong was gone, I spent my days in the hospital resting, grading my students' final exams that Lacy brought to me, and obeying the doctors and nurses. I wanted to get out of there to go home to my family. Dr. Hackney came to examine me during his rounds, along with his med students, and he had a lot of questions for them and for me about my symptoms and the pneumonia. He said he had looked at my X-rays, had some questions, and would talk to Dr. Armstrong about that. He ordered some more tests, one of which was a tuberculosis test. I was like, "You gotta be kidding me! Where could I have gotten that?"

An older doctor, Hackney was fatherly and seemed to be more traditional in his approach to medicine and with his patients than Dr. Armstrong. I did my homework on the two of them. Hackney was Howard-trained in the tried-and-true methods of medicine, and Dr. Armstrong was Johns Hopkins-trained in the newer, more experimental methods. I guess you could say that Dr. Hackney was old school and Dr. Armstrong was new school. I thought they made a good team. Hackney said there was no such thing as walking pneumonia, so to speak. He said, *"pneumonia is pneumonia,"* and ordered me to stay in the hospital until the pneumonia was under control.

On that Sunday, Lacy brought little Gharun to the hospital to see me after Sunday school. I took the oxygen tubes out of my nose so as not to scare him. Dressed in his Sunday best, he charmed all of the nurses. The little guy brought me a fistful of flowers and was full of questions.

He inspected every gadget and item in my room. He told me he missed me and said, "You told me you would only be gone a couple of days. That was Wednesday. It's Sunday. That's more than a couple of days, Mommy! When are you coming home?"

Well, that didn't surprise me. My little fella was smart as a whip. I could see that he was concerned and that he knew things weren't as hunky-dory as I tried to make them. So, I was honest with him and told him that I wasn't sure. I told him my doctors would be back to see me the next day, and that his dad and I would be able to give him some answers soon. I got a big hug and high fives from the two of them, and they left to go home and change so they could go to the Capital Center to see a Bullets' game. We were big Wes Unseld and Bobby Dandridge fans.

My mother also came to see me after church also, and boy, did she give me an earful. Lacy had filled her in, and she came in hyper. "What the hell is going on?" she asked. "What did you do to yourself to wind up in here? Pneumonia? How in the hell did you get pneumonia?"

Softly, I said, "Calm down, Ma. Watch the cursing! Remember, you just got out of church. I have just as many questions as you do, and so do the doctors. Obviously, I got run down and need some rest."

She calmed down, and we got caught up a bit. I told her about my trip and my defense. She told me about everything that was going on in our extended family and at church. She said that she would put me on the prayer list at church. She said she was planning a graduation party for me and before leaving, she said, "I need you to get better and get out of that bed and go home. I don't plan on raising any more children in my lifetime," and she gave me one of her sassy looks. I knew exactly what she meant.

I responded, "I don't plan for you to either," and added, "I love you too, Ma," as she was leaving.

And with that, she was gone. Nothing more needed to be said. I knew exactly where she was coming from. I knew she had my best interest at heart and she wanted the best for me. That was just her way of saying it. I spent the rest of the day reading, grading papers, watching basketball, and resting. I was still coughing, especially at night.

MORE QUESTIONS THAN ANSWERS

I couldn't wait until Monday morning and for Dr. Armstrong to get back to his rounds. I kept watching the clock on the wall and waiting and waiting and waiting. Finally, around ten o'clock, he came in with a gang of his male med students, with my X-rays under his arm. He introduced me as I would introduce a case study to my students.

He said, "Good morning, Dr. Lacy. Please allow me to present your case to these interns. Here, we have a twenty-eight-year-old, relatively healthy young African American woman who doesn't smoke and rarely drinks. She is married, with one young toddler. She lives in Northeast, Washington, in a heavily wooded area with lots of trees, called Woodridge. She works here at Howard as a professor in the School of Business and just returned from Madison, Wisconsin, where the weather was very cold and where she dealt with the very stressful ordeal of defending her dissertation—successfully, I might add, so she is now Dr. Lacy. She has been coughing like crazy for months, especially at night, and has lost a significant amount of weight, also in recent months. Here is her X-ray that Dr. Hackney and I have been studying. What do you see? What do you think is wrong with her, and how would you treat her?"

He put the X-ray up on one of those X-ray readers that was in my room and waited for an answer. One young intern said that looking at the lungs, there were clearly signs of pneumonia and that he would treat me with antibiotics. Dr. Armstrong said he was somewhat correct and that the intern could see that I was on an antibiotic drip.

Another intern, with an African accent, asked, "Have you tested her for TB?"

Dr. Armstrong said that Dr. Hackney had done just that, and that the TB test had come back negative. Dr. Armstrong then went up to the

X-ray and said that there was clearly something more than pneumonia going on. He pointed to what he said were *granulomas* on both lungs. One intern asked whether I could be having an allergic reaction to the trees in my neighborhood. Another suggested that I could be having an asthmatic episode that was affecting my lungs, and that I could have gotten worse from the extreme cold weather in Madison. Dr. Armstrong said that they were somewhat right.

Dr. Armstrong then asked the students, *what was the worst-case scenario?* One intern said cancer, and another said pulmonary fibrosis. Dr. Armstrong said that he didn't think it was either of those, but that clearly there was something else there. Before leaving with his entourage, however, Dr. Armstrong said, "Dr. Lacy, this is not just a simple case of pneumonia. There is something else going on that we must get a handle on. I'll be back later to talk to you one-on-one. You will not be going home today."

I said to myself, *What the hell?* I immediately called Lacy and told him what had taken place and that I would not be coming home. He said he would pick up Gharun and take him to Mama Lacy's house and get to the hospital as soon as possible.

A DEVASTATING DIAGNOSIS AND TREATMENT

Dr. Armstrong and Dr. Hackney came back to examine me before leaving for the day. Dr. Armstrong said that he had a suspicion that I had a relatively mysterious autoimmune disease called *sarcoidosis*, where inflammatory cells called granulomas had formed due to an overreaction of my immune system, resulting in my cough and pneumonia. The doctors explained the diagnosis to Lacy when he arrived.

Dr. Armstrong went on to say that sarcoidosis occurs most often in women of childbearing age between twenty and forty years old, mostly of African, Scandinavian, and Japanese descent, with certain inherited genes. A high level of stress is a risk factor that can cause the immune system to go haywire and bring on symptoms. He said that in the US, most cases occur in African American women in my age group and that I was in the high-risk category, given the amount of stress I had been under while working on my doctorate. He had heard that joke about Ph.D.s too. He said that in order to confirm his diagnosis, he wanted to conduct a minor surgical procedure called a *bronchoscopy*.

By then, I was getting overwhelmed, so I was glad Lacy had gotten there to hear everything about the procedure. Dr. Armstrong explained that the bronchoscopy involved inserting a flexible tube down my nose with a bronchoscope at the end to examine my airways and collect tissue samples from my lungs to be used in his diagnosis.

I agreed to have the procedure done the next day, if they could promise me that I would be able to go home in time for Christmas, which was a week away. Although they wouldn't guarantee anything, they said that if all went well and their suspicions were true, I probably would be able to be home for Christmas, with a treatment plan. I was told not to eat or drink anything after midnight and to get plenty of sleep—and with that it was time for everyone to leave. I asked Lacy to keep everything under wraps so as not to alarm the family unless absolutely necessary.

The next morning, the nurses came in to get me ready for my procedure. As usual, they connected me up to sensors to track my blood pressure, heart rate, and oxygen levels. They also inserted another IV tube into my vein with medication to make me sleepy and relaxed, but not enough to completely put me to sleep, because they needed me to be awake to answer questions during the procedure. They also gave me a sedative, Valium, and put a numbing gel up my nose.

Once everything was ready, Dr. Armstrong came in and inserted the bronchoscope down my nose and talked to me the entire time, through every stage of the procedure. Although it was a little uncomfortable and I coughed a couple of times, it was not too painful. He took a specimen of lung tissue and ended things with what he called a bronchial washing and suctioning. After about forty-five minutes, it was all over, and they wheeled me back to my room, where I went to sleep. I woke up later that afternoon and threw up. The nurse said I was having a bad reaction to the medications I was given.

After dinner, I dozed off again from those crazy drugs they had given me. When I woke up, my minister was standing at my bedside. I could have sworn I saw a halo over his head. I absolutely adored him. He was like a second father to me. After all, he had baptized me, performed my wedding, and blessed my baby. He had marched with Martin Luther King Jr. in the March on Washington and was a soldier of the civil rights movement. Still in a haze, I asked him, "Why are you here? Am I going to die or something? Are you here to give me my last rites?"

He said, "Oh, no, my dear. I hope not. They do that in the Catholic Church. In fact, the nurse at the desk told me to come on in and that you were not critical. No dear, I saw your mother and she told me you were here, and I visit the sick after prayer meeting every Tuesday night. I'm just making my rounds and thought I'd stop by. Allow me to pray for you!"

Mama had arranged the whole thing. That was just like her; always looking out for her baby girl. Reverend Patterson took my hand and prayed for my recovery and good health. It was a lovely prayer. I always loved his prayers. He could really put one up there.

Then we talked a bit. He told me that Mama had told him that I had received my doctorate. He said that the Good Lord wasn't through with me yet and that He had a lot of work for me to do. So, he told me to hang in there and to fight to get well. He said he would announce my latest accomplishment to the whole congregation when I returned to church. He asked me about Lacy and Gharun and wished us a Merry Christmas.

I also sent season's greetings to his wife, Mattie, and their three kids. His family was so much like MLK's family. He said that Mattie, who reminded me so much of Coretta Scott King, was busy at home and at the church, getting things ready for Christmas. After that, like Santa, Reverend Patterson took off to see his next child of God. With that visit and prayer, somehow, I knew that eventually, I was going to make it through and that this was just another hurdle in life that I would have to jump over.

The following afternoon, Dr. Armstrong came by to see me, alone this time. He had put a rush on the results of my bronchoscopy, and as he suspected, the biopsy showed signs of sarcoidosis. He said, "So let's work out a treatment plan so you can go home on Friday. I know how badly you want to get home to your family before Christmas."

The treatment plan he had for me was a shock and totally unacceptable. The thing that bothered me most was when he said he wanted to put me on a steroid called prednisone for a year, starting with a high dosage and then weaning me off of it over a year's time. I had heard of that drug from friends and knew about several side effects that he confirmed: weight gain, a moon face, and mood swings.

On top of that, he said that because of the prednisone, I shouldn't get pregnant, because the drug might adversely affect the unborn fetus. In addition, he said, I should not take birth control pills or several other medications that had adverse interactions with prednisone. I said to myself, *What kind of craziness is that? Don't get pregnant, but don't use birth control pills, which I wasn't using anyway?*

I was totally stressed out, and my reaction showed it. I told him I didn't like what I was hearing, and I asked if there was any other treatment regimen I could consider. I told him I was sorry, but I could not agree to that one, and I explained why. First, I could not agree to a drug that would have such negative effects on my body internally and externally and change my emotional well-being. Second, I told him that I had planned to give my son a sibling as soon as possible so that they wouldn't be spaced too far apart. So, I said, "Thanks, but no thanks" to his treatment plan.

In response, Dr. Armstrong said, "Well, if you won't agree to my protocol, I won't be able to continue as your doctor. So, I tell you what. Think about it and give me your answer on Friday. I will come by with your discharge papers then."

To say the least, I was devastated. I started to cry but quickly got myself together. First, I called Lacy and asked him to stop by the hospital before picking up Gharun so we could talk. After all, my decision would affect our entire family. He could tell how upset I was, so he said he would rearrange his afternoon schedule and come as soon as possible. First, I called Dr. Edwards, and he agreed with Dr. Armstrong: no babies.

I then got on the phone for a second opinion about the prednisone. I called my Aunt Freddie, who worked at the National Institutes of Health. If I could get an honest expert opinion, it would be there. I explained my entire situation to her on the phone. She said, "Wait, let me get my boss to talk to you, Dr. Anthony Fauci."

At that time, Dr. Fauci, an immunologist, was the head of the Clinical Physiology Section in the Laboratory of Clinical Investigation at the National Institute of Allergy and Infectious Diseases. Responsible for conducting basic and applied research on infectious and immune-related illnesses, he took the time to speak to me on the phone. I repeated my diagnosis and the treatment plan that was being recommended by Dr. Armstrong.

Dr. Fauci said that he knew of Dr. Armstrong, his Johns Hopkins background, and that Armstrong had an excellent reputation. He said that the proposed treatment plan was standard procedure for sarcoidosis. He recommended that I follow the protocol, in that research showed that it worked and that most patients got better.

He asked if I knew that Dr. Armstrong was treating Elizabeth Taylor for sarcoidosis. At the time, Taylor was married to Sen. John Warner of Virginia. I told him that I did not know she was one of Dr. Armstrong's patients. Fauci told me that Taylor probably didn't want people to know that, so mum was the word. Dr. Fauci said that if he were me, he would take the prednisone and work with Dr. Armstrong to get off of it as soon as I was better. I thanked him for his advice and thanked Aunt Freddie for arranging for me to talk to Dr. Fauci.

Weeping off and on, I told Lacy everything when he got to the hospital. I told him all of my concerns and hesitations. It was one of the toughest conversations we'd had in our seven years of marriage. I was upset with myself for getting so sick. I was upset with the crazy, mysterious disease I had, and I was upset about the treatment plan that had been mapped out for me. I told Lacy I just couldn't do it.

He said to me, "Hold up, wait a minute! Remember when you wanted to quit on getting your doctorate? Don't be such a stubborn Taurus the Bull, crybaby!"

Well, that got me to calm down. Then, lawyer that he is, in a logical yet jovial way, he said, "Being the math whiz that you are, you see things in black and white, with one answer. Well, medicine and science aren't like that. We're dealing with a lot of unknowns here, like in your math formulas. Don't get so frustrated that you don't have all the answers you want. Let's just break each thing down."

So, we did. First, he said that he knew I was frustrated because I didn't have all the answers for my disease. He told me to take the bull by the horns, use my *determination*, and decide that I was going to beat it—that I wasn't going to let some strange disease with a funny name get me down.

Second, he said that the doctor wanted me to take a drug that I knew little about that had wacky side effects that weren't appealing to me. He said to *hope* that it would work on the disease. He said, "So what if you gain a little weight, you can use a little meat on those bones, and besides, you can always go on a diet afterward."

Finally, he repeated that old adage: good things come to those who wait. "Although we had planned to have another baby right away, you can't always have what you want when you want it. You gotta *persevere!* You know how to do that!"

Lacy knew that was really what was bothering me the most. I had so much wanted to have another child right after getting my degree. So, he said we'd have to put that on hold for a while and use the Catholic method and other old-fashioned methods of birth control. We had done that before. We could do it again. Just put off until tomorrow what you can't get done today. Besides, I had a few more years on my side.

He said, "Look, you just got over a major hurdle of getting your Ph.D. Those hurdles don't stop in life just because you have new letters and a fancy new title behind your name. Here's another hurdle, called illness, in front of you. Use those same letters in your degree to jump over it: *PHD, perseverance, hope, and determination.*"

I asked him how he had gotten so wise all of a sudden, and with that, we laughed and shared the Jell-O that was on my dinner tray. Lacy always knew how to make me laugh and feel better about myself. Together, we could get through this next storm in life. All we had to do was hunker down and prepare to ride it out.

That Friday, Dr. Armstrong came with backup—my friend, Carolyn—and my discharge papers. I apologized for being such a jerk and so uncooperative the day before and said that I would take the steroids and other medications he needed me to take. He said that he understood how overwhelming everything was and that most of his female patients are reluctant at first. He assured Carolyn and me that he would take good care of me, gave me my prescriptions, and said, "Let's get on with it. I promise you, it'll all work out OK. Just work with me, hang in there, and give it time."

I couldn't wait to get out of there. Lacy picked me up around lunchtime. On the way home, I asked him to drive by Howard's business school so I could drop off my grades. It was the last day to get them in before the Christmas break. He took them to the dean's office for me and gave everyone an update on how I was doing, told them I was on my way home from the hospital, and that I would be back to work when everyone returned from the holidays in a couple of weeks.

The dean told him how concerned everyone at the school had been about my well-being. He understood what I had been through, given that he had undergone the ordeal of getting a doctorate as well. He sent his best wishes and told Lacy to take good care of me so that I could return to Howard in good shape. He told Lacy that he and the school had big plans for me.

When I got home, we had exactly three days to get everything ready for Christmas. There was no tree up, and my two guys had made a mess of things at the house. I immediately called Barbara, our housekeeper, and begged her to come the next day to help me whip our house into shape for the holidays, and she said she would. Thank goodness I had done all my Christmas shopping before Thanksgiving, as I always did.

Mama Lacy, my mother, and Vee said they would come to a potluck Christmas dinner at our house to celebrate little Gharun's Christmas, as we had done the Easter when Gharun was born. All Lacy and I had to do was put up the tree, wrap gifts, and play Santa, and that was a lot within a few days' time, given my illness.

Christmas fell on a Tuesday that year, so we had the whole weekend to prepare. We got the tree up and pulled the house together just in time to play Santa. Although I was still tired and coughing off and on, I was beginning to feel a little better. And nothing warms the heart more than to see a child's face light up on Christmas morning. Happy to have his mommy home, my little Gharun was beginning to learn the true meaning of Christmas.

Of course, my dad came by that morning to play with his grandson and slowed us down a bit, but the table was set and my part of dinner was ready before our other guests arrived. Kat came by, and we paused for a champagne toast to the newest Ph.D. in the family. Then we sat down to our traditional Lacy Christmas dinner. It was *delicious*.

So, 1979 turned out to be a year of triumph and pain. I came out of it with a diploma that had the degree title of Ph.D. on it, signed by the president of the University of Wisconsin–Madison and dated December 22, 1979. I was the first and only black female ever to receive that title from the Industrial Relations Research Institute, for that program no longer exits. Yet, I was left with a chronic disease sitting in my chest that would haunt me like a ghost, something I would have to wrestle with until it went into remission, leaving scars; a disease that could come back any time it wanted to, and that I would have to learn to live with for the rest of my life.

On the other end of my life's spectrum was my wonderful, understanding husband and my beloved children, born and unborn. I had no other choice than to chalk it up as I have said so many times in my life before: *"C'est la vie*, that's life!"

After the birth of 1980, I celebrated my accomplishment in several ways, first at the Wright family New Year's Day reunion at my Aunt Freddie's house. I got to celebrate with my loving family, especially my maternal grandmother and my aunts, uncles, and cousins who helped bring me through my journey from childhood to the Ph.D. We joked, made light, and poked fun at that skinny little girl in the family picture books we passed around who grew up to be a Wisconsin-bred Ph.D.

That Sunday after New Year's Day, Reverend Patterson announced my receipt of the Ph.D. to the entire congregation in his announcements during the church service. He had me stand up to the applause of my fellow church members: some who had watched me grow up, some who had taught me, some I had taught in Sunday school, and many who had attended my wedding. I must say, I blushed to be honored by the village that helped raise me, gave me values, and cheered me through my Ph.D. journey with their prayers. Afterward, many members, old and young, came up to me to shake my hand. I felt like a rock star.

After church, Mama and Vee hosted a brunch in my honor at a famous restaurant in Silver Spring, Maryland, known as Mrs. Kay's Toll House. It was an all-girl hen party of sorts with my sorority sisters, college buddies, and other close girlfriends and family members in attendance. Lacy and Gharun were the only males that were invited. I will remember the pink champagne toasts in my honor for the rest of my days.

A TRIUMPHANT RETURN

As with all New Years, January 1980 also ushered in the second semester for most college campuses, and Howard University was no exception. The faculties usually return to campus at the end of the second week in January, prior to the students returning the following week to start classes. In 1980, the School of Business held a one-day retreat that Thursday, hosted by the dean, along with continental breakfast and a luncheon, as usual, as we prepared for our upcoming semester and accreditation.

During our morning session, the dean talked about the standards to be covered in our accreditation report, one by one, including the faculty qualifications standard. Just before lunch, he said that he was proud to announce that the Department of Management and Marketing was 100 percent terminally qualified because I had completed my Ph.D. as of December 22, 1979—the same day I was released from Howard University Hospital. He joked and said that he had received too many copies of my transcript from the University of Wisconsin and for me not to have any more sent to the school, *please.*

The dean said that we were the only department in the School of Business where every faculty member held a Ph.D. He asked me to please stand up, as the youngest and first African American female member of the Department of Management and Marketing to hold that honor. That statement drew thunderous applause, especially from my male colleagues, and to my shock and surprise, a long standing ovation followed from everyone in the room. That was quite an honor from a usually very reserved group of colleagues.

On the way to the luncheon, which was held on campus at the Blackburn Center and was usually a classy, catered affair, I stopped off at the ladies' room to freshen up my make-up. Overwhelmed by the outpouring of love and support, I had teared up and didn't want anyone to see the tracks of my tears; that wasn't a businesslike thing. When I got myself together, I entered the Gallery Lounge a couple of minutes later. Again, my colleagues applauded me and stood up to give me a standing ovation. To my surprise, the staff had decorated the room as a graduation celebration and hung a banner that read, "Congratulations Dr. Lacy: A Job Well Done!" Their applause was genuine and real, for truly the Ph.D.s in the room had experienced and understood the journey that I had just completed, which was no easy task. They then yelled, "Speech, speech!"

I wasn't expecting that, but I went up to the podium in the front of the room and gave the usual acceptance speech. I thanked all those on whose shoulders I stood: my parents and family, my wonderful husband who had stuck by me through thick and thin, and my children, born and unborn. I thanked the dean and all of those in attendance, both faculty and staff, who understood, watched, encouraged me, and prayed for me through the formal educational stage of my journey, and I vowed that one day I would tell my story.

Every Ph.D. has a story, and this one is mine. This is just one part of my story, for one's story is never truly over until one's life is over. The rest of my life was just beginning, and getting a Ph.D. was a comma, not a period.

After getting my Ph.D., to my delight, there would eventually be another baby (a girl, named Gayna) and many more students who would come and go and do well—some whom would become famous, too many to name, many whose names you know. There would be higher positions, a bigger house, consulting jobs, and interesting projects that would take me all over the United States and to other parts of the world, such as Haiti, Europe, and South Africa. Even now, I hope that there will be many more tasks and stories to tell, many more hurdles to clear and barriers to overcome, and many more lessons to teach and to learn. *C'est la vie*! That's life!

ABOUT THE AUTHOR

Gwynette Ford Lacy grew up in inner-city Washington, DC. After graduating magna cum laude from Lincoln University (PA), marrying, and working as an auditor for the federal government, she earned an MBA and Ph.D. at the University of Wisconsin-Madison, eventually becoming the first African American female Ph.D. to earn tenure and serve as chair of the Department of Management of the School of Business at Howard University, and later as the Associate Provost. Today she is an international management consultant, trainer, and motivational speaker.